All God's
Children

BY JAMES KELLER

JUST FOR TODAY

GOVERNMENT IS YOUR BUSINESS

ONE MOMENT PLEASE!

THREE MINUTES A DAY

YOU CAN CHANGE THE WORLD

CAREERS THAT CHANGE YOUR WORLD

MEN OF MARYKNOLL

ALL GOD'S CHILDREN

All God's Children

What Your Schools Can Do for Them

by James Keller, M.M.

HANOVER HOUSE, GARDEN CITY, N.Y.

The Purpose of the Christophers

The aim of the Christopher movement is to stimulate at least a million individuals to assume a personal responsibility for restoring to the market place the spiritual truths upon which this nation is founded and without which it cannot survive.

Those who hate God, a few at most, have done much to upset the world by concentrating on the vital fields that touch the lives of most people: (1) education; (2) government; (3) the creative end of newspapers, magazines, books, radio, motion pictures, and television; (4) labor relations; (5) social service; and (6) library work. The chief strength of the evil-doers has been the failure of the average good citizen to fulfill his individual responsibility.

Little is accomplished by complaining or criticizing. We frequently repeat, "Better to light one candle than to curse the darkness." We are convinced that even a comparatively small number working as individual Christophers, or Christ-bearers, in these vital spheres of influence can do much to bring lasting peace to the world—that a few living for peace may, with God's help, save millions from dying for peace.

A unique feature of the Christopher movement is that we have no meetings, no memberships, no subscriptions, no dues. Each person participates as much as he can and will.

Christopher programs emphasizing personal responsibility are presented each week on more than 100 television stations and 450 radio stations.

Christopher News Notes are sent free of charge to any adult who requests them. Nearly a million individuals now receive them. No charge is made because many who are "doers" cannot be "donors." We depend entirely upon voluntary offerings for all expenses.

James Keller

THE CHRISTOPHERS
18 East 48th Street
New York 17, N.Y.
Father James Keller, M.M., director

Contents

Introduction

This is a book* about God and our American schools. What it says about God is obvious—that He is a part of our American life, a part of that tradition which makes America what it is. What this book says about our schools is obvious to some, although perhaps forgotten or overlooked by many American people.

In the American ideal, all human beings are reverenced as children of God by their very creation. In theory, therefore, it is all very simple. The education of our youth should include God. Not many people in this country would argue about it. Parents, teachers, and school administrators generally agree that all of our schools, both public and private, should be imbued with this basic ideal. Every one of us can do something about securing it. The difficulty is that in practice we have not fully measured up to our ideal. And that is a problem we have to face.

This book is talking to you, individually—whoever you are—about this problem. The message here is plain; essentially it comes down to this:

1. America is founded on a belief in God, most Americans believe in Him. Our American way of life today recognizes Him. Therefore, it is reasonable that America's schools should give the same attention to Him.

*Whatever value this new Christopher book may have is due in no small part to the important assistance given us by teachers, administrators, and numerous other authorities in the educational and related fields. Our appreciation at best is very inadequate. God will reward them in a way that we cannot.

xi

2. School officials, as a rule, are willing to do this.
3. It is up to you to support them.

That is the whole story in its simplest terms.

We acknowledge, of course, that the story has its difficult and complex side. And we recognize that something has been done by our educators to solve this problem. Our position is that there is much more to be done, and that our schools are still somewhat out of line with our traditions and with our other institutions.

The experts seem to be agreed on this too. Just recently the American Council on Education published its latest report (1953) entitled, *The Function of the Public Schools in Dealing with Religion*. It declared that although it is rather rare to find any deliberate avoidance of religion in our schools, and while in most schools there are many ways in which religion is recognized and encouraged, there remains great room for improvement. We read on page 82:

To assume that the school is meeting its full responsibility for religious literacy, intelligent understanding of the historical and contemporary role of religion in human affairs, and developing a sense of personal obligation to achieve convictions and commitments, merely by conducting devotional opening exercises, reading the Bible without comment, recitation of prayers, and observance of religious holidays, seems to us to be a misunderstanding of the requirements of a fundamental general education.

EDUCATORS WELL DISPOSED

School authorities and teachers, as a general rule, want to teach their students about God. Recognition of God has been removed from many schools in the past twenty-five years because a few people wanted Him out—or more accurately because the majority of people did not back up the teachers who are convinced that education is incomplete without God.

The vast majority of Americans believe in God and they want Him in our schools. But they must make their voices heard to get the results they desire. You, the individual citizen, must let your educators know.

They are waiting. It is your move.

A CHANGELESS TRUTH

First of all, why should our schools pay attention to Almighty God? There are a number of answers to this question. We try to give some of them in this book. In a recent decision of March, 1952, Justice William O. Douglas of the United States Supreme Court said, "We are a religious people whose institutions presuppose a Supreme Being." In this he was merely reaffirming what Justice Brewer of the U. S. Supreme Court said many years before: "We are a religious nation." In a historic decision in 1892, while summing up a survey of our noteworthy national documents and declarations, he declared: "There is no dissonance in these declarations. There is a universal language pervading them all, having one meaning. They affirm and reaffirm that this is a religious nation. These are not individual sayings, declarations of private persons. They are organic utterances. They speak the voice of the entire people."

The statements of Justice Douglas and Justice Brewer present nothing new. The idea was not new when the Declaration of Independence was written, and it was not new even when the earliest settlers left their ships and walked into an unknown land. Many of those settlers had left their homes because their right to religious freedom had been restricted. They were willing to face a strange continent and a new life so that they might worship God according to the dictates of their own consciences.

That kind of moral courage and devotion to God was still intact in this country when our forefathers wrote the Declaration of Independence. At the beginning of a revolutionary war and in the very act of founding a new nation, these men accepted what Thomas Jefferson had written clearly and decisively in the second paragraph of the Declaration of Independence: "We hold these truths to be self-evident, that all men are created equal; that they are endowed by their Creator with certain unalienable rights . . ." From its birth as a nation, the United States acknowledged the sovereignty of God, the Creator.

Today, as in our past, the United States is conscious of its religious tradition. Our government has always recognized God publicly. We have already read the statements of Justices of our Supreme Court. Our coins and our public buildings are inscribed with messages declaring our trust in the Creator. The Armed Services, too, include religious instruction in their basic training program. Our President and our legislators ask God's guidance in public addresses and at the opening of Congress.

An American Responsibility

In all these cases, the American people as a whole are represented. When their leaders speak, for example, they are not speaking for themselves alone. They speak in the name of the American people whose faith in God they uphold. The artists who designed our coins are not responsible for the phrase, "In God We Trust," on every coin that is turned out. The American people are.

The American people are essentially a religious people; yet religion is often ignored in the people's schools. The importance of religion is given due recognition in all areas of our national life, except in the schools where our children are being trained to participate as good citizens in that life.

Plainly, it does not make sense. Many of the teachers in our schools—elementary, secondary, and college—are not satisfied with the exclusion of religion. They want to change the situation; but they are powerless to do so. They look to you for help.

Many ways have been suggested for the inclusion of God in education, and probably all of these ways can contribute toward the complete solution of this great problem. We leave it, therefore, to the experts to work out the best method of returning God to His rightful place in American education.

For our part, we offer in this book suggestions for ways of restoring God to the place that should be His. They can and should be included, regardless of what other means are adopted. They are not meant to supplant the other methods but to supplement them.

The basic need is simply the *recognition of God in the very subject matter of the curriculum whenever the facts themselves require that recognition.* In other words, we ask only for complete and honest teaching of all the facts. We believe that this approach will bring God, and religious values, into the curriculum many times and in many ways, because our whole American history and culture are basically religious.

We find that this fundamental approach has been accepted by those groups which have studied the matter. The American Council on Education in its report mentioned above, referring to this "factual study of religion when and where intrinsic to general education," stated (p. 83):

This approach has distinctive merits. It is thoroughly consistent with modern educational theory and practice. It is applicable to any school, college, or university. . . . Its justification lies principally in the requirements of a fundamental general education. Such practice need not supplant planned religious activities, but it will tend to fill a vacuum caused by avoidance of religion.

The American Council on Education has further pointed out (p. 84): "So far as we have been able to discover, no tax-supported school, college or university has yet attacked the central task in any comprehensive fashion, namely, how to deal with the facts and implications of religion intrinsic to all aspects of the curriculum. Until this is successfully accomplished, the problem will remain unsolved."

In this book we attempt to make a small but constructive effort toward the solution of a pressing problem. We are confident that many rank and file Americans would gladly participate, each in his own way, if they realized the important contribution that they, individually and personally, can make.

Important difficulties that baffle even the experts must not be oversimplified. On the other hand, we feel that there are a few minor steps along positive lines which can be taken here and now. However inadequate they are, they may bring about some slight gain.

If this book, therefore, does no more than offer a word of hope and encouragement and present a few practical suggestions that will result in even one step in the right direction, we will rejoice in the thought that we may have rendered at least a small service to God and country.

If Education Is to Be Complete

The teacher sees the problem in its most concrete, day-to-day terms. He knows the primary duty of the schools is to provide our young people with a complete education—mental, moral, and physical. This is impossible when there is no mention at all of religion. If your child were studying history, could he fully grasp the concept of the Holy Roman Empire, or understand the Reformation, or the founding of the modern state of Israel, without some idea of the religions or religious beliefs involved?

A literature class in college, reading Milton's *Paradise Lost*, would surely be confused if the professor deliberately avoided any mention of God.

Education without any reference to religious influences is incomplete education, for it treats only a portion of our history and culture. Many public school officials in this country want to make the education of your child as complete as possible. They wish to supplement, not run counter to, that portion of religious training provided by the home and the church. But they need assurance from you that you want it, too.

UNFAIR TO THE STUDENT

In a recent pronouncement, Justice Robert H. Jackson of the United States Supreme Court (1948) said the following about the question of religion in public education:

. . . it would not seem practical to teach either practice or appreciation of the arts if we are to forbid exposure of youth to any religious influences. Music without sacred music, architecture minus the cathedral, or painting without the scriptural themes would be eccentric and incomplete. . . .

Certainly a course in English literature that omitted the Bible and other powerful uses of our mother tongue for religious ends would be pretty barren. . . .

The fact is that, for good or ill, nearly everything which gives meaning to life, is saturated with religious influences . . .

One can hardly respect a system of education which would leave the student wholly ignorant of the currents of religious thought that move the world society . . . for a part in which he is being prepared.

When a teacher maintains silence about God in class he cannot rightfully claim to be impartial. To say nothing about God is to say God does not matter. If a teacher of history never mentioned the name of George Washington, the students might learn of him from some other source, but they would probably think that George Washington was of only minor importance to them and to their country. The young person who does not hear of God in school may easily assume that God is insignificant. As a rule, whatever the school ignores, the student also ignores. Therefore, it is decidedly unfair to the student to exclude God and religion from education.

WAITING FOR YOU

Most people are waiting for someone else to make the first move. It is your duty to make the move where and when you can. It is the duty of each individual to lend support and assurance to those who are in charge of the American schools.

This book attempts to suggest to you, the American parent, teacher, or citizen, some of the things you can do to include awareness of God in education. With positive effort, you can work toward the well-rounded training that you want for your own child and other American children. Through your efforts, the youth of this country can receive an education based upon American traditions and ideals—an education that is, in all justice, the due of young citizens of "this nation, under God." From the very beginnings of our nation, Americans have for the greater part recognized that all men are children of one God Who is their Father, and are destined to be truly brothers with Christ, His Divine Son.

MANY FACETS

Our educational system is a pluralistic one, comprising three main branches: the public, the private, and the church-sponsored schools. In turn, each of these subdivisions divide into lower, intermediate, and higher grades, from primary classes to university lectures. We recognize that what we have to say in this book does not apply equally to all these divisions and subdivisions of our whole system. To some parts it does not apply at all, to others almost entirely. Each individual reader must decide upon its applicability to the individual case.

The Basic Issue

The outcome of the issue of God in our schools is a grave one. At bottom, the issue is America itself. Unless we adhere to our religious traditions and loyalties, there is little doubt that sooner or later the United States of America will go down the road of those nations which have forsaken God. The future of our precious liberties will be decided in the American classroom.

It is your duty to see that your children receive their full birthright, so that they too may pass on to the next generation those fundamental truths which have made America great in the past, and which alone can ensure its future greatness.

All God's Children

Section One

The general public, as well as educators, is becoming more and more aware of the fact that our classrooms can be a powerful instrument for strengthening or weakening our nation.

In this first section we attempt to touch upon some of the fundamentals essential to an education which will assure a stronger America.

We also cite the Inauguration ceremonies of 1953 as striking a keynote that should be followed in all spheres of American life, especially in our schools.

one

Keep First Things First

ONE EVENING IN NEW YORK, I HAD DINNER WITH a group of fifteen college students. Among them was a young man named Tom,* a senior at a leading Eastern university. He impressed everybody with his clever comments on current topics.

He was doing fine until he began to talk about rights. Then, without realizing it, he made several statements which, to say the least, were out of line with American concepts.

"Tom," I said, "I'm a little confused about your interpretation of the rights of man. Where do you think they originate?"

The young man seemed to grope for words, not quite sure of what he should say.

One of his friends, endeavoring to help him out, said: "Tom, aren't you trying to say that man's rights come from the state?"

"Yeah, that's it!" Tom replied gratefully, "I suppose they do. I don't know where else they would come from."

Another voice from the end of the table broke in: "But that's just what Hitler said—and what the Communists say now."

Tom was embarrassed. To relieve the situation, I asked another question: "Well, Tom, what about the sixty-three mil-

---

*Personal names are used in relating incidents whenever the information has already been made public. In all other instances, full names have been withheld, usually at the request of the individual concerned.

3

lion displaced persons in the world today? They have no country, so what about their rights?"

Quick as a flash Tom brightened up and said: "Well, I guess they haven't any rights."

I was taken aback at this. I asked Tom how he had ever reached that conclusion.

"Well, if you can't exercise your rights, you don't have any rights," Tom replied.

I smiled. "That's a new twist on rights."

Aware of some personal difficulties the young man was having, I saw an opportunity to bring home to him just what I meant.

"Suppose," I said, "you had inherited a million dollars, and it was tied up in an estate for several years. Do you mean to say that because you couldn't exercise your right to that money, that you had lost your right to it completely?"

Tom blurted out: "That's my money!"

I had hit on a sore spot with Tom. For he had been left an inheritance which had been held up for three years pending the settlement of the estate. But he had not the slightest doubt that the money was still his, even if he could not obtain possession of it for years. Seeing the fallacy of his argument, he turned to me and said: "O.K., what's the real story on rights? Where do they come from?"

"Well, Tom," I replied, "the answer is as old as the hills. Every human being gets his basic rights from God. That means the highest and the lowest Americans possess the same rights and they derive these rights from their Creator. That's the essence of democracy as we know it in this country.

"That was the idea on which this nation was founded. The men who settled our country were sufficiently wise and farsighted to put the God-given concept of rights down in black and white in the Declaration of Independence. They made it clear that man gets his rights from his Creator—not from the state. They also made it clear that the state exists to protect and preserve the God-given rights of every individual."

It was evident from the expression on Tom's face that he agreed. He said quietly: "That certainly makes sense to me! But here I am finishing college. How come somebody didn't pound this into my head a long time ago?"

What makes this story remarkable is that a young American like Tom could go all the way through school—from primary grades to his senior year in college—without really understanding the basic fact so well expressed in our Declaration of Independence—that our basic rights come from God, not from the state.

A Strange Situation

Unfortunately, Tom is not an exceptional example. His case is becoming all too common; common enough to make us ask ourselves if we are depriving our youth of their full heritage in our schools.

On the other hand, Tom is typical of most American students. Like him, they gladly accept a true and reasonable position once it is shown to them. Since practically all American citizens have some belief in God, one would naturally expect that all our schools, without exception, would show Him the recognition that is His due. Otherwise America's youth is being cheated or short-changed.

The fact that there has been a serious neglect in giving God His proper place in the field of education is due both to neglect on the part of most of us and to the relentless efforts of a handful who make it their business to eliminate God from all spheres of influence, the classroom in particular.

Education Can Be Good or Bad

Nowadays, when so much attention is given to the training of the young, we have come to look on almost any form of education as a magic cure-all. Because of a deep confidence in the vital role that education can play in their lives, people in general have unconsciously concluded that all education is good, just because it is education.

The sooner we wake up to the fact that education can be good, bad, or indifferent, the sooner we are likely to do all we can to promote the best in education, to see that our classrooms do an orderly, well-balanced job in developing the physical, intellectual, and spiritual side of each young American.

Too often the world has learned that what is labeled a "step forward" in education is really a "step backward." The atheistic regimes have shrewdly used education to fool the people time and time again. They have excelled in turning out men and women who are bodily superior and endowed with powers of physical endurance that put most others to shame. They have erected countless educational institutions that are the last word in modern equipment. Their schools have gleaming scientific laboratories on which no expense has been spared.

But it has been education for death—not for life. It has concentrated on the physical or animal side of man, distorted his intellectual outlook, and removed anything and everything that would remind him that he is a child of God.

Bring Back What They Put Out

Regardless of their labels, the one thing that all totalitarians have in common is their determination to banish God from all spheres of public and private life. They openly admit that the least recognition of Him slows up their objective of reducing man to the level of a puppet of the state. The more they succeed in eliminating any thought of a Higher Power, the easier it is to *depersonalize* and *brutalize* their helpless victims.

The fact that, first, last, and always, the godless banish

from the classroom any teaching which reminds a young person that he is made in the image of Almighty God should be argument enough, even for those who belong to no faith, for restoring to education what the anti-God forces strive so furiously to eliminate.

If you are in a room and the oxygen is used up or otherwise withdrawn, you begin to feel drowsy and languid. If this condition continues you may lose consciousness and eventually die. You don't have to be a scientist to know that the cure for this condition is to restore what is missing—the life-giving oxygen.

Easy to Overlook

The story of a motorist in Minnesota is significant.

One day he drove up to a service station in St. Paul and asked for ten gallons of gas. Three station attendants sprang into action immediately. One wiped the windshield, the second checked the air in the tires, and the third put water in the radiator. When they finished the motorist thanked them and drove off.

A few minutes later the same driver came back, with a puzzled look on his face.

"Did any of you put gasoline in my car?" he asked.

The three attendants consulted, and found to their surprise that no one had pumped the gas. They had been so busy with incidentals that they had all overlooked the one thing needed to make the engine run.

Attention to Fundamentals

In our busy modern world with its many distractions, it is easy for us to become so preoccupied with effects that we forget the First Cause of all.

As America grows in size and complexity there is the

danger that we may lose sight of those fundamentals upon which our country is founded. Similarly, American education could become so preoccupied with incidentals that the essential ideas and values would be forgotten.

To avoid this possibility, it is of greatest importance that we have a fair idea of what the ultimate objective of education really is.

Education in America has rendered a tremendous service. And it can play an even greater role in the decades ahead if it does not miss primary truths by becoming bogged down in secondary objectives. It is so easy to seek attractive effects and at the same time to overlook or to eliminate the very cause of those effects, or to become so involved in techniques that one loses sight of the chief purpose of education. Difficult as it is to keep "first things first," we must do so or pay a heavy penalty for generations to come.

EDUCATION AND LIFE

Education should be a preparation for life. That sounds simple enough but we know that life is not simple. It is very complex. It embraces all our physical, social, intellectual, and spiritual needs. No education is adequate which neglects any of them.

1. If education is to be a true preparation for life, it must take account of man's physical needs. It should prepare him to earn a living so that he can provide for himself and his dependents those necessities and those conveniences and comforts which will enable him to live in reasonable dignity.

2. Education should cultivate the art of social living. Man does not live alone. He must live with others and he must share the responsibilities of social living. He must be taught those tenets of morality which will govern his relationships to God, to his neighbor, and to himself. There must

be impressed upon him the obligation to shoulder conscientiously his share of maintaining public law and order. His duty to vote intelligently and to make his voice heard in public affairs must be clearly made known to him. Only in this way can there be a healthy society.

3. Education must provide for the intellectual needs of man. It is not enough that he be given great stores of information. He must be taught how to use that information. He must be taught how to think, how to relate his knowledge to the world about him. He must become familiar with that which concerned the great minds in the past.

4. Education must nurture and cultivate man's spiritual side. The noblest part of man is his spiritual soul. It marks him off from the rest of the animal kingdom. To ignore the soul is to degrade man. It is not enough to delegate to the home and to the church the cultivation of man's spiritual qualities. The school must play its part, within its competence, in this great work.

Since God is the Beginning and the End of all things, to exclude Him from any area of life, particularly education, would be like leaving the mainspring out of a watch. Our students must be made acquainted in school with the great facts of human life—God, man's nature and destiny, and what the wisdom of the ages teaches us about these facts. There will be difficulties in working out this preparation for life, but these difficulties should not become obstacles. We must aim at educating the *whole man* for the *full life*. This can only be done when all the aspects of man's nature are taken into consideration in his education.

KEEPING THE GOAL IN SIGHT

I shall not forget one occasion on which this lesson was pointed up to me in a striking way. I was on the *Queen Eliza-*

beth, returning from a speaking tour in Europe, when a violent storm arose.

The way in which the captain handled the ship during the stormy weather left a lasting impression on me. His singleness of purpose and direction stood out in an unusual manner.

Not for one moment did this captain forget where he was going and how he would get there. Day and night he was alert to his one objective on the other side of the Atlantic, New York harbor.

During the stormiest part of the trip he remained on the bridge, eating and sleeping only a few feet from the helm. Too much was at stake for him to take the slightest chance.

One night when the lashing storm was at its height, I stood behind an enclosure near the bow of the ship, which was lost at times in the engulfing waves. Watching the huge vessel plunge on despite the battering of the seas, I was forcefully reminded that one should never lose sight of a high purpose when doing his life's work. Particularly in education should this be constantly kept in mind.

THE ROLE OF EDUCATION

True education, then, aims at the full development of each human being so that he may have a happy, peaceful, and meaningful life on earth, while preparing for his eternal destiny. It should aim at turning out citizens of highest character.

On page 11 of Ernest R. Hull's book, *Formation of Character*, there is presented one of the best comments on this matter we have seen. He points out that most citizens expect youth will be intellectually well-informed, clever, conscientious, morally upright, sanely religious, strong and healthy, energetic and enterprising, cultivated in taste and feeling.

But then he warns:

Our boy may become a very Hercules of physical health and strength, and yet a perfect dolt. He may be as clever as the devil—

and yet as wicked. He may be as good as gold and pious as a saint, and yet a flabby helpless creature. He may be the pink of aesthetic refinement and yet a sensual libertine. He may be a perfect genius and yet as fantastic as a goblin. The best qualities in one line may be discounted or even cancelled by some glaring disability in another—the head of gold and the trunk of brass and the legs of iron and the feet of clay—a bundle of disparities rather than a man.

A Man of Principle

There is much that education can do in conjunction with the home and the church to draw out the power that is in a young person. The greatest achievement is to make him a *complete person* whose intellect and will are so well developed that he has both self-reliance and self-control. He has a right to training that will prepare him for a life dominated by principles, not whims. The deeper his values are, the richer his life becomes, and the more he enriches the lives of others.

With God in education it is difficult enough to instill character in young people. Without God it is virtually impossible.

Far more dangerous today than the Communists are those who prepare the way for moral disintegration by excluding God from education. In most instances, these are well-meaning people who little realize the consequences of the ideas they foster. They remove God from the lives of the young and put nothing substantial in His place. They leave the student an incomplete person. There is a vacuum that is often filled with false values. *Those who stand for nothing, easily fall for anything.*

Too frequently the godless man turns out to be confused, frustrated, and floundering—in short, a "lost soul." He goes through life without ever going deep into life. Seldom does he discover the greatness hidden within him. Because his power for good has never been developed, it stagnates within him. Sooner or later, he finds himself leading a dull, monoto-

nous, unfruitful existence when so easily he could have shared
the joy of "having life and having it more abundantly."

PUTTING BACK WHAT WAS ALWAYS THERE

Bringing God back into all American education is not adding
anything new to the life of our nation. It is merely restoring
the recognition of the Creator that characterized American
education from its very beginnings until recent years.

The first teachers in America were the family and the
church. Then came the private religious schools. Next came
the religious schools aided by the state. Finally emerged the
state-supported and state-controlled public schools which
strove to include a proper recognition and respect for both
God and country in their curriculum.

Only in the last quarter of a century has there been a
slow but steady trend towards a form of teaching that is completely secularistic and materialistic.

Yet, in all fairness, it should be stressed that this has not
been the aim of most educators. Horace Mann, considered by
many as the founder of the public school system, said in a
letter to the Reverend Matthew Hale Smith: "Every one who
has availed himself of the means of arriving at the truth on
this point, knows that I am in favor of religious instruction in
our schools to the extremest verge to which it can be carried
without invading those rights of conscience which are established by the laws of God and guaranteed to us by the Constitution of the State." (Quoted in Raymond B. Culver's
*Horace Mann and Religion in the Massachusetts Public
Schools*, p. 297.)

Present-day school authorities have recognized the problem for some time. In the American Council on Education
report of 1953, referred to above, we read (p. 6):

. . . to be silent about religion may be, in effect, to make the public
school an anti-religious factor in the community. Silence creates

the impression in the minds of the young that religion is unimportant and has nothing to contribute to the solution of the perennial and ultimate problems of human life. This negative consequence is all the more striking in a period when society is asking the public school to assume more and more responsibility for dealing with the cultural problems of growth and development. Therefore, it is vitally important that the public school deal with religion.

Thus, the experts agree for the most part that it is not enough for the home and the church to teach religious truths while the school completely ignores them. Such a procedure really indicates a conflict—especially to the mind of the impressionable young person.

THE HIGHEST COURT

In the Zorach decision, 1952, allowing the released-time program in the New York public schools, Supreme Court Justice William O. Douglas wrote:

We are a religious people whose institutions presuppose a Supreme Being. We guarantee the freedom of worship as one chooses. We make room for as wide a variety of beliefs and creeds as the spiritual needs of man make necessary. We sponsor an attitude on the part of government that shows no partiality to any one group and that lets each flourish according to the zeal of its adherents and the appeal of its dogma.

The Justice continued:

When the State encourages religious instruction or cooperates with religious authorities by adjusting the schedule of public events to sectarian needs, it follows the best of our traditions. For it then respects the religious nature of our people and accommodates the public service to their spiritual needs.

To hold that it may not, would be to find in the Constitution

a requirement that the government show a callous indifference to
religious groups. That would be preferring those who believe in no
religion over those who do believe.

ALL FAITHS EXPRESS CONCERN

Representatives of the three major denominations in America
recognized our national tradition in their recent expressions on
the need for religion in education.

Their demand for the recognition of religion was based
both upon American tradition, and upon the present-day problems our country faces. They all emphasized the one paramount thing—religion must be restored to its proper place in
the classroom.

A JEWISH OUTLOOK

First, here is a Jewish view: In the book, *American Education and Religion*, edited by F. Ernest Johnson, Simon
Greenberg wrote "A Jewish Educator's View." He said (p.
56):

The schools cannot be said to be teaching history at all, if they
eliminate completely whole areas of vital human experience. Religion and religious institutions have been determining factors in the
evolution of civilization. To omit a study of them in a course of
history, is to pervert history. The same is true of the relation of the
great religious literary monuments to the history of literature generally. Nor can one honestly dodge the religious issue in the teaching of science and philosophy.

In those matters it is the public school educator rather than
the religious leader who should be the active proponent of the proposal. He should maintain that he perform his task as an educator
whose duty it is to evaluate objectively the forces at work in human
history, without including the factors of religious institutions and
religious literature into his curriculum. It is most unfortunate that
so-called secular educators have not spoken up vigorously in behalf

of the inclusion of the Bible in a course in literature, and of Church history into the courses in history.

THE PROTESTANT POINT OF VIEW

In December, 1952, the National Council of Churches of Christ in the U.S.A. meeting in Denver, Colorado, said:

A way must be found to make the pupils of American schools aware of the heritage of faith upon which this nation was established. . . . On no account must an educational system which is permeated by the philosophy of secularism, something quite different from religious neutrality, be allowed to gain control of our public schools. . . . In some constitutional way provision should be made for the inculcation of the principles of religion . . . within the regular schedule of a pupil's working day.

THE CATHOLIC POSITION

A month before, in November, 1952, the Catholic Bishops of the United States made the following statement at the close of their annual meeting:

To teach moral and spiritual values divorced from religion and based solely on social convention . . . is not enough. Unless man's conscience is enlightened by the knowledge of principles that express God's law, there can be no firm and lasting morality.

Without religion, morality becomes simply a matter of individual taste, of public opinion or majority vote. The moral law must derive its validity and its binding force from the truths of religion.

Without religious education, moral education is impossible. . . . But if religion is important to good citizenship—and that is the burden of our national tradition—then the State must give recognition to its importance in public education. The State therefore has the duty to help parents fulfill their task of religious instruction and training. . . .

The Part You Can Play

You, whoever you are, can strengthen the entire educational system in your country by doing something to restore to every classroom the basic truth upon which our nation is founded.

This undertaking is beset with many delicate problems, of a legal, pedogogical, and religious nature. Because you cannot solve everything you should not be discouraged from "lighting your candle." Every little flame counts in removing the darkness.

There is a minimum that you can insist upon here and now. We are convinced that this minimum must include: (1) the recognition that God and religion permeate our American culture, history, laws, institutions, and traditions; and (2) the transmission of these essentials to every student as a birthright which is due him in strict justice.

Too often we tend to forget that every citizen has a serious obligation in conscience to help pass on intact the heritage of the past to our citizens of tomorrow. It is a heritage, to use the forceful language of President Franklin Pierce (term, 1853–1857), "which we are sacredly bound to transmit undiminished to our children."

two

A Pattern for All

FEW NATIONS IN THE WORLD TODAY COULD WIT-
ness within their boundaries what recently took place in the
United States. Not only was there a peaceful, orderly transfer
of power from one administration to another, but both the
incoming and outgoing Chief Executives, speaking in their
official capacity, humbly professed faith in God. Both President Eisenhower and former President Truman made an explicit declaration of our nation's dependence on God.

From our beginning as a nation our leaders have publicly
acknowledge our dependence on God, the Source of our rights
and our many blessings. Every President from George Washington to Dwight D. Eisenhower made this profession of faith
in his inaugural address. (See Chapter 17.)

A DAY OF DISTINCTION

What distinguished the Inauguration Day of 1953 was the
deep spiritual theme that characterized it from beginning to
end.

As his first act on January 20, 1953, the new President,
accompanied by Mrs. Eisenhower, attended a special morning
service at the National Presbyterian Church in Washington.

A definite historical link with America's tradition of the
acknowledgment of God was to be found in this church. The
Eisenhowers occupied Pew Forty-seven, three pews in front of
the one once occupied by President Benjamin Harrison and

17

three rows behind the pew where other presidents have worshiped.

A SPECIAL PRAYER OF HIS OWN

After church services the Eisenhowers returned to their Washington hotel to prepare for the Inauguration at noon. General Eisenhower excused himself and went into a room alone. In solitude and meditation he wrote what he called "a little private prayer of my own." He prayed:

Almighty God, as we stand here at this moment my future associates in the Executive branch of government join me in beseeching that Thou wilt make full and complete our dedication to the service of the people in this throng, and their fellow citizens everywhere.

Give us, we pray, the power to discern clearly right from wrong, and allow all our words and actions to be governed thereby, and by the laws of this land. Especially we pray that our concern shall be for all the people regardless of station, race, or calling.

May cooperation be permitted and be the mutual aim of those who, under the concepts of our Constitution, hold to differing political faiths; so that all may work for the good of our beloved country and Thy glory. Amen.

At his Inauguration, General Eisenhower changed the usual procedure. Before delivering his Inaugural speech to the people, he addressed his "little private prayer" to Almighty God. Those in the huge crowd bowed their heads in supplication to the Father of all as the President spoke the simple, reverent words. By putting his prayer first and foremost, the President emphasized the dependence on God that is so basic to American life.

ON TWO BIBLES

On a platform built on the East Capitol steps, where the solemn ceremonies were to take place, there were assembled

2,200 special guests, including congressmen, justices of the Supreme Court, diplomats, members of the incoming and outgoing Cabinets, and State governors.

As the audience of more than one hundred thousand looked on, together with the tens of millions following the proceedings over television and radio, the President put his left hand on two open Bibles, raised his right hand, and then slowly, firmly, repeated the words of his oath of office, phrase by phrase, after they were spoken by Fred Vinson, Chief Justice of the Supreme Court of the United States.

One of the two Bibles on which President Eisenhower solemnly swore that he would "faithfully execute the Office of President of the United States" was the same one used by George Washington at the first Inauguration. It was opened at his request to the first verse of the 127th Psalm:

"Except the Lord build the house, they labour in vain that build it; except the Lord keep the city, the watchman waketh but in vain."

The other Bible, President Eisenhower's own, was opened to II Chronicles, 7:14.

"If my people, which are called by my name, shall humble themselves and pray, and seek my face, and turn from their wicked ways, them will I hear from Heaven, and will forgive their sins, and will heal their land."

President Eisenhower's use of our First President's Bible is eloquent testimony to the continuous importance of religion in the official acts of the United States Government—from the days of Washington to the present time.

AMERICA WAS PLEASED

The vast majority of Americans were pleased by this reverent approach of the new President to his high office. It was a public and official expression of a belief which is, and always has been, that of most Americans.

Overseas other peoples and nations were edified, and they expressed their approval. They could not but contrast the religious tone of this inaugural in the United States with the attitude of present-day secularist leaders in Europe. For instance, *Osservatore Romano*, the Vatican newspaper, commended it in a special editorial on January 23, 1953. It termed the President's action "a solemn and humble homage to God." In commending this action by the President, the editorial went on to contrast it with the "advanced Europe of today" where for the head of a state "to raise one's mind to God at the exalted and fateful moments of life, and to do so before a believing people, means to get out of bounds."

ONE WOMAN'S EFFECT

The fine impression made on so many on Inauguration Day was not enough for one high-minded woman in New York City. To make sure that the good effect would last she sent a letter to the *New York World-Telegram and Sun* and signed her name, Adelaide R. Rosenfeld. It was published in that newspaper on January 27, 1953, just a week after the Inauguration. It was an answer to a letter appearing in the same paper from a man who objected to the singing of the fourth stanza of "America" in the public schools. He said it violated the principle of separation of church and state. He was really challenging the unanimous decision of the New York City Board of Education directing all public schools to begin each class day with the singing of the last stanza of "America," an officially approved patriotic hymn.

Educational authorities felt that singing the following few lines each day might help, in a small way at least, to remind all students of the spiritual values needed in their training:

> Our fathers' God, to Thee,
> Author of Liberty,

> To Thee we sing;
> Long may our land be bright
> With freedom's holy light;
> Protect us by Thy might,
> Great God, our King.

Miss Rosenfeld knew there was no church-state issue here. But, fearing many might be misled by the issue raised in the letter to the newspaper, she saw an opportunity to clear up a misconception that has been spread far and wide by some sincere but misguided persons and by the anti-God forces. She decided to go right to the people with facts that would not only disprove, but might help in a positive way to encourage others to do something to restore God to all phases of American public life.

SHE CLEARED THE ISSUE

You may wish to read a portion of her letter:

I have just finished watching the inauguration of Dwight D. Eisenhower as President of the United States. This awe-inspiring ceremony, certainly the embodiment of American tradition beyond any shadow of doubt, and I am sure violating no American principle of separation of church and state, belied Mr. Reice's concept of what our American tradition is, so much more eloquently than anything that I might write, that I beg leave to run briefly through the program:

1. Most Reverend Patrick A. O'Boyle, Roman Catholic Archbishop of Washington, D.C., opened the ceremonies with a prayer.
2. Dorothy Maynor followed with our national anthem including, "Let this be our motto, in God is our trust."
3. Richard Nixon took his oath of office—his hand on the Bible and the oath ending, "So help me God."
4. Eugene Conley gave a stirring rendition of America, the Beautiful, concluding with "America, America, God shed His grace

on thee, and crown thy good with brotherhood from sea to shining sea."

5. Rabbi Abba Silver then offered a prayer. . . .

6. Next, General Eisenhower, placing his hand on two Bibles (the one used by George Washington), took the oath of office as President of the United States. (Not American tradition?) This oath also ended, "So help me God."

7. President Eisenhower then asked leave to preface his inaugural address with a prayer to Almighty God for divine guidance, and at his request all heads were bowed and all silently prayed with him and for him.

8. The Most Reverend Henry Knox Sherrill (Presiding Bishop of the Protestant Episcopal Church) gave the benediction.

Eight events on the program and every single one bore testimony that the American doctrine of separation of church and state is not synonymous with a doctrine of separation of state and religion. The former is our American tradition. The latter, a rather recent concept held by a small but very articulate minority, has never been a part of our American way.

It Couldn't Be Plainer

Just four weeks before the Inauguration of President Eisenhower, Harry S. Truman, the outgoing President, gave his last Christmas Message. Again, it was an open profession of our nation's faith in God and in the Prince of Peace. Mr. Truman said:

As we go about our business of trying to achieve peace in the world, let us remember always to try to act and live in the spirit of the Prince of Peace. He bore in His Heart no hate and no malice —nothing but love for all mankind. We should try as nearly as we can to follow His example.

We seek only a universal peace, where all nations shall be free and all peoples shall enjoy their inalienable human rights. We believe that all men are truly the children of God.

As we worship at this Christmastide, let us worship in this spirit. As we pray for our loved ones far from home—as we pray for our men and women in Korea, and all our servicemen and women wherever they are—let us also pray for our enemies. Let us pray that the spirit of God shall enter their lives and prevail in their lands. Let us pray for a fulfillment of the brotherhood of man.

Through Jesus Christ the world will yet be a better and a fairer place. This faith sustains us today as it has sustained mankind for centuries past. . . .

At Our Peril

Just a few weeks previous to this Mr. Truman had stressed the dependence of our democracy on a religious concept when he spoke at the laying of the cornerstone of the Westminster Presbyterian Church in Alexandria, Virginia, just across the Potomac River from the Capitol.

Two portions of his remarks deserve the attention and the thoughtful reflection of all Americans, and especially of students, in expanding and fortifying their understanding of the essence of democracy.

"Democracy is first and foremost a spiritual force," the then President frankly stated. "It is built on a spiritual basis— on a belief in God and an observance of moral principles. And in the long run only the Church can provide that basis. Our founders knew this truth, and we will neglect it at our peril."

A little later in this same address, Mr. Truman was even more specific when he said: "The only hope of mankind for enduring peace lies in the realm of the spiritual. The teachings of the Christian faith recognize the worth of every human being before Almighty God. The teachings of the Christian faith are a sure defense against the godlessness and brutality of ideologies that deny the value of the individual."

What Does It Mean?

Two lessons emerge from this which are of major importance to our schools today.

First, Inauguration Day, 1953, was nothing extraordinary
or new. It was simply the most recent of a long series of mani-
festations of the American spirit which comes down to us
from our Founding Fathers, from our Declaration of Independence, and even further back.

Second, it is of greatest importance that these facts both
present and past be included in our teaching.

*If the President of the United States can officially recog-
nize God in his Inauguration ceremony or at any public function in which he speaks as the highest representative of our
government, certainly every teacher is entirely within his or
her rights in voicing religious sentiments in school.*

Our democracy is bound to grow weak and disappear if
its spiritual foundation is neglected or eliminated. To guard
against this danger, every American should see to it that our
spiritual roots are protected and nourished. Most teachers, administrators, and boards of education would like to see recognition of God emphasized in our schools with the same clarity
with which it has been voiced by our Presidents. They look to
you for help to make this recognition a reality.

Section Two

In the United States, the strengthening of our schools is everybody's business. The objective of all education, of course, is the student. The primary responsibility rests with the parent. But it is the teacher that makes the school.

Nevertheless, our school system also belongs to every American. Both as a voter and a taxpayer, he has a vital stake in seeing that the schools fulfill their great trust.

In the following section it is our aim to point out the part that all must play, if our schools are to meet the task before them.

three

Every American Has a Part to Play

NO MATTER WHAT YOUR POSITION IN LIFE MAY BE, you can say or do something that no one else can to strengthen your schools. There is no substitute for you.

When movie actress Loretta Young was invited to speak to five thousand teachers at the Shrine Auditorium in Los Angeles in March, 1952, she hesitated to accept because she could speak neither with authority nor from experience. One of her close friends reminded her that she could still render a real service by sharing her own convictions with the teachers.

Miss Young not only accepted but paid such an eloquent tribute to the power of a teacher that she was soon besieged by educational groups in many parts of the country to come to them and make a similar talk.

Miss Young spoke frankly and sincerely. In the closing portion of her talk, stressing the tremendous influence exerted by the teacher in determining the future of all of us, she said:

As you teach today, our children will think and act tomorrow. What a power! What a magnificent opportunity!

As I rejoice to think of what one good teacher can do—I shudder to think of the endless harm that can be done by a bad one. I have seen the result in Nazi Germany and Communist Russia. I can measure what would happen in an escapist America. . . .

All the world loves a lover. I'm no exception. I'm very happy to be here tonight because I stand in the midst of the greatest lovers in the world—those men and women who love God and country so much they have turned their backs on the obvious

27

material advantages of other careers in order to help mold our vulnerable youth of America into the kind of citizens every mother and father would hope for.

For in these future citizens lie the blessings—or the scourge—of our future.

So I beg of you—as a mother—teach them well—teach them the love of God—the love of country—and the love of their fellow men.

Teach them—the truth!

A ROLE FOR YOU

You will find that most school authorities and teachers welcome the thoughtful and constructive interest of the public. You may know of several instances of this appreciation. Here is the statement of the Superintendent of Schools of New York City, William Jansen, issued in anticipation of "Open School Week" of 1953:

"The teachers and principals join me in inviting your inspection and examination of our stewardship. We believe that we are doing well, and we could like you to be the judges. We want to do even better. You can help by showing us that you are interested."

In his open letter, Dr. Jansen urged everyone to manifest an active concern in education, because, as he put it:

"The lifeblood of a democracy surges strongest when citizens are active and interested in community affairs."

Any time and effort that you as a citizen spend in making sure that the truth—and nothing but the truth—is taught in your schools, will be a sound investment for the years ahead. The future of our nation—and of the world itself—depends to no small degree on what is taught in your schools.

As enrollments increase in schools on all levels, the job of staffing classrooms becomes a larger and more important task. At the present time there are 36 million young people

in the classrooms of America, with approximately 2 million
more being added each year.

The erection of buildings to handle this enormous expansion is a tremendous problem in itself. But as we have
stated many times, far greater consideration should be given
to the persons who teach in these buildings and to what they
teach.

Where Are Our Teachers?

About two years ago I was invited to speak on the Christopher movement to a group of a hundred business executives in
Chicago. During the discussion period that followed the talk,
one man rose and stated that he was greatly impressed by the
constructive, affirmative Christopher approach to the crisis of
our day—"doing something about it" instead of merely complaining. He then asked for a specific suggestion showing how
a businessman could do something to benefit the educational
field.

Fortunately, I was able to make a concrete proposal. That
very morning I had seen a brief item on the front page of the
Chicago Tribune stating that four thousand teachers were
needed in the public schools of Illinois. I pointed out that
this shortage was largely due to the failure of the average
good citizen to concern himself with getting the best type of
person to teach in the schools of his community; and that this
indifference left the way open for the "next best" to move in.

Many of us unconsciously take a "let George do it" attitude. We think that all we have to do is sit on the sidelines
and wait for someone else to serve up good education, good
government, good television, and good everything else. We
don't pay much attention until things go wrong. Even then
we habitually do little more than scream: "Why don't *they* do
something about this?"

Too seldom does it even occur to us to turn the searchlight

on ourselves and say: "Why don't *I* do something about it myself?"

Still worse is the almost disdainful attitude that many otherwise good people take towards those who muster enough courage to forsake the attractions of a more gainful career and dedicate themselves to the public good by embracing a teaching career.

He Discouraged His Own Son

It occurred to me that it would be well to tell these hundred businessmen of a specific instance in which one splendid prospect for college teaching was stopped cold by his own father, who happens to be the head of a business corporation.

Jack was a boy of high ideals. Upon completing his junior year at a well-known university, he had almost decided to become a college teacher. Two factors had considerable influence upon his decision. One was his father's continual criticism of the type of teaching in colleges today. The other was the repeated emphasis made in Christopher literature that no field can be any better than the people in it, and that the best way to strengthen education is to increase the number of good teachers in that important sphere of influence.

After considerable reflection, Jack decided that he, personally and individually, might be able to improve the situation by becoming a teacher himself. It had taken prolonged wrestling with himself to bring him to the point where he was ready to pass up the lucrative business position that could be his upon graduation. But his unusual sense of purpose helped him over that hurdle. Finally he decided to talk the matter over with his mother and father before going ahead with any definite plans. He felt sure they would be elated and that their encouragement would bolster him in overcoming any minor obstacles which might remain.

Knowing his father's critical attitude towards modern

education, Jack was positive he would be glad to hear of his decision. And so, one night at dinner, he said: "Dad, I have some news for you and Mom. I've decided to become a college teacher."

WHAT COLD WATER CAN DO

He got no further. His father almost had a stroke. Dropping his knife and fork, he turned to his wife and exploded: "Did you ever hear of a sillier idea than that? A son of ours wanting to waste his life teaching!"

Taken aback by this attitude on the part of his father, Jack was deeply hurt, as well as confused. He determined to put off until later his decision to become a teacher.

Over two years have passed since then. A year after graduation, we find Jack working with his father's corporation. He is making a lot of money. But his heart is not in his job. He has the makings of an ideal teacher who could accomplish much good.

He may still summon enough courage to "leave all things" and devote himself to the teaching career in which men and women of his type are so badly needed. But the chances are that, having been sidetracked this long because of the bitter opposition of his own father, Jack will gradually become so absorbed in immediate preoccupations that he will forget his original desire.

Little does Jack's father realize that instead of lighting one candle, he has blown one out—and he probably still continues "cursing the darkness" to which he has added.

A CHANGE FOR THE BETTER

It had taken about five minutes to give this somewhat lengthy answer to the businessman's simple request. In concluding my talk, I suggested that each of those present make it his business to encourage at least one person to undertake a career in the teaching field, in addition to showing a constructive and continuing interest in all phases of education.

Immediately the gentleman who had asked the question got to his feet, and turning to his associates said: "This makes sense to me. Frankly I've never encouraged one person to become a teacher. I'd never make a teacher myself, and have no one in my family who would. But that doesn't prevent me from doing something personally.

"As soon as I get back to my plant, I am going to write an open letter to everyone on our payroll from top to bottom. First of all, I shall state quite candidly that I have been unintionally neglectful. But I'll add that I am convinced that each and all can do something to relieve the shortage of four thousand teachers right here in our own state. More than that, we can all show a personal responsibility in promoting the proper respect and support for the dedicated men and women who devote themselves to this most important task of shaping the lives of our own children."

It is typical of most Americans that once they are reminded of their responsibility in conscience toward public affairs, they begin to move in the right direction. But much remains to be done to convince persons in all walks of life that their personal and individual interest is a determining factor in whether the American school system will be good, bad, or mediocre.

One Housewife and Eighteen Public Schools

In February, 1950, a housewife in Stamford, Connecticut, all on her own, decided that if we Americans put "In God We Trust" on our coins, the least we can do is put it in our schools, too.

She felt so strongly about it that she was determined to do something single-handed if nobody else pitched in. As things turned out, that was just what she had to do. For a year and a half—and practically alone—she battled against discouraging odds.

Today, thanks to the perseverance of this one woman, all eighteen public schools in Stamford display in a prominent place a bronze plaque with the words, "In God We Trust" inscribed on it.

This amazing achievement is another striking instance of what one person can do when fired with a strong sense of purpose.

This zealous housewife, Mrs. William H. Cleary, had been thinking of the idea ever since she had heard a talk on the Christopher movement. The speaker had emphasized the power for good that God has put in even the least of His children. Mrs. Cleary came away resolved to do what she could to restore recognition of God to public life.

Her first move was to visit the principal of the new three-million-dollar Junior High School which had just opened in Stamford. He received her cordially, and personally showed her through the elaborately equipped school. When he told her of the increasing problems with young people, she suggested that it might help to develop a sense of responsibility among them if there was a more open recognition of God.

Others told her: "You're crazy—why bother? What good will it do?" A public official assured her it was "a hot potato" and that she "wouldn't get far with it."

These comments didn't stop Mrs. Cleary. A Protestant minister told her she was on the right track. A Catholic priest called it a wonderful step in the right direction. A Jewish rabbi expressed complete sympathy.

During the following twelve months, Mrs. Cleary carried the campaign to thousands of citizens, to groups and individuals. But, in all that time, she received only one letter containing a specific offer of help.

Mrs. Cleary was tempted to be discouraged, but her own children spurred her on.

"Just as I began to wonder if I had taken on too much and was sorely tempted to give up," she said, "the Lord sent me fresh courage from an unexpected source. I overheard my eight-year-old daughter praying one night that 'Mommy's plaques get in the schools so boys and girls who never knew God will at least know there is one.'

"And then my little boy of five came to me and asked, 'Mommy, why don't you buy those signs for God and put them in the school?' Without the understanding and encouragement of my children, and my husband, I might have given up."

Sparked with a renewed sense of purpose, she decided to present her plan to the Board of Representatives—the legislative body of the city.

She found that these lawmakers already knew something of the proposal. The groundwork that she had laid among the people had not been in vain. On December 4, Mrs. Cleary was granted a hearing.

She said:

"When I got the floor, I gave all the arguments I could think of for putting the inscription, 'In God We Trust,' in our schools. A discussion followed, but before long a motion was made and passed unanimously. This was a wonderful step forward, but it did not necessarily mean that the inscription would get into the schools."

The recommendation also had to have the approval of the Board of Education. After a month of deliberation, this group approved the project, with the proviso that the plaques be made of bronze.

"The annoying part of this," said Mrs. Cleary, "was that bronze was to be 'frozen' within the next week. Couldn't it be in wood or cement or any of the other 'easy-to-get' materials? As far as I was concerned, they could make the plaque of cardboard as long as they put the word God on it."

Four more months of complete inaction passed. But then

a seed she had planted in a talk before the Appropriations Board suddenly bore fruit. A member of this Board publicly denounced the delaying tactics. He declared that until the directive calling for the plaques was carried out, he—for one— would approve nothing further for the Board of Education.

That did it! Within a matter of days the plaques bearing the words "In God We Trust" were ordered—in bronze. In the summer of 1951, they were installed in all eighteen public schools in Stamford.

At the dedication ceremony of the plaque in one of the schools, a student, Briscoe Smith, speaking for his fellow students, said in his public address: "It is an honor to have this plaque in our building."

Then turning to Mrs. Cleary he continued: "We wish to express our gratitude to you for your work which led to its installation in our school."

It seems safe to say that the majority of students want "In God We Trust" in their schools.

Because she deeply believed in the full implication of the great American motto, "In God We Trust," the lofty objective of one housewife became a reality. The accomplishment of this one woman in Stamford, small in one sense, may have far-reaching results.

If one woman could put "In God We Trust" in eighteen schools, think of the possibilities if a hundred thousand other Americans would each work as hard as she to bring some recognition of God into the schools of their locality.

ENCOURAGE, DON'T DISCOURAGE

Whoever you are—a taxi driver, scientist, housewife, fireman, banker, waiter, editor, typist, clerk, or professional worker there is something you can do. Our teachers need your encouragement. They ask for no favors no "special handling," but they don't want to be overlooked or belittled.

Never forget, the better the teachers do their job, the better for you and everybody else.

A passing word of encouragement may have far-reaching effects. We see repeated instances of this. In our Christopher television programs, presented once a week on over one hundred stations over the country, we frequently touch on the important role played by the teacher. Here are just two of thousands of reactions that have reached us:

A teacher in Milwaukee sent this brief comment on a postcard: "Saw your TV program last night. I was about to resign my job as teacher next Friday. After hearing the Christopher message, I have changed my mind. I feel I ought to continue 'taking it,' rough as it gets at times."

From Brentwood, Tennessee, came this message: "After seeing the Christopher television program, I feel compelled to write and tell you how it has given our whole family new strength and courage to do our part as Christ-bearers. One result is that I have decided to go into the teaching field."

Something to Be Guarded

One thing that you can do to guard our heritage is to help keep education under local control. There are many advantages to be gained by centralizing certain features of education, but there are great dangers, too. By relegating or abandoning authority to those who are far removed from the locality, the average citizen may deprive himself of having any voice at all in educational policy. In totalitarian states, control of schools is quickly and completely centralized in one supreme authority which has little regard for the individual rights of parents, teachers, students, or other citizens.

The Schools Are Yours

Every American citizen has a stake in every American school. Whether he has any direct connection with a school or not, he has a particular responsibility to the schools that are supported by public funds. As a taxpayer, small or large, he is a stockholder in the public educational system of the United States and has an obligation to see that the best possible teaching is provided for the young people who are being trained in our schools.

You are a part owner of the American school system. If you and enough good citizens like you make it your business to see that every student is taught all he has a right to know, you will do a great service. You may be the means of saving the educational system of our country from lapsing into the plight of schools elsewhere in the world where the freedom of God has been banished and replaced by the rigid enslavement of mind as well as body.

Regardless of your age or walk of life you can do something to make sure that your schools are staffed by Americans who are motivated by a love of God and country.

Not long ago in San Diego a retired admiral of the United States Navy did something very personal about it. He started a new career for himself—as a grade-school teacher.

"I'm fifty-four now," Rear Admiral Elliott M. Senn told an Associated Press reporter. "I figure I should be good for ten or twelve years more, at least, as a schoolteacher."

The admiral's pupils will get firsthand reports of some historic events. Senn was captain of the heavy cruiser *Quincy* when it fired the first shot in the preinvasion bombardment of the Normandy coast in World War II.

His cruiser took President Roosevelt to the fateful Yalta conference in 1945. As captain, he was host to such other notables as Winston Churchill, Emperor Haile Selassie of Ethiopia, and a score of top Allied commanders and diplomats.

Senn retired from the Navy three years ago. He attended San Diego State College for two years and "was astonished at how much I didn't know."

The idea of teaching school had come before his retirement, when he was commandant of the Treasure Island Training Center in San Francisco Bay.

"We had ten thousand sailors there, taking instruction of various kinds," he recalled. "They wore uniforms, but they were really just schoolboys. I began to realize I was a sort of a schoolmaster.

"At first it surprised me, but I got to thinking how important it was that they should have good teaching."

There is a large number of men and women in America with many useful years still ahead of them who could well be used to strengthen education. Most of those interested devote their energies almost entirely to fund raising and to the material needs of their local schools or alma mater. This support is important. But far more significant is what is to be taught within the school buildings. If more citizens paid attention to that, they would render a big service that would pay rich dividends for all.

Some people feel, because they have no children of their own in a school, they have no right to make suggestions. This is a mistake. As a citizen and taxpayer—or as a donor to a private school—you have a stake in this project, and therefore you have not only a right but a responsibility to make your voice heard.

OUR EDUCATIONAL SYSTEM

To see just how much education is a local affair in the United States it would be well for us to look briefly at our system as a whole.

There is no national control of education. In fact, our Constitution does not touch on education at all, the intent being to leave the entire matter to the states and localities.

There is, for example, no national education board. We have a *United States Office of Education* (Department of

Health, Education and Security) with a commissioner appointed by the President, but its function is limited to research and service. There are *state and county boards*. But even these are not always governing bodies, since they are often limited to an advisory or co-ordinating capacity.

Our American educational system as such really begins at the *local level*. And here it divides into its main parts.

The first major division is between *public and private* schools. The private schools are made up of those endowed by private groups or institutions and those supported by the churches.

In *public education* we must distinguish between local public-school systems on the one hand, and state colleges and universities on the other. Local systems include elementary and high schools, as well as two-year junior colleges. These systems provide universal free education for every boy and girl in America, regardless of creed or economic status.

The public school system is usually built on a city-wide basis, or on the basis of some identifiable community that is not a city, such as the county or the town.

The most important element in the *local system*, not to mention the teachers and students themselves, is the *board of education*, often called the school committee, the board of school trustees, and the like.

The school board is a governing board of lay citizens. The control and management of our schools resides in these boards. The interesting thing here is that these local governors are not professional educators. They are elected respresentatives of the people of their community, who in most instances receive no financial remuneration for their service. In some places they are elected directly by the people, in others they are appointed by the mayor or by a duly elected official. There are seventy thousand of these school boards in the United States.

In this way, our school system is the closest thing to *home rule* that exists in the country. The board of education is a sort of teacher-trustee team, by means of which our schools remain not only in contact with the people, but responsible and responsive to the will of the community.

This feature of our system is not sufficiently understood and appreciated. Too many citizens believe that they have nothing to do with the schools, and that the schools have nothing to do with them, unless they are parents and have children in school. They have to realize that the schools are *their* schools, not only as taxpayers, but also as governors of them—through their chosen representatives.

Our legislatures and our school departments are recognizing this more and more. The general trend is to make the school boards fiscally independent, on the grounds that public education is, as one expert, Edward M. Tuttle, put it, "a continuous, constructive, nonpartisan service to all the people in which they should have a direct voice not complicated by any other consideration than the greatest possible good to children and youth."

Ten Steps to Better Schools

Since the public is nothing more than you multiplied over and over again, it follows that you are important, that you count very much in determining how effectively the school system in your community is training the coming generation. Here are some specific steps within your reach which can help you strengthen your schools:

1. Acquaint yourself with problems of the schools in your locality. You cannot act intelligently unless you know the facts.

2. Do all in your power to assist teachers by:

a. Doing what you can to see that they are provided with adequate salaries which will assure them of the decent living you would expect if you were in their position.

    b.   Helping to make economic and social conditions as pleasant as possible for every teacher.

    c.   Doing your bit to increase respect for teachers all the way from kindergarten to university.

    3.   Make yourself a committee of one to interest competent young persons with a Christlike purpose in a teaching career.

    4.   Be sure to vote in local school board elections. Before casting your vote, satisfy yourself beyond any question of a doubt that your candidate is an upright person with experience and ability.

    5.   Focus attention on the good aspects of your school system and encourage these. It is far better to do something positive, no matter how little, than to confine yourself to criticizing.

    6.   As a citizen, you have rights which must be respected. But remember, too, that you have responsibilities which should be discharged.

    7.   If you cannot become an active member of your local school board, encourage other God-respecting citizens to do so.

    8.   Notify others when important educational matters are being considered. You can do this by a telephone call, by contacts at your office, in your shop, at luncheons, while doing your marketing, and so on.

    9.   Encourage good performance by public recognition of it. You can write to your paper expressing approval of a good job, or propose a resolution at one of your local organization meetings commending those who are doing good work in education.

    10.   Show the courage of your convictions. Do whatever you can to bring about the proper recognition of God in your schools.

four

The Parent Comes First

A BUSINESSMAN IN HOUSTON, TEXAS, SENT HIS daughter to a college in New England. After six months he wrote to her dean asking for information on what she was studying.

The reply astonished our friend. The dean indicated rather stiffly that the college was not accustomed to having parents question the institution's ability to decide what was best for its students. The dean's letter conveyed disappointment that this parent should challenge the college program.

The Texan was astonished, first of all, that the majority of parents showed so little interest in the academic work of their sons and daughters. Still, he could see no reason why he should fail in his own duty as a parent. He wrote another note saying:

"Sorry that you misunderstand my inquiry. Nothing in it was critical. It was merely a request for information that I am entitled to as a parent."

Then, to make his attitude clear to the college authorities, he continued:

"I rely on you to provide training for my daughter that I cannot give her myself. But that does not mean that I can throw the whole load upon you. It's still my responsibility to see that, as far as possible, she gets the schooling I feel she should have.

"I know what kind of a room she has, what she eats, what the classrooms look like, and the kind of tennis racket she uses. But I still don't know what's going into her head. I'm her Pop . . . and it's my job to know."

This father was right. Parents hold the first rights in the education of their children, and furthermore, they are the child's first teachers. Their rights as teachers are established not only by natural law, but by American law and traditions as well.

The First Teacher

Long before school or state came into existence, the individual family was the agency which educated children. From his parents the growing child gets his concepts of right and wrong. He learns the difference between danger and safety as a toddler. His first knowledge of words, objects, and thoughts comes from his father and mother.

Educators are quite correct when they maintain that the school cannot educate the whole child without assistance from the home. Our professional educational authorities are on sound ground when they say that the school should supplement and expand the primary training which the home gives the child.

Before a child goes to school there are certain aspects of training which should be taught at home. For example, parents should teach the necessity of religious faith, prayer, and churchgoing; the difference between right and wrong; obedience to authority; and good manners.

How can our schools function properly unless children come to school with a fairly good background of morals, obedience, and good manners? What teacher can handle a class in which one child believes it wrong to steal; another says it is right to steal; and a third says: "It's all right if you get away with it." Lack of home training in these essentials is responsible for many so-called "problem children" in school. In most cases their "problem" is rebellion against a home which shows neither understanding nor sympathy for them.

The home is duty bound to provide the teacher with a student who has been fortified with the essential foundation and preparation that parents alone can supply.

THE SCHOOL AN EXTENSION OF THE HOME

All parents have a serious obligation to give their children the best education they can in fundamentals. Then parents exercise their right to choose the kind of education they want for their children. And thirdly, parents are obligated to maintain an interest in what the child learns after he enters school.

One day recently I happened to be talking with a high-school teacher about some of her problems in dealing with difficult pupils. She told me one instance which opened my eyes still wider to the clear need for complete co-operation between home and school, parent and teacher.

Jane had become unmanageable in class. Her indifference to study made it necessary for the school to summon her mother.

When the mother came to school, the teacher told her about the difficult time the school was having with her daughter. The mother could not understand why her daughter was causing trouble.

"She doesn't go out nights," the mother said. "It is true that I don't see her very much since I work all afternoon and evening, but she's always there when I phone her every night at ten o'clock."

The mother's statement brought the interview to a speedy end. The teacher saw how useless further discussion would be and decided that she would have to manage Jane by herself. It was a case where the good influence of the parent on the child was almost completely absent.

This mother no doubt had satisfied herself that she was

"doing right" by her child in working and keeping Jane at school. What she failed to see was that the parental influence on her daughter was just as essential to the child's education as her formal schooling.

Expecting too much of the school is a mistake made by some parents. A prominent businessman, for instance, who was enrolling his son in a well-known university, shook his head dubiously when he began to examine the institution's catalogue of studies. "Does my son have to take all these courses?" he asked the dean. "Can't you make it shorter? He wants to get out quickly."

"Certainly he can take a shorter course," replied the dean. "But it all depends on what he wants to make of himself. When God wants to make an oak He takes twenty years, but He takes only two months to make a squash."

HOME AND SCHOOL ARE PARTNERS

On the other hand, the school should not assume that parental rights disappear as soon as a child reaches school age. The ideal that both home and school should strive for is a happy medium: a harmonious working relationship between home and school to advance the child.

To assume that control over a child passes from home to state at school age is dangerous; recent experiences in totalitarian countries show us the pitfalls in such an assumption.

While the great majority of teachers welcome the interest and co-operation of parents, some few do not. This latter group seems to believe that teaching is so highly specialized a field that only professional educators are competent to make judgments.

These few forget that ultimately all the aims of education rest on primary principles in which parents are as competent to teach as the school. It is in pedagogy or teaching techniques that the parent must yield to the educator.

DISAGREEMENT ON ESSENTIALS

Because there is such close connection between home and school, it is harmful to the child if there is a radical difference between what is taught in one and in the other. Just as there would be confusion if a child came to school having been taught that $2 + 2 = 5$, that all men are thieves, or that arson is not a crime, so also there is conflict in the child's mind if he is taught the importance of God and religion at home and finds either a belittling or an ignoring of Him throughout his years of schooling. Unconsciously at least, the child wonders at the hostility or omission and is liable to end up suspecting that the parents are wrong—that religion is not too important.

The famed British educator, Sir Walter Moberly, has pointed up this danger in his book, *The Crisis in the University* (p. 56):

It is a fallacy to suppose that by omitting a subject you teach nothing about it. On the contrary, you teach that it is to be omitted, and that it is therefore a matter of secondary importance. And you teach this not openly and explicitly, which would invite criticism; you simply take it for granted and thereby insinuate it silently, insidiously, and all but irresistibly.

PARENT VERSUS STATE IN EDUCATION

In the past, efforts have been made from time to time to deprive parents of their God-given right to educate their children as they see fit.

In our day, as government increases in size and as many phases of life become more complex, the danger of the state encroaching on the rights of the individual is bound to increase. It seems highly important, therefore, that not only parents, but educators, trustees, students, and citizens in general be reminded of the basic rights of the parent as clearly defined in many court decisions.

Perhaps the best known of those was made as a result of an attempt by the State of Oregon to close all private schools and require parents to send their children to public schools. This case is called the *Oregon Case;* or the *Pierce Case,* after Oregon's governor at the time.

The story began in November, 1922. Oregon voters had approved a bill to change the compulsory school attendance law into a compulsory *public*-school attendance law. Under the change each child from eight to sixteen would be compelled to enter the public schools of the State of Oregon before September, 1926.

Because this change departed radically from both the United States' and Oregon's traditional position on education, and the position of every other state in the Union, the new law was challenged in the United States District Court. The lower court issued an injunction against the Governor, the Attorney General, and the District Attorney of Multnomah County, forbidding them to put the new law into operation.

The State of Oregon then appealed the lower court decision through the appellate court and up to the United States Supreme Court. The case was argued on March 16 and 17, 1925. On June 1, 1925, came the historic decision.

The nine-member Supreme Court decided unanimously against the State of Oregon. The country's highest tribunal held that the new school law was unconstitutional in requiring compulsory attendance at public schools. The court viewed this requirement as an illegal invasion of the rights of parents to educate their children as they saw fit.

Fundamental Rights Affirmed

The Supreme Court's opinion provides a timely reminder of the rights and duties of parents in educating their children. The opinion reads in part:

The Act of 1922 unreasonably interferes with the liberty of parents and guardians to direct the upbringing and education of the children under their control . . . The fundamental theory of liberty upon which all government in this Union reposes excludes any general power of the state to standardize the children by forcing them to accept instruction by public teachers only.

The child is not the mere creature of the state; those who nurture him and direct his destiny have the right, coupled with the high duty to recognize and prepare him for additional obligations.

In other decisions, notably in the *Meyer vs. Nebraska* case, the Supreme Court upheld the wishes of parents in educating their children. The rights of parents over their children's education are grounded in the Declaration of Independence and in the United States Constitution. They are among the "unalienable rights" guaranteed to every American. The Constitution protects them against interference by either the Federal Government or any state government.

THE STATE CANNOT INTERFERE

In numerous other cases our courts have held with the parents and against the state in educational disputes. In the case of *Prince vs. Massachusetts* in 1944 the Supreme Court held:

It is cardinal with us that the custody, care and nurture of the child reside first in the parents, whose primary function and freedom include preparation for obligations the state can neither supply nor hinder.

In the *Levison* case in Illinois, the State Supreme Court again upheld parental rights against a threatened invasion by the state. The Levisons withdrew their son from school in the belief that they could educate him better at home. They maintained that "the atmosphere of the home cannot be obtained in the public school" and held that competition in school would produce a "pugnacious character" in the child. The father was a minister in the Seventh Day Adventist Church. The mother had had two years of college with some training in education.

When they began their home teaching, they were charged in Greene County Court with violating the Illinois compulsory school law.

In the Supreme Court of Illinois, the parents were upheld. The state statute which required parents to send children to a public, or outside private school, was held unconstitutional. This decision found that a "private school" can be understood as a school set up at home, providing parents could teach well enough to meet the requirements of the state.

THE PRIMARY RIGHT

In one of the strongest court decisions ever written in an educational case, Justice McReynolds upheld parental authority in vigorous language. In his opinion in the case of *Commonwealth vs. Armstrong* (Supreme Court of Pennsylvania) he wrote:

The authority of the father results from his duties. He is charged with the duties of maintaining education. These cannot be performed without the authority to command and to enforce obedience.

The term education is not limited to the ordinary instruction of the child in pursuit of literature. It comprehends a proper attention to the religious and moral sentiments of the child.

In discharging this duty it is the undoubted right of the father to designate such teachers either in morals, religion, or literature, as he shall deem calculated to give correct instruction to the child.

No teacher, either in religion or in any branch of education has any authority over the child except what he derives from the parent or guardian and that authority may be withdrawn whenever the parent, in exercise of his disciplinary power, may think proper.

THE ROLE OF THE STATE

While the state under our system has a definite and proper interest in education, the state's authority is not only secondary to that of parents, but also to that of the locality. We have no national educational system. Our Constitution leaves it to states and their political subdivisions to maintain educational systems.

The state's interest in education rests upon the need in a democracy of a literate, well-informed electorate. Democracy can neither thrive nor survive in ignorance. The State Constitution of Texas puts it this way:

A general diffusion of knowledge being essential to the preservation of the rights and liberties of the people, it shall be the duty of the Legislature of this state to make suitable provision for the support and maintenance of public schools.

The role of the state is chiefly that of a supervisory agency. Each state government makes provision for general free education according to the will of parents residing within the state boundaries, as expressed in the school boards, and other agencies on the local level.

HOW IT HAPPENS

Recent reports show how the Red China government is turning children against their parents. In primary schools the Communist motto learned by all children is: "I have no father, I have no mother, I have only the state."

Chinese parents were stoutly resisting this attempt at encroachment on their rights over their children, but they had little redress against the all-powerful state.

From Red China comes another disturbing account concerning Dr. Hu Shih, former Chinese Ambassador to the United States and an international leader in education. He is here in the States as an exile from his native China; his son is living in Peking under Communist control. Once the son loved his father dearly, and said: "I felt deeply insulted when my father was criticized."

Now, after only a few years, the son expresses his attitude toward his distinguished father by saying: "Until my father returns to the people's arms, he will always remain a public enemy of the people, and an enemy of myself. Today, in my determination to rebel against my own class, I feel it important to draw a line of demarcation between my father and myself. . . ."

Join Your Local P.T.A.

Your local Parent-Teacher Association is the one community organization which can draw teachers and parents together to the greatest benefit of the student.

The P.T.A. organization is there. It may be used for good purposes, or for bad. How it is used depends upon you and thousands like you. You cannot influence education for your children unless your voice is heard. It is important for those directly concerned to join their local Parent-Teachers group, attend meetings, and state their views. School authorities generally heed the voice of the P.T.A. before policies are set, or courses are prescribed.

A teacher in Alabama writes:

From personal experience I can vouch for the fact that Parent-Teachers Association meetings present splendid opportunities for speaking to public school teachers about religious concepts of education. Far from resenting the parents' attempts to align education with God, most teachers welcome this cooperation and assurance.

FIRST THINGS FIRST

If it is important that parents join the P.T.A., it is equally important that after joining they (both fathers and mothers) press for the right things. The material and cultural welfare of our schools is important, but the spiritual welfare is even more important. Any P.T.A. which ignores this is missing the essential.

We were told of the case of a large city in which the Communist-inspired teachers used to refer to the P.T.A.'s of the city as "the paper and towel committee." While the teachers injected subversive ideas in their children's minds, the parents busied themselves with incidentals.

From one teacher comes an expression of regret that the P.T.A. in her school seems to be more concerned with pleasant social evenings than with the work of the schools. To her mind, these parents have missed golden opportunities to aid teachers in bringing spiritual values into the school.

"I have never seen a P.T.A. concern itself with what is taught in the classroom," she says. "Parents groups can be a powerful force for good when they work with their schools and local organizations. But they must have a constructive purpose, otherwise they accomplish little or nothing."

Happily all stories are not like this. In California one parent reported about a meeting where the topic was: "What Makes Home and School Partners in Education?" The audience was divided into six groups, each with a spokesman. All six agreed that religion was the binding force which tied home and school together.

In some localities Communists and fellow travelers have deliberately sought control of the local P.T.A. If they can control the P.T.A. and work with pro-Communist teachers, it is obvious that the combination can stifle the voice of the average good American who has a child in school.

The Communists are keenly aware of the value of the P.T.A., and try to use it to promote their own ideas in education. The Communist Party in Milwaukee, Wisconsin, recently stated:

Progressive women must join and work in the Parent-Teachers Association. This is one of the main points on the agenda of our Communist Women's Commission here for the Fall. . . . This is a real battle for the minds of our children.

The most powerful force in the educational picture is the parent. By reason of his rights before the law and his natural status as the first teacher, he can perhaps more than any other individual help to keep our school system in line with our highest spiritual, intellectual, and patriotic traditions.

five

The Teacher Makes the School

FORTY YEARS AGO A PROFESSOR AT JOHNS HOPKINS University told his class of graduate students to go to the worst slums in Baltimore and pick out two hundred boys between the ages of twelve and sixteen. The assignment was to look into the living conditions and attitudes of these youngsters and then to make a prediction about their future.

The students investigated as thoroughly as they could and consulted statistics. They came to the conclusion that most of the boys would be failures in life.

Twenty-five years later the professor had retired and been replaced by a younger man. In going through the files the new professor came across the records of this survey. He decided to carry it further and find out how correct the study had been. So he put his own students on the job.

After extensive searching they found 180 of the original 200 boys. Only four had gone to the penitentiary.

Why was it that this group, which had been raised in the slums with everything against them, was able to achieve a record so much better than the average? The students continued asking questions and found that they kept getting the same answer: "Well, there was a teacher . . ." Further investigation revealed that in 75 per cent of the cases it was the same teacher. They then went to the school board to learn that the teacher had retired and was living near by. They plied her with questions about why she had such a strong influence

54

on the boys, what she had taught them, and why they remembered her.

The teacher seemed puzzled and could not give any reasons for the splendid record these men had made as citizens. Finally, as the past flashed through her mind, she spoke as if thinking out loud: "I loved those boys . . ."

Those few words answered all the questions and helped to solve the mystery of the astonishing report.

This story, as told by Milton Britten, is a forceful reminder of the great influence for good which one teacher can exert.

Time Cannot Destroy

When Daniel Webster, the renowned statesman and orator, spoke at Faneuil Hall, Boston, in 1852, he underlined the important service rendered by one who dedicates himself to teaching:

If we work upon marble, it will perish.
If we work upon brass, time will efface it.
If we rear temples, they will crumble to dust.
But if we work upon men's immortal minds,
If we imbue them with high principles,
With the just fear of God and love of their fellow man,
We engrave on those tablets something which no time can efface,
And which will brighten and brighten to all eternity.

Those who have dedicated their lives to a career in teaching, with a sense of real devotion, find that seemingly major difficulties become incidental. They clearly recognize and enjoy the privilege of being instruments of God in bringing His truth to youth. For them, purpose makes the difference.

Another example of a devoted and tireless worker is Miss Mary Elizabeth Vroman, a Negro teacher from Montgomery, Alabama. In February, 1952, she was given the $2,000 Chris-

topher Award for the best magazine story of 1951, entitled
"See How They Run." This, her first magazine article, appeared in the June, 1951, issue of the *Ladies Home Journal*.

You may wonder what a magazine story has to do with
teaching. Simply this—the warm tale, based on personal experience, told what one teacher, inspired with a Christlike
motive, did to help a class of small Negro children who were
less fortunate than most others their own age.

The great appeal of Miss Vroman's beautifully written
story lay in the unadorned account of a good teacher at work.
Her devotedness, her individual attention to the problems of
her students, and her joy in working were eloquent and moving
enough in themselves.

Bruce Gould, editor of the *Ladies Home Journal*, wrote
us: "We have seldom published a story which had such an
enthusiastic reception as did this story by Miss Vroman."

In accepting her award at the Beverly Hills Hotel, her
talk, only a minute and a half in length, so stirred the audience of over two hundred writers, producers, directors, actors
and actresses, that all acclaimed it as the best of the fourteen
given that night in acceptance of Christopher awards.

Immediately after she finished, Dore Schary, the head of
MGM in Hollywood, came to me and said: "We want to
make a full-length movie of Miss Vroman's story."

The film was completed in April, 1953, and played over
the country under the title, *Bright Road*.

An excerpt from Miss Vroman's brief speech will show
you her deep love for the children and her heartfelt concern
for their well-being:

. . . When I wrote "See How They Run," it was with the primary aim in view to make an effort to develop a talent that I believed I had, and secondly to bring an awareness to a reading public
(if I should be so lucky as to have my story published) of how boys
and girls in a Negro school are identical with children everywhere
—lovable, sometimes exasperating, and completely wonderful in

their ability to grow like French weeds through the rocks and stiflingly infertile soil, of conditions not of their own making. As a teacher in a Negro school I know them well . . .

When my story was accepted by the *Ladies Home Journal*, I felt that I had reached the ultimate in happiness so I was unprepared for the wonderfully warm reception given "See How They Run" by the readers. When the lovely, encouraging letters came pouring in, I felt with surprised humility how far that little candle throws its beams. How over-rewarded I am for a small effort that truly gave me only pleasure in the writing.

I feel that this award is being given me not only as encouragement to a would-be writer but as an expression also of encouragement to these children, whose story you loved, that you do love and believe in them as you love and believe in children everywhere. So for them and for myself whose heart is very full, let me say thank you and God bless you everywhere.

OUR GREATEST HOPE

If, as the saying goes, our hope for the future lies in our children, we can add, for the same reason, that our future is in good measure in the hands of our teachers. A million teachers in the United States with Miss Vroman's high ideals and competence would leave little concern about the next generation.

At the present time in the schools, colleges, and universities of America there are many such teachers who are working hard to give their students a deep realization of the spiritual values necessary for a complete education.

Even though all teachers may not have the high sense of dedication Miss Vroman has, the majority are genuinely interested in serving the best interests of the young people who look to them for inspiration, guidance and training. Teachers who are indifferent or inarticulate can often be encouraged to greater effort once they realize how much each of them can do personally.

FOR TIME AND ETERNITY

Year after year 36 million young Americans have their view of
life largely determined by teachers. For many the teacher is
the source of knowledge, the standard of good and evil, the
students' ideal and sometimes even their idol.

Henry Adams once said: "A teacher affects eternity; he
can never tell where his influence stops."

One day Michelangelo was strolling through a back street
of Florence with a friend. He stopped to examine a block of
marble half buried under dirt and rubbish. He started to clear
away the filth and tried to lift it from the slime and mire.
When his companion asked him what he wanted with the
chunk of rock, he gave his famous answer:

"Oh, there's an angel in that stone, and I must let it out."

He had the block of marble transported to his studio.
Then he set to work, and after patient toiling with chisel and
mallet, he "brought the angel out." What to others was a
shapeless, useless, dirty mass of stone, was to the master's eye
a hidden glory and a challenging possibility. The stone might
have become part of a wall or road. But the artist changed it
into a work of genius, a work of value for ages to come.

That is the thrilling challenge for the teacher—to see *the
potential power in each student* and to chisel and sculpture
the marble of character into something worth while, something precious for time and eternity.

Many teachers are deeply conscious of the power they
exert in the lives of their students. A few excerpts from some
letters show this very clearly.

One professor in a college in Ohio wrote:

. . . in my belief the oft-neglected moral and spiritual values
must be kept foremost. As a member of a college administration,
my influence can be great on students, in their training to meet
the materialistic factors in the world. As a business officer, my

example and my statements may perhaps carry more weight in convincing future businessmen that high ethical standards are necessary, than if I were a religion or philosophy professor. . . .

An Episcopalian college teacher in Denver wrote this to us about the power of a teacher:

I sincerely believe that millions of people of good heart can in countless small ways achieve miracles, just as a number of small creatures can and do build coral islands.

Another wrote as follows:

I am just an average American man, married, loyal to my country, family and church. Tonight I write this from a college dormitory. Perhaps you may wonder why a man of thirty-five years of age would quit a good paying job and go to college. Over two years ago I decided that I ought to do something that would build a better world. I read *You Can Change the World* and decided to take the leap, quit my job as a worker in a furniture factory and finish my college work. I am taking my Master's Degree in elementary education because I believe that much good can be done in that field and I like to work with children.

I believe that just ordinary people like me can do a lot, with God's help, to change the world for the better. We will never be famous, but we will have the satisfaction of knowing that our influence has been on the positive side.

Another teacher in the South, deeply impressed by her responsibility, made the following remark:

There is no more exalting profession in the world, except that followed by those who preach the word of Jesus. I quake in my boots when I think of my responsibilities. I feel I am rendering a service to humanity—and Lord knows it needs it.

A California teacher said:

I don't see how people can be helped unless, we, who know Christ, can go to them, share their problems with them, teach them. We who have been more fortunate haven't any right to use what we have just for ourselves. I feel strongly about that. We've got to get out and share. I can do that by teaching.

MORE THAN A BUILDING

The tendency of most persons is to think of a school as just a building with some classrooms filled with young people. Too little thought is given to the most important factor in the school—the teacher.

In the strict sense of the term, the school *is* the teacher. It cannot be stressed too frequently that no matter how elaborate the building and equipment, no school will ever be any better than its teachers. As a matter of fact, a good teacher, teaching the right ideas, could teach the students anywhere.

Teachers can be divided into three categories—good, bad, and indifferent. A large number are unquestionably good. Many, if not most, of those who are "indifferent" might shift to "good" if they realized the important part they can play from their own classrooms in shaping the destiny of the country. Teachers who are bent on evil are comparatively few, thank God. But they exert an influence far out of proportion to their number.

THE QUALITIES EXPECTED

Much more than scholastic competence is needed to fulfill the trust that parents, students, and the public place in one holding the responsible position of a teacher.

All these people who depend so much on the teacher certainly have a right to expect that he or she should be strong in the love of God and country and conscientious in the devotion to duty.

So much good or so much harm can be done by one individual in teaching. As one veteran in the educational field so well summed it up:

"If the teacher really believes in God and wants to bring God into her classroom, there are countless ways in which it can be done. The teacher must be strong in her convictions. There isn't anything that a good teacher can't do. . . ."

How They Do It

One college professor who has observed at close range the Communists at work in the teaching field sent us the following "play by play" account of how thoroughly they cover the ground, which we present here in its entirety:

1. Indoctrination in classroom.
2. Censoring of books and materials—pushing some and omitting others deliberately.
3. Conferences after class with students.
4. Working with student clubs to promote their program. They use political clubs, social clubs and religious clubs.
5. Fighting in department meetings for their program or attempt to wreck the meeting.
6. Drafting syllabi for courses.
7. Organizing "protest meetings," "peace mobilizations," "student strikes."
8. Writing material for student protest meetings.
9. Black-balling certain courses, departments and teachers and vigorously promoting others who are friends.
10. Use of words—(a) words to label those who do not go their way: "reactionary," "conservative," "dogmatic," "ancient stuff," "abysmally ignorant," "neurotic," "schizophrenic." (b) good words for an evil end: "progressive," "liberal," "modern," "democratic."
11. Infiltration into all organizations and offices of schools, to get information or disrupt them.
12. Attempt to control student newspapers and use them to promote program.
13. Trying to control professional journals. It is difficult for even some of the top scholars in certain fields to get an article in some of the journals in the field.

14. Directing and helping Communist students to infiltrate and
gain control of student organizations to attack and smear instructors and courses and to influence other students against
them.

These methods are indeed shocking. But much as we
disagree with them, they furnish a striking example of devotion to a cause which is so often lacking in the loyal teacher
who has much more to give. Christ Himself said, "The children of this world are wiser in their generation than the children of light." (Luke 16:8.)

THE POWER OF THE GOOD TEACHER

A substitute teacher in a school in the desert of Southern
California has furnished a striking example of what one teacher
can do.

When she was assigned to take over the fifth grade of a
particular school during the illness of its regular teacher, she
was afraid at first that she would not be able to cope with the
situation that confronted her. There had been considerable
trouble in this school due to racial conflicts and background
differences.

She found it difficult at first to keep order in the class
because there was a general disrespect for authority. In des-
peration she decided to try out on them an idea that she had
picked up in a Christopher book.

One day the worst ruffian in the class was disrupting
things more than usual by making fun of an underdog.

In the midst of it she singled him out and said: "Paul,
you shouldn't treat Bob that way. He's your brother!"

Paul looked at her in consternation: "That guy my
brother? You're crazy. He's not my brother."

The teacher stood her ground and said: "He certainly is
your brother. You claim to be an American. Well, if you're a
good American you believe what the men who founded our

country said, don't you? They put right in the Declaration of Independence that all men came from one Creator. You can figure that out for yourself. If God made all of us that means he is the Father of all of us. If He's our Father, doesn't that mean that we're all brothers and sisters? So that makes Bob your brother."

Paul looked startled and his face lighted up: "Gee, that's right isn't it! I never thought of it that way before."

Not only did Paul learn a new lesson but the whole class was impressed, too. From then on they thought of each other in a different way. Gradually the friction began to disappear.

The teacher continued to show in every way that she had a deep personal interest in each child. When it came time for her to leave, the children pleaded with her to remain. They said she had taught them things they had never heard before, and they wanted her to stay.

How It's Done

Any teacher has endless opportunities to integrate a recognition of God and spiritual values into her work. Provided she has the conviction and a little determination, the occasions will multiply.

Following are ways in which some teachers tell us they have brought God into the lives of their students. We pass them on to you:

1. In one case a wife wrote in to tell about her husband's efforts in the field of education. She wrote:

A year ago A—— completed work for his Ph.D. and joined the faculty of B—— University, where he gives courses in Genetics, Cytology, and General Biology. This field is especially gratifying for Christopher work since it is so often invaded by pseudophilosophers who, because it suits their convenience or salves their pride, marshal their facts and theories in such order as to disprove the existence of God. Without invading the field of theology, my husband finds that he is able to give credit where credit is due, and to direct the thinking of the students along positive lines. It was his purpose to exert this kind of influence. . .

The most surprising development, however, was that students consulted him on problems concerning morals. He was able to instruct these people who had no clear reasoning to guide them, but only a vestigial conscience capable of instilling in their minds sufficient doubt to cause them to seek outside help when they were in danger of pursuing a morally questionable course.

2. A sociology professor in a large university in Ohio was suddenly struck one day by the realization that hundreds of students pass through his classes each year without any knowledge that their rights as human beings come from God. He outlined a plan which met with the hearty response of the students. He organized a nine-day institute composed of 141 high-school juniors and seniors from six states to study the life of American youth.

—he introduced films and recordings to assist the young men in their group and individual discussions;
—then three days were spent in discussion of three main topics:
  1). The reason for brotherhood (emphasizing the Fatherhood of God);
  2). Why this land is free (showing by study of the Declaration of Independence that our rights come from God);
  3). The place of the young man in the community (showing the young man's responsibilities as a child of God);
—the next three days were spent in factories, radio stations, newspaper offices and television studios, showing America at work;
—another two days were spent in a mock political campaign and election, in order to give the students the "feel" of the responsibilities and privileges of the citizen;
—the last day was spent in analyzing and evaluating the program.

The professor was most gratified by the effects the program had on those who took part.

3. Another college teacher told us:

Some of my best teaching has been done—not in the class-room—but in my office. Students know my door is always open to them. We just talk about anything and everything.

I do not hesitate to refer to moral and religious values. So many lack confidence, need to be reassured—to be inspired to greater heights. It is a great thrill to me when a student with whom I have worked finds himself and goes on to make his life worth-while. There is no greater satisfaction than to know that you have helped—even in a small way.

Hidden Hunger

The following parts of letters received from educators make this clear. One is from a professor in an Eastern University who writes:

I am a teacher, an instructor of English at A—— University. It seems to me that I find two qualities constantly appearing among my students; a surface cynicism, which is apparently deemed "popular"; plus an underlying desire to believe in Christian vir-tues and moral principles which they are not quite sure how to express. The help that the Christophers give in clarifying their searchings is so very necessary.

Another wrote:

Most students seem actually eager to be convinced that high ideals are worthwhile, and we in the colleges are missing a great opportunity if we fail to recognize this, and let them settle for a tarnished code of ethics, when we could so easily show and teach them the ways in which they can best adapt these ideals to the everyday needs of business. . . .

In our investigation into this subject we have found that in practically every case where attempts have been made, the teacher has discovered that the students *want* to hear about spiritual truths. Some teachers are afraid that their words will

fall on deaf or hostile ears. They would be surprised to find
that God has implanted in every heart a hunger for truth and
for Himself. This is very strong in the hearts of the young—
though it is sometimes partially hidden. It is for the teacher
to bring this out.

six

The Power of the Student

SCHOOLS OVER THE WORLD GRADUATE 20 MILLION students a year. The vast majority of these young people would like to do something to make the world a little better for their being in it. Unfortunately, in the past few decades, the idealism of youth has been misused and abused by those who would enslave all mankind.

You will read in a subsequent chapter (Chapter 14) how the Nazi system brought death and destruction to countless millions of innocent persons. Young people were victimized in a particular way. Too late they learned that they were accomplices in catastrophe.

Because the mistakes of the past can provide a valuable lesson and warning for the future, we feel that you might profit from the experience of a group of German youths who sacrificed everything in an effort to make amends for the frightful tragedy that they had unwittingly helped to make possible.

Let us turn the pages back, briefly, to see how the Nazi student of the 1930's compares with American students in the 1950's.

First, every dictator tries to enlist youth in his cause through false promises, sham slogans, and half truths. Shrewdly, the totalitarians capitalize upon youth's love of peace, justice, and liberty, together with youth's natural rebellion against existing authority. The would-be dictator knows how to sell "old stuff" as "progressive new ideas," even though his material may be as old as the hills. So we saw in

67

Nazi Germany a "new religion" based on old Teutonic gods, which represented a paganism ages old before Germany was even civilized.

Early in 1942 seven young Germans gambled their lives— and lost—in a vain effort to destroy the Hitler Germany that had enslaved their bodies and had tried to enslave their minds. William Bayles tells their story in his book, *Seven Were Hanged.*

The seven youths fought against tremendous odds after they had seen their ideals betrayed by the Hitler machine. They realized too late that they had been swindled out of their birthright, and had been made unwitting accomplices in bringing endless tragedy to themselves and their fellow men.

American students who know how German youths were duped and disillusioned can be alert for the signposts on the road that leads to destruction.

He Started at Twelve

The story begins in 1932 when Adrian Probst, a twelve-year-old schoolboy, found his dreams come true. The Nazis gave him a uniform and a place to march in a brass band. They made him feel important.

In the Hitler Youth, he held a treasured rank. With his comrades, he fought pitched battles with boys who were "outsiders." They broke into church basements, and raided meetings of "sissies" who didn't have the manly courage to disobey their parents. His training and education stressed "the body" and material things, played down the "spirit" and the spiritual side of life.

Adrian was so overcome with his good fortune that he failed to notice that God and everything connected with religion were thoroughly excluded from his schooling. Bit by bit he was being prepared for his role in life as a perfectly disciplined German soldier. He was taught that religion was nothing but a racket. He showed a growing contempt for all spiritual values. Though his conscience hurt a bit when he was cruel to old men and women, he drew comfort from Baldur von Schirach's slogan: "Conscience is a Jewish invention."

At seventeen he went into the labor service. Outdoor work hardened his body, and his mind was steeled against softness in talks with youth leaders at evening sessions. They proclaimed the "New Germany" to him and induced him to idolize Hitler as its patron saint.

DECEPTION UPON DECEPTION

For Adrian, the experience was thrilling and exalting. He learned his Nazi lessons well, for that was the surest way to promotion. Five years of his young life had already been devoted to the godless ways of the Hitler Youth. For him, family life had virtually ceased to exist.

His first doubts came when he passed his eighteenth birthday. Suddenly, it seemed, he had grown into manhood. Now he was in the Army under the stern and impersonal discipline of officers who had no concern with the Hitler Youth.

One day his Army post was visited by a Nazi official of prominence. After the military inspection had ended Adrian heard one of his sergeants say: "They make the wars, and we are the idiots who get killed in them."

GRADUAL AWAKENING

After a solid year of military training, Adrian was ordered to the university. Unlike American students, he had no choice as to where he would study. In the form of official Army orders, the university and his courses were prescribed for him.

He was deeply disturbed and embarrassed when he heard a student younger than himself, clad in the uniform of a Hitler

Youth, tell the faculty: "One young German inspired with the ideals of Adolf Hitler is wiser than the lot of you."

A few days later he got another shock when a detachment of brown-shirted troopers tore German maps out of the library atlases, because the maps were based on the Versailles treaty. Two old men looked on in dismay, and one whispered to the other: "Soon sane men will again be compelled to retire to the monasteries to find freedom."

And Mr. Bayles, the author, comments: "A few years ago the Young German would have denounced the two old men; at twenty, he felt strangely ashamed."

Soon Adrian saw that his university education was a travesty on learning, for all the German universities had been enrolled in the Nazi cause. Professors extolled war at great length in their lectures. The life of a fighting man was held out as the realization of Germanic life. One history professor told Adrian's class: "The inevitableness, the idealism, and the blessing of war as an indispensable and stimulating law of development, must be repeatedly emphasized."

In his biology course Adrian heard Professor Dr. Kindler say: "War is a biological necessity of first importance, a regulative element in the life of mankind which cannot be dispensed with. It is not only a biological law, but a moral obligation."

After university training, Adrian found himself at twenty-one fighting in Russia during the second winter of the German campaign there.

FINAL DISILLUSIONMENT

There he speedily reached the climax of disillusionment. The terrible toll of suffering inflicted on Russian and German alike shook his spirit. Fear and disgust clutched at him when he heard that only one-tenth of the supplies sent from Germany reached the front. The rest had been stolen or sold.

All at once, everything seemed to be wrong. This was not the glorious struggle for a free Germany about which his professors had talked. What did teachers know about the hardships of war? He thought about them, living their quiet, comfortable lives, and "believing first in their pensions and then in the German Army."

Frostbitten feet took him out of the front line. Cynical, bitter, and now unbelieving, he watched as thousands of other young Germans came to the front eager to find this so-called "glorious career in uniform." Only a short time before, he reflected, he had been as eager and as full of illusions as any of them.

From this point on, Adrian's life rapidly approached its climax. One night he heard the idol of his youth, Baldur von Schirach, declaiming over the radio: "We want fearless, vigorous, commanding, cruel young men—young men with the strength and beauty of young beasts of prey."

The voice he had once respected now seemed to him to mouth nothing but hysterical mockery.

Adrian Probst was just twenty-two years old when he returned to Munich from the Russian front. He was a broken man, fit only for the scrap heap. At a time when most young lives begin, his was ended. Few of his old friends even recognized him. One said of him: "His face was drawn like a dried sheepskin. When he laughed, it didn't sound like a laugh. His feet were clumsy bundles in bandages covered with shapeless canvas boots, and he hobbled along with the aid of two heavy sticks."

Ordered back to study at his university, Adrian was told by his Nazi officer-in-command: "The fact is, we don't want you in the university or on the streets. We want you kept out of sight. Why they sent you back here I do not know. At times like these we have no place in the Reich for cripples. You are ruining the general picture."

Doing Something about It

With six other student-veterans, Adrian decided to rise against the power that had transformed him in ten short years from a vigorous boy of twelve to an old, useless man of twenty-two. Secrecy was essential, for the eyes of the police were everywhere. Detection meant immediate death. Working at night in a secluded spot the students printed thousands of copies of their message to the students of Germany.

STUDENTS!

Our people is in ferment! Are we going to entrust parvenus with the fate of our nation? Are we going to sacrifice the remainder of German youth to the lowest power instincts of a Party clique?

NEVER!

In the name of the whole German nation, we demand from the State of Adolf Hitler the restitution of personal freedom, that most precious possession out of which we have been cheated.

FREEDOM AND HONOR!

Hitler and his confederates have twisted and abused these two beautiful words until they have become loathsome. They have thrown the highest ideals of a nation into the gutter. What they mean by freedom and honor they have shown only too well in ten years of destruction of all personal freedom, all freedom of thought, all moral principles.

The eyes of even the most stupid have now been opened by the terrible blood bath in which they endeavor to drown all Europe. The name of Germany will remain forever dishonored if German youth does not arise at last, revenge, atone and destroy its tormentors and help build up a new spiritual concept in Europe!

STUDENTS!
THE GERMAN NATION IS LOOKING AT YOU!

The daring call-to-arms of that handful of students spread like wildfire. They had planted a seed which could not be rooted out by all the agencies of the secret police.

But the price they paid was the highest anyone could pay. One by one, they were tracked down. After summary trials, each of the seven was condemned to death by hanging—a felon's death. Deprived of even the last consolation of a soldier's death—by shooting—their lives were terminated at the end of the hangman's rope.

STUDENTS CAN LEAD THE WAY

The Nazi effort to dominate the world has come and gone. Like a latter-day comet, it flashed through the skies with initial brilliance, only to sputter out in blackness darker than night itself.

But it left a stark lesson that American students might well ponder. We are all reasonably sure that the same disaster cannot happen here. But so were the students and young people of pre-Hitler Germany! Yet, it happened to them.

Only a few years ago, laughing, hopeful, idealistic students held pro-Communist demonstrations in Shanghai and other Chinese cities. Simultaneously, American students on one campus demonstrated for Communist China. Like students everywhere, these young men and women were afire with zeal for a new experiment, courageous in their determination to try something which seemed new and better to them. But was it better?

No, sadly, it was not. Neither here nor in China did the enthusiastic young people realize that they were promoting the enslavement of 800 million human beings. Formerly free, these people have passed under Moscow control since the end of World War II in 1945.

To our students here, we say: Beware of any theory that omits God by deliberate plan or neglect. No matter how alluring it may sound, consider well that godlessness never works out in practice, especially if power-drunk and corrupt human beings are in the driver's seat. Use your own God-given soundness of mind to get facts. Use your reason, instead of becoming unwitting tools of a conspiracy that may turn out to be more cold and brutal than the Nazi conspiracy was.

STUDENTS TAKE A STAND

You as a student can do much to shape the destiny of the world. Do not underestimate for one moment your own power for good.

If you have the courage to take a stand for God and country, even during your school days you can make your voice heard in favor of good and against evil. In your own way, you may be an instrument in bringing peace to millions on this troubled earth.

Ordinarily we think of students as those who sit in the classroom, and of teachers as those who teach from the platform. Thus, we sometimes forget that many of our qualified teachers become students themselves, after school hours, so that they may improve their professional standing. It is of one of these teachers turned student that we relate the following account:

This high-school teacher, with a number of others, was taking graduate work in a large Eastern university. One day their professor declared: "There is no power in democracy—bar none—greater than the majority."

Our teacher-student, a social studies major, challenged this statement with the question: "Does not even the majority have to comply with a law higher than itself?"

"No," the professor said flatly.

"Then how," the student pursued, "do you account for such evils as the murder of six million Jews by the Nazis? If the majority decides it is all right to be anti-Semitic to that extent, does that make it all right?"

"Of course not," the professor replied. "But that would not happen here."

"What's to prevent it?" the student demanded.

"It's against the democratic process," the professor said.

"Precisely," said the student. "But it simply proves the point that majority rule is not the essence of the democratic process. The saving virtue in democracy is that the people in it receive their rights and duties from a Power higher than themselves or the state. The evils of Nazism came when this Higher Power was abandoned. Then it was easy for mob rule to take over. To me, it's obvious that God is the basis for the democratic process."

As those in the class murmured agreement, the professor speedily changed the subject to less challengeable matter.

This experience of one student in a class teaches us a valuable lesson. If we remain silent and do nothing when a misstatement is uttered, we contribute to the strength of the untruth. Only by challenging it and stating our own views can we hope to "set the record straight."

ONE SPARKED THIRTY-FIVE HUNDRED

Here is another story. When our Federal government was considering whether or not to recognize the Red Chinese government, one college student decided to make his voice heard in Washington. He felt that one lone letter from him opposing recognition would carry little weight. He obtained permission to address his class on the subject, and found that many others agreed with him. These students encouraged him to spread his views over the entire campus. As a result, in the words of the student himself: "What started out as a mere plea to forty students has now turned into a project enlisting the aid of thirty-five hundred students. Truly, one candle lights another."

REVERSED THE FIELD

A young lady studying in California noticed that a trend away from God and country was being fostered on her college campus by a small group in the Student Council. Like most of us, her first inclination was to "mind her own business" and stay aloof.

As she thought about it, however, her conscience would not rest. Thinking along Christopher lines, she came to realize that she would be "minding her own business" in a truer sense if she acted to correct the abuse. She told classmates that they all had an obligation to keep student activities on a high level, free of domination by a minority that was obviously working to destroy the truths on which our country was founded. Instead of remaining quiet, our student induced a leading student with high ideals to run for the Student Council. Her friend was elected easily.

Immediately, the two began to stimulate fellow students to take an active interest in student government. With help from all sides, the minority's influence on all phases of student activity diminished. Its strength diminished in proportion.

Not content with her own achievement, this courageous student made another constructive contribution. She and a few other seniors, before they were graduated, fired several undergraduates with their own enthusiasm. In this way they made sure that their program would be carried on.

WHEN IT WAS TOO LATE

From the Communist zone of Eastern Germany comes another illuminating episode. Here, a Communist high-school teacher undertook to prove to his students from the Bible itself that there is no God.

Since most of the students came from good Christian

families with religious training, they were not so easily convinced. However, the teacher held a Bible aloft and said: "You can see for yourself! This is a Lutheran Bible. And on Page 246 it says: 'There is no God!' "

Next day, one student brought the Lutheran Bible to class with him. He had been chosen by his schoolmates as the most courageous, to represent them.

"About the quotation . . ." the spokesman asked the teacher.

"From the Bible?" the teacher asked.

"Yes, from the Bible," the student said.

"Well, what about it?" the teacher demanded impatiently.

"Well, sir," the student said, "it seems you have read but part of the sentence. Clearly, you referred us to Psalm thirteen, the first verse. Is that correct?"

The teacher said he did not remember.

"Indeed, sir," the spokesman went on, "there it reads: 'The fool says in his heart: "There is no God . . ."' "

The spokesman got no further. His teacher went to the principal who saw that all students in the protesting group were dismissed from the school for having "caused a severe disturbance of the democratic order." In Communist parlance, that means they were automatically excluded from all higher education.

Here was an instance of student heroism where God had been officially and completely banished from education. Unfortunately, this display of courage came too late to be effective. It recalls the old adage that "an ounce of prevention is worth a pound of cure."

In every country that has been betrayed into slavery, the power of the classroom has been employed to abuse truth rather than support it.

If justice, integrity, morality, and all the other basic foundations on which freedom is built are eliminated from education, the bottom soon falls out of every other phase of life as well.

WHAT ONE STUDENT CAN DO

Our mail at Christopher headquarters contains a goodly number of letters from students in all parts of the country. Many of these young people write in to relate their own experiences or seek more information about our movement. Some express frank bewilderment in their search for a faith to follow.

Here is a letter from an eighteen-year-old girl, a freshman at a Colorado university, which recounts how she made her voice heard for God.

"My university is a pretty nice place," she tells us. "The social activities are swell, the kids super, and the professors about as fair as they can be. All in all, the university is tops! There's just one thing that's missing—a person known as God. Try as you might, you can't find Him anywhere."

An Episcopalian, this young lady reported that no one seemed to be doing anything about the absence of God on the campus. So she wrote a letter to her university newspaper pointing out that the university had been founded on a religious basis, yet was promoting "downright atheism."

"Our Lord should be more evident on the campus and in people's hearts," she wrote. "Where is religion at this university?" she demanded.

Then, as she writes us, things began to pop.

"I was besieged with calls asking for my views of religion and why I wrote the letter in the first place," she says. "I began to wonder myself. Then, it became clear to me. I was trying to be a Christopher. You know it's rather difficult to 'keep smiling' when people think you're either a fanatic or a moron. However, everyone has unwittingly paid me a compliment by saying: 'Well, I guess if you can write stuff like that, you believe in something.' That is the highest praise a person could ever receive. I believe that everyone, Catholic, Protestant or Jew, can try to be a bearer of Christ. Even an eighteen-year-old girl can help a little."

If only a few, a mere handful of students in each school in the United States, had the courage to take a stand as this girl did, the course of history might well be changed.

With world tensions as tight as they are, and the forces of anti-God and godlessness pressing upon us, it is more essential than ever for each American to fight for his religious heritage. Parents, teachers, and citizens can do much in this respect. But there is something irresistible about an enthusiastic college student, a peppy teen-ager, or even a lively child in grade school, if he has the courage to stand up for his rights and to recognize the responsibilities that go with his place in the world.

While You Are in School

Most of us find out too late that we have muffed many a chance to prepare for the future. Too many young Americans complete their education with no place in particular to go and with little or no meaning in their lives.

There are countless opportunities to help young people who are groping and floundering. No matter what your position in life, you can do something to give at least one student a sense of purpose and direction.

Here are a few reminders that you might care to pass on to some young person:

1. Keep ever before you the big purpose of your life— why you are here, where you came from, and where you are going. The more God-centered your life is, the more meaningful it will be for you and for everybody with whom you come in contact.

2. Remember always the school is for you, whether you

are just beginning or completing your studies. In a very real sense, everybody in the whole educational setup is working for you—parents, teachers, and administrators.

3. You have the right to know the fullness of truth. Every teacher has an obligation to transmit to you your complete American birthright, especially the very heart of it which defines your relationship to God. No teacher should impose agnostic or atheistic theories on you or your classmates. To do so is to violate the academic freedom of both teacher and student.

4. Start early to prepare for the part you will play in life. If you can, choose a career where you can do more than earn a living—a career with a purpose. The average person works 2,000 hours a year. In forty years that mounts up to 80,000 hours. It is within your power to make those hours useful.

5. Keep always in mind that your power for good during school and in the years ahead, will be more or less in proportion to how deep you sink your roots spiritually, as well as intellectually. Your judgment will never be any better than your values. You must decide for yourself how to develop your inner strength by reflection and prayer. All that you say and do can be little more than an outward expression of your interior life.

seven

Academic Freedom
Is Everybody's Business

AN ELDERLY LADY ONCE HANDED ME A DIAMOND, expressing her desire that any money derived from its sale be given to the poor. Thanking her and commending her charity I placed the diamond for the time being on my desk. My guess was that it might bring about a hundred dollars, which could be used for the sick and afflicted. I was free to do with the diamond as I liked. But my conscience reminded me that with this freedom went responsibility.

Several days later I showed the diamond to a man who knew something about diamond exchange. He told me I'd probably get eight hundred dollars for it. Without delay I removed it from my desk and locked it in my drawer.

Again I had it priced, this time by professionals. I was offered eleven hundred dollars. Things were looking up, so I had it carefully locked in a safe. For the sake of the poor I felt obliged to get the best price possible for it.

A little shopping around finally brought the matter to a successful conclusion: fifteen hundred dollars. This amount was given to the poor.

The incident taught me a lesson. Had I presumed to adopt the role of a diamond appraiser, the poor would have lost fourteen hundred dollars. Fortunately, I realized my limitations in time and put the case into the hands of those more experienced in the field.

I have often thought of this in connection with the great responsibility resting in the hands of those entrusted with the education of our youth. Academic freedom must be theirs if they are to be true teachers. But accompanying that freedom is academic responsibility. Every teacher has an obligation in conscience always to use it in a way that will help, not harm, the youth of our country.

True Freedom No Risk

The vast majority of American teachers have a safe and sound appreciation of both the breadth and limitations of academic freedom. They need not be reminded that they have a right to discover and present in class all facets of truth related to a subject under discussion and at the same time to point out the errors. They would not dream of saying there is no more difference between truth and error than there is between vanilla and chocolate.

When a young man enters medical school his instructors teach him first the basic principles of health so that he will be in a safe position to make correct judgments on the nature of disease. The medical student, like his instructor, must have the largest amount of academic freedom for extensive investigation of his own. But he, like his teacher, must proceed scientifically. He cannot brand all the proven results of previous medical and surgical experiments as of no value and take the attitude that he has the right to label diseases as health, and health as disease, as he pleases.

Not long ago, when Dr. Henry T. Heald became Chancellor of New York University with its 68,000 students, he emphasized the moral obligation that must accompany academic freedom:

It is necessary that a faculty have a full degree of academic freedom, that a university be representative of various points of view. You don't expect them to be propaganda agents. You expect them to teach the truth, to be free to seek the truth in their investigations. You certainly do not expect to control their thinking. You expect them to have a responsibility to themselves and to the university.

ACCEPTED ELEMENTARY TRUTHS

Responsibility on the part of a teacher, whether in kindergarten or university, requires respect for the truth. It does not require more than a moment's reflection to recall to mind a few of the basic truths that lie at the very heart of our society. They are:

1. That there is a God Who is respected by most Americans.

2. That each individual is responsible to God and country for his actions.

3. That murder, stealing, and dishonesty in any form are evil.

THE FEW CAN DO MUCH HARM

Although abuses of this power entrusted to the teacher are limited to a small handful, yet they are occurring with such frequency as to jeopardize all levels of education. It is up to parents, teachers, students, and those in every other walk of life to insist that the whole truth about American ideals be presented without any slight, slant, or distortion.

A young lady told recently of how a fellow student in one university in New York was the victim of unfair pressure on the part of such a teacher. The student had included in the bibliography of one of her papers a book on educational psychology which happened to have been written by a minister of religion. Her paper was literally tossed back at her by the professor, who said: "This is America, and you have no right to present such a biased and unfounded opinion in a most important field!" She was then told that if she did not omit the listing of that book, she would be "flunked."

A mother in St. Louis remarked that it was only by accident that she found out that her teen-age son had been assigned a month previously, along with the rest of his high-school classmates, a book to review that favored a man whose loyalty to his country has been repeatedly questioned. The lady claimed that her son, still in his impressionable years, had been influenced by that one book to such an extent that he favored the theories and practices of a man linked with disloyalty and treason.

It is often too late when parents discover the harm that has been done to their children. Their sons and daughters are at the mercy of those few teachers who use the classroom as an effective working ground in which to sow seeds of atheism, treason, and immorality under the cloak of academic freedom.

No father or mother sends his child to school to be corrupted, yet this is happening to more than a few, because those who use the classroom to destroy our freedom have lost no time in getting into positions of influence in the educational world. They have already succeeded in bringing about many trends and policies that restrain and neutralize the good that the rank and file of teachers are doing in their schools.

What You Do Is Important

It is dangerously late, but not too late to do something about this. What you as an individual do in correcting this abuse may have far-reaching effects for your country and your world.

Whether you are parent, teacher, student, or in any other category of American life, you should act quickly and firmly to see that academic freedom is used to uphold American truth, not to undermine and destroy it.

Find out ways and means of your own. It is the policy of

the Christopher movement merely to point out the opportunities, then to leave you entirely on your own to decide for yourself where and how to act. The more you investigate and discover for yourself, the more you will exercise your own academic freedom of insisting on the full truth in every classroom. In clubs and organizations to which you belong encourage talks and discussions among your friends on what constitutes the proper use of academic freedom.

Keep on the alert and observe points of discussion. For instance, you may have noticed in the newspaper that one of our leading university presidents is forever repeating that he is "searching for the truth." But for some strange reason we have never heard him refer to the "self-evident truths" that our Founding Fathers stated most explicitly are the very cornerstone of American life.

It might be well for you to write a letter to such an educator and remind him that one of his first responsibilities in an American school is to "uphold" the truths which are the foundation of our nation. Encourage him to use as much freedom as he likes in pursuing or searching for new phases of truth, but urge him to pay the same respect to the "self-evident truths" that the signers of the Declaration of Independence did.

WHAT STUDENTS FACE

A university student in California pointed out that most of his teachers were a credit to the school, but that a few frequently made disparaging remarks about religion. One anthropology instructor, in particular, continually insinuated that man was nothing but an animal and therefore had no responsibility beyond that of a beast.

This instructor went to great lengths to avoid class discussion on the subject. He used various means of intimidation that indicated he was not quite sure of his position. He seemed to sense that a latent disagreement by some members of the class might voice itself when he was off guard and thus embarrass him.

To anticipate this, one day he asked the class if any of them belonged to a church. He presented the question in such a way as to put at an uncomfortable disadvantage anyone who would admit that he had church affiliations.

Only one student stood up. He was a young man who later told the incident. Clearly and emphatically, he said: "I do!" That was all. He sat down, ready for the worst.

But the worst never came. Like most who take advantage of their position to intimidate those under them, this professor was a coward at heart. Fear of what this one courageous student might do apparently induced him to give up his diatribes against religion.

Another case that has come to our attention is one of a young lady who attended a university in Illinois. She claims that her sociology teacher played safe by writing the correct view about man's responsibility on the blackboard. Anyone viewing it without hearing the verbal discussion on the subject would agree that this statement was safe and sound, for it read: "We do have free will."

However, when she said "That's correct" in reply to the professor's request that she comment on the truth of the statement, he turned on her immediately and exclaimed: "I cannot accept your answer. You are wrong. The answer should be that the statement is false."

This student did not let the matter rest. She countered with the truths that she had been taught by her parents and her church. She said that the rest of the class, about fifty in all, were far from convinced by his claims but remained silent for fear of receiving low marks.

Commenting on the approach of this professor who allowed no one to have an opinion on the subject of free will that differed with his own, the young lady said that he was a cynical, proud atheist who proclaimed democracy while being most undemocratic. "He screamed at me before the whole class as being dogmatic simply because I believe that I have free will, and yet he could not have been more dogmatic himself. He did more than offer his opinion, he tried to shove it down our throats. Parents have little idea of how their children are being 'atheized,'" she added.

She spoke of another sociology professor who is a strong Methodist and openly proclaims that "God's law is basic, the foundation of America." Then she continued: "Get more like him in the teaching field and they can easily offset those who work hard to root every trace of God out of the hearts and souls of every student they can reach."

LIGHT A CANDLE

In all that you say and do, be positive and constructive. Do not merely complain and bemoan dangerous trends. Above all, keep ever in mind as well as on your lips that the great percentage of American teachers are honestly anxious to transmit to every young American full appreciation of his material, cultural, intellectual, and spiritual heritage. Encourage these teachers to make their voices heard, to insist on keeping first things first, to see that the basic values remain unchanged in our changing times.

If you happen to be a student, there is much you can do. Remember the Christopher motto: "It is better to light one candle than to curse the darkness."

Young people can be most effective in unmasking those who parade under the banner of freedom and yet are working relentlessly to deprive one and all of their God-given liberty.

In Los Angeles, a group of such students provided a practical pattern that can be followed in any classroom or on any campus in showing up the betrayers of academic freedom. When one agitator outside of City College exhorted the students leaving their classes to join a leftist front, a few of his listeners began to question him and ask him for factual proof on some of his assertions. He refused to allow members of his audience to debate his views.

Two weeks later the leftist propagandist appeared again at the same place. Again he exhorted the curbstone audience of students to join his organization. In an extreme effort to win them, he made the mistake of shouting that the students had long been oppressed, denied free speech and the right of debate.

Recalling his own flagrant abuse of free speech on his previous visit, some of the young men decided to test him again. They tried to get him to answer their legitimate questions. He once more refused to discuss the issues with the students and insisted on their accepting his position without a word. They all laughed at his daring to refuse them the very freedom of debate that he claimed they were being denied by others. The agitator soon left. By insisting on the truth, the students effectively focused attention on what was false.

What Educators Say

Communists constitute only a small number of those who abuse academic freedom. The attitude of educators themselves regarding this problem offers a sensible pattern for the treatment of all who would prostitute academic freedom by withholding the truth or imposing on students opinions and theories that are hostile to accepted American doctrine.

During his inaugural address as President of the University of North Carolina, Gordon Gray said:

Frequently academic freedom, which must be preserved at all costs, has been used as a cloak to give a sort of immunity to Communists and their side-car passengers. I cannot believe that any university must reach into the ranks of those who are disloyal to American principles to develop a dedicated, independent faculty. . . . We shall not provide asylums for those who would extinguish the lights of liberty.

In similar vein the Board of Trustees of Ohio State University not long ago declared:

The University favors the fullest academic freedom consistent with its educational program and national security. It believes that steadfast adherence to the principles of free discussion and investigation, with equal responsibility, is the cornerstone of such an institution in a free society. . . .

AN AUTHORITATIVE STATEMENT

The Association of American Universities has forcefully declared that its staff members should be loyal citizens. The *New York Times* of March 31, 1953, summarized:

To protect its members and their faculties against Communist infiltration, the association [Association of American Universities] laid down these principles for universities to follow:

—Loyal citizenship, integrity and independence as well as professional competence should be required in appointing and retaining faculty members.

—Loyalty, integrity and independence are incompatible with membership in the Communist party or adherence to the Soviet Union and its satellites. Therefore present party membership "extinguishes the right to a university position."

—Those who follow the party line and silence criticism of it in classrooms also have no right in American universities, and forfeit the protection of academic freedom.

—Cooperation should be extended to legislative investigating committees, and abuses should be met by appealing to public opinion rather than by non-cooperation or defiance.

—Academic freedom does not include freedom from criticism, and is not a "shield" to protect violation of the law.

—Not only governing boards but also faculties have public obligations because of the public benefits they enjoy, including support of state universities by funds and aid to endowed universities by tax exemptions.

—Even in the face of popular disapproval timidity should not lead a scholar or teacher to stand silent when he must speak in matters of truth and conscience, particularly in his own special field of study.

—The spirit of the university requires "investigation, criticism and presentation of ideas in an atmosphere of freedom and mutual confidence," relying upon "open competition as the surest safeguard of truth."

—Academic freedom and freedom of expression are not merely faculty rights, but are vital to the American system and the general welfare.

A Significant Ruling by the Supreme Court

On March 3, 1952, the United States Supreme Court upheld the Feinberg Law which aimed at preventing employment or retention in the public schools of the State of New York of officials or teachers of subversive influence.

There are three portions of this momentous decision that should have particular interest for you. It makes an important distinction between the free speech guaranteed to a private citizen by the Constitution and that allowed one employed by the state to teach in the schools.

We cannot emphasize too strongly the great care and delicacy that must be used in seeing that the innocent do not suffer. We quote at length from this Supreme Court decision simply because it spells out in no uncertain terms that there are definite limitations to freedom and that no one has a right to use the classroom to spread subversion. You would do well to read slowly and reflectively the following excerpts from the decision by the highest court in the country:

It is argued that the Feinberg Law and the rules promulgated thereunder constitute an abridgment of speech and assembly of persons employed or seeking employment in the public schools of the State of New York.

It is clear that such persons have the right under our law to assemble, speak, think, and believe as they will. . . . It is equally clear that they have no right to work for the State in the school system on their own terms. . . . They may work for the school system upon the reasonable terms laid down by the proper authorities of New York. If they do not choose to work on such terms, they are at liberty to retain their beliefs and associations and go elsewhere.

Has the State thus deprived them of any right to free speech or assembly? We think not. Such persons are or may be denied, under the statutes in question, the privilege of working for the school system of the State of New York because first, of their advocacy of the overthrow of government by force or violence, or secondly, by unexplained membership in an organization found by the school authorities, after notice and hearing, to teach and advocate the overthrow of the government by force or violence, and known by such persons to have such purpose.

RESPONSIBILITY OF THE STATE TO THE STUDENT

Emphasizing the moral responsibility of the teacher to the student and the obligation of the state to see that this is fulfilled, the decision of the high tribunal continues:

A teacher works in a sensitive area in a schoolroom. There he shapes the attitude of young minds towards the society in which they live. In this, the State has a vital concern. It must preserve the integrity of the schools. That the school authorities have the right and the duty to screen the officials, teachers, and employees as to their fitness to maintain the integrity of the schools as a part of ordered society, cannot be doubted.

One's associates, past and present, as well as one's conduct, may properly be considered in determining fitness and loyalty. From time immemorial, one's reputation has been determined in part by the company he keeps. In the employment of officials and teachers of the school system, the State may very properly inquire into the company they keep, and we know of no rule, constitutional or otherwise, that prevents the State, when determining the fitness and loyalty of such persons, from considering the organizations and persons with whom they associate.

Whether you are a parent, a teacher, a student, or are in any other sphere of American life you might set aside a little time and study the far-reaching implications of this decision, for it is an official pronouncement on the part of the Federal government in regard to the limitations of academic freedom.

It can serve as a pattern of authority for you or any group in clarifying what is allowed and what is not allowed under the heading of academic freedom.

To Protect the Child

Note in this further excerpt from this decision how the Supreme Court specifically sustains the New York Legislature's contention that children should be protected from harmful teaching:

The preamble of the Feinberg Law makes elaborate findings that members of subversive groups, particularly of the Communist Party and its affiliated organizations, have been infiltrating into public employment in the public schools of the State; that this has occurred and continues notwithstanding the existence of protective statutes designed to prevent the appointment to or retention in employment in public office, and particularly in the public schools, of members of any organizations which teach or advocate that the government of the United States or of any State or political subdivision thereof shall be overthrown by force or violence or by any other unlawful means.

As a result, propaganda can be disseminated among the children by those who teach them and to whom they look for guidance, authority, and leadership. The Legislature further found that the members of such groups use their positions to advocate and teach their doctrines, and are frequently bound by oath, agreement, pledge, or understanding to follow, advocate and teach a prescribed party line or group dogma or doctrine without regard to truth or free inquiry.

This propaganda, the Legislature declared, is sufficiently subtle to escape detection in the classroom; thus, the menace of such infiltration into the classroom is difficult to measure.

Finally, to protect the children from such influence, it was thought essential that the laws prohibiting members of such groups, such as the Communist Party or its affiliated organizations, from obtaining or retaining employment in the public schools be rigorously enforced. It is the purpose of the Feinberg Law to provide for the disqualification and removal of superintendents of schools, teachers, and employees in the public schools in any city or school district of the State who advocate the overthrow of the Government by unlawful means or who are members of organizations which have a like purpose.

JUDGE FOR YOURSELF

Most Americans are blessed with a sense of fairness. Whether you realize it or not, you probably have a sufficient appreciation of the difference between *academic freedom* and *academic license* to judge in most cases what is honest and what is dishonest.

You know, for instance, that while a man is free to sell good oysters, he is not free to sell bad oysters. One is free to drive an automobile down the street. He has no right to speed it over a crowded sidewalk. He is free in a court of law to tell the truth. It is certainly an abuse of freedom to swear falsely, even if not detected in doing so. A person has a right to speak in a crowded theater, but he has no right to shout "fire" when there is no fire.

When the teacher takes certain undemocratic prerogatives to himself, trouble is usually the result. If he regards himself as the transmitter of truth, he will find endless opportunities to investigate further and to give his own personal interpretations in order to develop and heighten the truth. But he has no right to decide for himself what the student should or should not know. If he deliberately omits, distorts, or withholds portions of the truth, he is violating the trust placed in him by the parent, student, and state alike. They expect him to act as a "transmitter," not as a "falsifier" or "withholder" of the truth.

You know how you would feel if your letter carrier suddenly took it upon himself to hold up mail sent to you, to throw away some letters, to rewrite others, and add or subtract words in others that would give them the opposite meaning to that intended by the sender. Or what if your grocer removed the top cream from every bottle of milk he sold because he didn't believe in cream? No, as transmitters, teachers have an obligation to pass on to you, whole and undiminished, all that is your due. Then you are at liberty to do as you like, whether you are right or wrong.

The chief purpose of academic freedom is that a teacher may better serve his students in transmitting the truth. The more he learns about the truth and conveys his findings to them, the better off they are. Neither teachers nor students have anything to fear from the truth, provided it is completely and objectively presented.

Section Three

The factual information that we present in this section testifies clearly that a recognition of God and moral values has been an essential part of the American idea from the beginning of our nation. To be sure, the teaching of these facts would be no substitute for the fullness of truth to which every child of God has a right.

On the other hand, they have a positive value, however small, in keeping in the classroom a minimum reminder that we are all God's children. Those who would enslave mankind realize that more than most. Invariably they strive to eliminate from all spheres of life, particularly education, the slightest reminder that each and every human being is made in God's image. This in itself should be a strong proof that the concept of God is at the base of our concept of liberty.

eight

Countless Opportunities for the Teacher

A FIFTH-GRADE TEACHER WAS EXPLAINING TO HER
Nature Study class one day that nectar was of no use to the
flower, but rather a substance which was useful for bees who
made it into honey for their own needs and for human con-
sumption.

She went on to tell the story of pollen, which prompted
one of the youngsters to say: "Say, that's pretty good! Who
thought that up?" The teacher did not hesitate. "God," she
answered, explaining that the design and intelligence in nature
was put there by God through creation. The children were
interested in all this because it confirmed the ideas they had
received at home and in church.

This little episode happened in the fifth grade. It could
have happened, and does happen, with appropriate differences,
from kindergarten to postgraduate university level. As a rule,
it will come up casually—in a discussion arising from a point
in the textbook, or from some new fact introduced, or from
a teacher's comment.

AN INTEGRAL PART OF THE CURRICULUM

In this chapter we attempt to show that the spiritual idea is
an integral part of the curriculum and should be included
whenever required by the subject. A full treatment of any subject will naturally and necessarily bring in an implicit or explicit reference to God and to spiritual values.*

*To understand just how much this is in keeping with American concepts

97

Complete education demands that a teacher bring out ideas and values of a religious nature when and where they are required by a full and unbiased treatment of the subject under discussion. This does not mean that a teacher should unduly seek opportunities to inject spiritual emphasis, important as it is, where it does not properly belong.

In *American Education and Religion*, F. Ernest Johnson quotes this statement of Simon Greenberg (p. 56):

The schools cannot be said to be teaching history at all, if they eliminate completely whole areas of vital human experience. Religion and religious institutions have been determining factors in the evolution of civilization. To omit a study of them in a course in history, is to pervert history.

The same is true of the relation of the great religious literary monuments to the history of literature generally. Nor can one possibly dodge the religious issue in the teaching of science and philosophy. In those matters it is the public school educator rather than the religious leader who should be the active proponent of the proposal.

From the multitude of courses offered students we have selected only a few of the basic ones—simply enough to suggest an idea of what countless opportunities there are to integrate the spiritual into all phases and levels of education. All the suggestions apply to some level of education. It must be left to the teacher to decide if, and to what degree, these suggestions apply to his particular class. We merely mention them briefly. Parents and students may be interested in glancing through this chapter in order to see to what extent God really does *belong* in every phase of education.

---

of education from the very beginning, you would do well to consult Chapter XIX, "The Beginnings and Development of Our Schools." The religious inspiration was just as much part of our educational system as of our national life in general.

History

From prehistoric times to the present, the religious or spiritual factor has been prominent in the story of man. *The history of a particular civilization or culture is fundamentally a history of its religion and morality.* No people in any age has been entirely without faith of some kind and the outward expression of that faith in religious practice. The various accomplishments of a people must be understood in the light of this faith.

Western civilization, for instance, is incomprehensible without Christianity. Eastern culture can be understood in the light of Buddha, Confucius, and Lao Tze. The historian of the Near East needs a knowledge of Mohammedanism.

To go into any detail in such a vast subject as world history would be a staggering task. A few suggestions may suffice to show how a teacher interested in presenting the whole story can include the spiritual ideas as an integral part of history.

One teacher wrote us listing material along these lines which he discusses with his students:

1. Evidence of man's intelligence; his religious propensities; his belief in a Power greater than himself; life after death as manifested in recent archeological discoveries in Egypt and Babylonia; and so on.

2. The development of moral sense in organized communities and in individuals where men learn to work together for the common good; where penalties are inflicted on those who violate the rights of others.

3. The Old Testament as a source of historical information about the ancient Hebrews, their wanderings, their ideals, their subjugations; the role of Abraham, Jacob, Joseph, Moses, David, Solomon, etc.; inspiration which the stories of these great leaders have given to writers, artists, sculptors; effects of the Jewish beliefs on lands which conquered them, or to which they traveled.

4. The influence of the Ten Commandments, the Psalms, the Proverbs, and Prophecies on the character of the Jewish people; their great religious feasts: Passover, the Day of Atonement, Purim and the story of Esther, Hannukah and the story of the Maccabees, and many others.

5. Ancient Greece: The search for truth; teachings of Socrates; his beliefs concerning God, conscience, best methods of choosing public officials, obedience to laws; the high ideals expressed in the *Dialogues* of Plato, in the Oath of the Athenian Youth, in the Hippocratic Oath.

6. Ancient Rome: Rise of slavery, decline of self-reliant family, dictatorship. Oppression of conquered peoples of Near East (refer to uprising of Jews under the Maccabees, and their rejoicing at the rededication of the Temple which had been defiled by pagan Syrians). Census of Jews at time of birth of Jesus, coin of tribute, position of Pilate, publicans, etc.

7. Rise of Christianity: Teaching of Christ; recognition of His influence, His teaching, preaching, etc., by His contemporaries; by later generations; in art and literature.

8. The spread of Christianity throughout the Roman world: Effects of persecutions; lessons to be learned; what the Catacombs represent. Barbarians: invasions and conversion.

9. Middle Ages: Age of faith. Unity of Middle Ages. Rise of Christian art and philosophy. Monasticism—its meaning; its effects on civilization in Western Europe. Why monasteries flourished in the fifth and eighth centuries. Symbols used in the illuminated manuscripts; monks of the continent as architects and artists, as well as teachers.

10. Crusades: Their aim; reasons for their failure as a spiritual undertaking; rise of towns; influence of Church on economic life, on the family, on literature, on art.

11. Renaissance: Our cultural heritage from the great artists and writers of this period.

12. The Religious Upheaval of the XVI Century: Causes. The Reformers and their objectives. The Counter-Reformation and the Council of Trent. General results.

13. Age of exploration: Missionaries in America; opening of West; religious growth.

Any thorough course in history will include a large amount of material of genuine spiritual inspiration such as this.

A teacher who has a firm faith in God and an earnest desire to arouse in pupils an interest in their heritage cannot fail to bring out some of the story of God's gifts to man and man's use of his opportunities for good or evil ends. The experienced teacher does this naturally, gradually, and unobtrusively.

SCIENCE

The notions of the First Cause, evolution, law and design in Nature, chance and purpose, are only a few of the many subjects that will come up for discussion in the classroom. And in the American frame of thinking there need be no hesitancy in giving the full story, the whole truth.

The study of science is, from one point of view, the study of Divine Intelligence in operation through the laws of nature.

A professor of chemistry, Dr. Harold Faigenbaum of Rensselaer Polytechnic Institute, used the following method to impress upon his students this fact. At the conclusion of some of his courses he would say:

As we reach the end of this course in chemistry, I trust that it has become clear to you that in science it is not sufficient to be able to distinguish fact from fancy; we must also be prepared to find, on occasion, that what we consider to be the truth today may turn out to be false tomorrow. To a degree, therefore, we are always dealing with relative truth and not with absolute truth.

It is important that we appreciate this distinction lest we assume for science a kind of omnipotence which it cannot achieve. Finally, I am hopeful that the pattern of knowledge which, together, we have unfolded during the past few months has impressed you with more than its utility. It is also my hope that you have sensed that some Divine Intelligence guides and directs that pattern, and that one of man's highest missions is to help weave that pattern, so guided and so directed.

It is true that science is science, that many of these subjects are philosophical or theological, and that the course ought not to be converted into something other than itself. It is also true that to suppress these points is artificial and forced. These subjects may occupy only a small bit of the scheduled time, yet it would be surprising if they received no time at all. The human mind does not think in air-tight compartments.

In a high-school science class one boy asked the teacher, "Don't you think that a hundred years from now science will take the place of religion?"

The teacher's answer was direct. "It never will," she said. She proceeded briefly to show how religion and science were on different planes. Science tells how things happen; religion tells why. Science deals with the world of phenomena; religion with the spiritual.

"Science," she said, "cannot answer the final questions about the universe, life and destiny; for these questions do not belong to the world of matter but to the immaterial world."

The boy looked thoughtful and murmured, "I think you've got something there."

In her letter to us the teacher said: "A week never passes that there is not an opportunity to guide some child's thought into the right channels."

VOICE OF THE GREAT

The great scientists saw God in their work. Humbled by the truths that were made apparent to them in their laboratories, the best of them were of religious temperament. They themselves attributed this to their scientific work.

Newton, Pascal, Pasteur, Copernicus, Galileo, and many others were men of deep faith.

Kepler, the founder of modern astronomy, said, "O God, I am thinking Thy thoughts after Thee."

Pascal kept the New Testament with him as a constant companion and unfailing comfort.

Gauss, one of the three greatest mathematicians of all time, said: "There are problems to whose solution I should attach infinitely greater importance than to those of mathematics, for example, touching ethics, or our relation to God, or concerning our destiny and our future."

George Washington Carver, the celebrated chemurgist, said: "I discover nothing in my laboratory. If I come here of myself I am lost. But I can do all things through Christ. I am God's servant, His agent, for here God and I are alone. I am just the instrument through which He speaks and I would be able to do more if I were to stay in closer touch with Him. With my prayers I mix my labors and sometimes God is pleased to bless the results."

The French scientist, Lacomte du Noüy, in his book, *Human Destiny*, considers "the materialistic conception of life" scientifically impossible (chapter 3).

Steinmetz, another great scientist, wrote: "I think the greatest discovery will be along spiritual lines. Here is a force which history clearly teaches has been the greatest power in the development of man, yet we have been merely playing with it. We have not seriously studied it as we have the physical forces. Someday the scientists will turn their laboratories over to the study of God, and prayer and the spiritual forces, a subject which has hardly been scratched. When this day comes the world will see more advancement in one generation than it has in the past four generations."

There is a story told of a young college student in France who was on his way home for a vacation. On the train he was seated opposite an elderly man fingering a well-worn rosary. The youth spoke to him and said that he was silly to believe in God and prayer. He scoffed and claimed that as a science student, he could prove that all things came from nature, that there was no God. He asked the man for his name and address and promised to send him literature that would enlighten his poor, uninformed mind.

The old man silently put his hand into a coat pocket, took out his card, and handed it to the student. The youth took the card and with some dismay read the name: "Louis Pasteur, Professor of Science."

MATHEMATICS

In discussing the problem of God and education, we have met with a variety of reactions. Many go something like this:

"I can see how all you say is true of American history, literature, economics, maybe even science, but how in the world does it apply to mathematics?"

That is a good question, and it will help to sharpen our particular stand on this whole matter.

It is probable that God will not find His way into the subject matter of a mathematics class very frequently or at any great length. Still, it is difficult to see how in the more advanced classes the various discussions (which are usually encouraged) concerning the nature and theory of numbers, the notion of infinity, the mathematical structure of the universe, the absoluteness of mathematical law, etc., can fail to lead to the Cause of all things. If this question comes up it should be dealt with realistically.

THE MASTERS' VOICE

The greatest mathematicians seemed to encounter the fact of God; and when they did they said so. Their mention of Him may constitute but a fraction of a per cent of their words, but when the occasion arose they did not fail to speak. Any mathematics professor can do as much.

Here are a few samplings:

Pythagoras said: "God is number."

Plato said: "God eternally geometrizes."

Jacobi said: "God ever arithmetizes."

Jeans said: "The great Architect of the universe now appears as a Mathematician."

Einstein, on the occasion of the publication of his recent formula for a unified universe, said: "I cannot believe that God plays dice with the cosmos. . . . God is subtle, but never mischevious."

Many others who have been deeply impressed by the order and beauty of mathematics have seen in its Source and Cause, God the Creator.

The Teachers Too

Teachers have told us they have had several occasions to discuss these things in mathematics classes in direct reference to the subject matter.

Let the teacher ponder deeply the superior certainty of mathematical knowledge! It is absolute knowledge. It is also truth. Such crystal-clear and changeless truth must have a source. Mathematics is an ideal infinity; it supposes a real infinity.

Economics

A teacher in Rhode Island challenges anyone to show him one case of economic trouble or labor-management unrest that cannot be reduced to a moral problem. Here are his own words:

I am constantly amazed to find that problems which are considered only technical or neutral have a moral foundation.

I can show by reasoning alone, whether it be in economics,

history or social studies, that in all cases every problem or difficulty finally can be reduced to a violation of moral law. It is always a question of some right which has been overlooked or some duty or responsibility which has been omitted.

For example in economics: Take the problem of production in a factory. If production is lower than it should be, it is because there is a moral violation somewhere, perhaps a series of them.

There may be waste in the picture. A workman, let us say, is deliberately wasting material. If you speak to him he'll admit that he is, but he'll excuse it by claiming that one of his rights has been denied—the employer or the foreman has refused a raise, or perhaps has simply been surly to him.

If you speak to the foreman or the employer, he'll admit all of this but will excuse it by blaming his union, his competitors, or someone else. If you speak to these others, it's the same story. They all admit they've done something wrong, or at least something short of what is good and they try to save themselves by "passing the buck."

He concludes:

I think that the coming of Communism, the great depression, and the great wars are not only results of economic laws, but of the immorality of man.

Don't Oversimplify

This teacher's approach does not, of course, tell the whole story. It would be false to assert that economics can be broken down into simple moral applications. Economics is a science based on valid principles; these principles should all be brought to bear on any problem.

But basically economic acts are also human acts, and therefore moral acts. The moral factor cannot be ignored. This point can and should be emphasized today, particularly since the materialistic approach to economic matters is so much in the foreground. Christianity has always taught that economics and morality are very closely related, and our economic and labor-management problems of today are eloquent proof of this truth.

All of this may give the teacher a wider and truer view of his work. Any teacher of economics or industrial relations runs into ideas of honesty, justice, right, wrong, Divine Providence, atheistic materialism, and the like. And if these ideas come up in the classes, on what grounds should they not be discussed?

The study of both Communism and Capitalism necessitates bringing up philosophical and theological points for a complete understanding. As an example we may take the question of private property. According to Christian and American tradition, it is a natural right with social obligations; a natural right is built on natural law; and natural law comes from God.

Civics

By definition, civics is a study of the workings and principles of government, and in our schools, of American government in particular. It should show how these principles are spelled out in the Constitution and in our political methods and practices.

The teacher of civics ought to be convinced of one important fact: that our American government is based on a philosophy of natural, unalienable, God-given rights as stated in the Declaration of Independence and that the function of the government is to protect these rights.

He can, for instance, show that the whole American system is one of checks and balances, from top to bottom, in such a way that no one agency, institution, or official may acquire an excess of power of influence over another or over all. The fundamental rights of individuals and minorities are above the government. Our government's very structure guarantees that these rights cannot be seriously violated for long.

Here is the reason why our government consists of parts, the executive, the legislative, and the judicial; why there are two houses in Congress; why there are federal and state constitutions; why the terms of office holders are limited, etc.

A TEACHER'S VIEW

One teacher of civics suggested the following ideas for consideration in class:

1. Correct concept of authority: The source not in the ruler, but in God. Duties and rights correlative; their limits, their scopes. Inalienable rights: rights that I have no right to give away or to surrender.

2. Liberty: The right to do as one ought. *Ought* is the past participle of *owe*, meaning to be bound by duty or conscience. It implies morality; morality implies law; law implies God. What liberty is; what it is not.

3. Law: Detailed direction by which people are guided along the road of life to the goal of happiness. Not a violation of freedom but, on the contrary, a positive guarantee to its inviolability. Teach laws as protective, not merely prohibitive. Pope Leo XIII, *On Human Liberty*: "In man's free will . . . lies the very root of the necessity of law."

4. Motivation for obedience as stated in the commandment: Honor thy Father and thy Mother: God made the world by His own creative act. He could govern the world all by Himself; but in His Divine Providence, He shares the government of the world with others: parents, superiors, officers of the law. When I obey I am helping God to govern His world.

LITERATURE

Many books could be written on the references to God in literature. Literature in every language offers thousands of examples. The reason is not hard to find. Man's relations with God from the beginning of time colored most of his important activities. Writers, whether spiritually inclined or not, could hardly touch on a situation or a theme without hitting upon the fact of God in human affairs. Literature is one subject where the omission of all references to the spiritual element would destroy its life.

A teacher of English presented the following questions to her class as a basis for discussing the characters in a novel previously assigned.

Were there any decisions or actions in which you think any character showed poor judgment?

Name some situations in which a character acted wisely.

Were there any decisions or actions that were morally wrong?

Name situations in which you would have acted differently. Why?

Which character led the most successful life?

What have you learned about life and people from reading this book?

What are the author's beliefs and ideals?

Discussion of these questions proved so lively that it had to be continued the next day. The teacher said:

It seemed apparent that some pupils were examining for the first time their own ideas and ideals regarding such topics as marriage, divorce, honesty, wealth, success in life, and religious beliefs. Their discussion was surprisingly serious and seemed quite mature. They recognized rather quickly the need for some basic guiding principles instead of the attitude "whatever you can get away with."

It has been said, for example, that all great literature owes its greatness to the fact that its theme devolves on the great questions of life and death, good and evil. The plot must consist in a conflict of these ultimate realities.

Professor Hoxie Fairchild, in an essay entitled "Religious Perspectives in College Teaching," published by the Edward W. Hazen Foundation, writes (p. 13):

In my opinion, then, the teacher of English who does not encourage discussion of the ideas expressed or implied in books is depriving the study of literature of precisely those elements which constitute its principle value for a liberal education. But as a matter of fact the students, if they deserve to be in college at all, will indulge in such discussion whether the instructor encourages it or not. . . .

Literature is not taught in our schools merely to impart an appreciation of literary style. The classics in every tongue are taught because masters of style have given interpretations of life to the peoples of all nations and of all time. Therefore, great literature constantly comes back to spiritual truths and experiences.

THE BOOK OF BOOKS

So much of our literary heritage is related to the Bible that the student of English literature should have a good working knowledge of it.

When a certain class in English literature began the study of "Paradise Lost," the teacher discovered that hardly any of his students knew the story of the creation and fall of man. He had to tell it to them in order that they might have the necessary background for understanding Milton's work. Then he directed them to read the story in the Old Testament book of Genesis.

Daniel L. Marsh, President of Boston University, said in this connection that "Shakespeare's writings contain more than 550 quotations from the Bible or allusions to it."

Senator Paul Douglas, referring to Lincoln's mastery of English style, has said, ". . . this mastery was largely due to study and reflection upon the two most penetrating analyses of life, namely the Bible and the plays of Shakespeare."

A thorough grasp of literature necessitates on the part of the teacher a wide familiarity with religious and moral beliefs

and practices. Without this familiarity, a course in literature
will be full of blind spots and omissions.

Professor Fairchild, in the above quoted essay, gives an
idea of how true this is on the college level.

We quote him at length so that a teacher can apply the
same procedure to his work in other phases of literature classes.
He writes on pages 8 and 9:

Let us ask an imaginary English major a few questions pertaining both to religion and to the field in which he has chosen to
specialize. What parallels between Old Testament history and
English history are involved in Dryden's "Absalom and Achi-
tophel"? Tell the story of Susanna and the Elders.

What is a "Job's comforter," a "doubting Thomas," a "Mag-
dalene"? What are the connotations of "the voice of the turtle,"
"barren fig tree," "went by on the other side"? What are the "two
massy keys" of St. Peter in "Lycidas"? Explain Wordsworth's line,
"Thou liest in Abraham's bosom all the year," and the titles of
Swinburne's "Super Flumina Babylonis," Ruskin's "Unto This
Last," Aldous Huxley's *Eyeless in Gaza*.

List, without "editorializing," the chief doctrinal differences
between Roman Catholicism and Calvinistic Protestantism. Define
"predestination," "transubstantiation," "puritanism," "deism,"
"theism," "pantheism," "atonement," "schoolmen," "Dissenter,"
"Puseyite," "Higher Criticism," "ritual," "agnostic," "Papal In-
fallibility."

Account for Chaucer's treatment of the Prioress, Monk, Friar,
Parson, and Summoner respectively.

Discuss the interdependence of theology and politics in Spen-
ser's "Faerie Queene." Wherein does Crashaw represent the
Counterreformation? What does Donne mean by "The new philosophy puts all in doubt"? Is there anything curious about the
fact that the main theme of "Paradise Regained" is not the cruci-
fixion and resurrection, but the temptation in the wilderness? To
what extent is the "Essay on Man" consistent with Pope's Catholicism?

Show how the Evangelical Revival is reflected in the poems

of Cowper, and how the conflict between "Auld Licht" and "New
Licht" helps to motivate Burns's satires. In Browning's "Christmas-
Eve," why is infidelity represented by a Göttingen professor, and
why may we suppose that his name is Strauss?

Why does George Eliot display all the moral urgency, but
none of the religious beliefs, of a Puritan? Explain Hopkins' line,
"And you unhouse and house the Lord," in relation to the Catholic liturgy. To what seventeenth-century religious community does
T. S. Eliot allude in "Little Gidding"?

It would be possible to extend a similar quiz endlessly.
It is not possible to list here the hundreds of pieces of prose,
poetry, or references in point, the understanding of which requires a real grasp of religious matters in general and of Christianity in particular.

This is the teacher's task—at least if he is to maintain a
high standard of competence, and if he is to pass on to his
students the full riches contained in the great writings of our
culture.

Art and Music

The fine arts are an interpretation of beauty in concrete form.
They are concerned with man's highest inspirations. Of all
subjects along with literature they are most intimately connected with God and the things of the spirit. The good art
teacher and the good teacher of music appreciation will respect
this and try to explain it to the students. The history of art
and music and literature is a vast study of the aspirations of
the ages.

An art teacher tells the story of how once on the occasion
of a discussion centered on Rodin's famous sculpture, "The
Thinker," a student declared:

"Do you know what he seems to be thinking of? He is
saying to himself: 'The cost of living is going up. Times are
very bad.'"

The teacher replied:

"No, I do not believe he is thinking of that. He is more likely thinking of eternity. He seems to say, 'Who put me here, and what am I here for?'"

The teacher went on to tell the student that we cannot interpret the past according to our present preoccupations. Rodin's "Thinker" is not a 1952 American. The sculptor tried to have him represent the deeper thoughts of all the ages.

And so it is with all the other great art subjects. A minority of them are free of some connection with the great questions that have always occupied men's better moments. From the earliest art to the present, the religious or the spiritual theme plays a dominant role. The competent art teacher will respect this fact, and will try to explain it.

A treatment of art cannot escape frequent reference to the things of God. Most of the greatest artists and most of their greatest works deal directly with these things. A listing of them would run into the thousands.

To the art teacher falls the task, if he is completely objective, of displaying these works in their fullest meaning.

It is the same in music. Whether it be the great operas, songs, choral works, anthems, spirituals, or popular music, the religious reference is paramount. Again the great ones bring out our point best. Our own American patriotic songs and our Negro spirituals are particularly a fertile field in this regard. To insist more on this thesis would be to belabor the obvious. The teacher need not search far to find many examples of the recognition of God in music. This recognition is too much a part of our American culture to have failed to enter into our music and song. To omit this element is to be untrue not only to the musical art but to our American culture as well.

Social Studies

Within the past ten years many radical changes have been made in the curriculum, especially in geography, history, civics, and current events. In the past emphasis in geography was placed on the physical and economic aspects of individual countries of the Eastern and the Western Hemispheres. As for history, the chronological and biographical phases of life through the ages were stressed. In civics the structure of government at all levels was the main consideration.

Today, history, geography, civics, and current events are woven into one complex whole under the title of "social studies," with emphasis placed on the role of the individual in human society, on how he lives, works, and plays with his fellow men. The following extract from the foreword of the *Course of Study in Social Studies of New York City* provides a clear definition of this course. It reads:

The social studies curriculum, as here presented, weaves together history, geography and current affairs, and emphasizes their mutual relationship. The program is developed through the study of major problems which make large use of historic, geographic and civic learnings as they are needed in the solutions of the problems. These learnings are interrelated through appropriate activities and experiences. Thus pupils understand the relationship of time and place, and the influence of people and events in city, state, nation and the world.

In the United States the principal aim of the social studies program is to train boys and girls to think and to act in full conformity with the American ideal of democracy; in fact, to develop American citizens with an inquiring mind in search of truth and a sound critical judgment, men and women who will dedicate themselves to a recognition of the dignity and worth of each individual regardless of race, creed, color, national origin, or economic status and thus bring to fruition and materialization the American heritage as voiced in the Declaration of Independence, the Constitution of the United States, the Bill of Rights, and the Emancipation Proclamation.

One can see at a glance how rich in opportunities the

social studies course is for showing in a factual way how deeply rooted in religious and spiritual values are the relations of man with his fellow man. For the brotherhood of man ultimately depends on the Fatherhood of God.

COUNSELING OR GUIDANCE

A teacher in a secondary school tells us about a young man who was, in her estimation, the most difficult case she had ever handled.

It was not a case of retarded development or the usual delinquency. Here was a boy with definite criminal tendencies. He had been caught stealing cars and molesting small girls, and had been involved in many acts of violence. All the usual techniques and treatments were applied. His unwholesome home conditions were looked into, special attention and many kindnesses were showered on him to help rehabilitate him—all to no avail.

The boy seemed only to advance more rapidly down the path that would most likely lead to a life outside the law and eventual imprisonment.

Only one thing stopped his rush toward destruction—a far sighted and inspired teacher.

She gave her finest efforts. Not considering herself a superior educationalist or psychologist, she knew she would have to rely on other resources yet untried. She decided to use what she herself considered her own greatest asset and power—her faith in God and her reliance on Christian charity. Perhaps these might succeed where the rest had failed.

A POSITIVE APPROACH

Her persuasive kindness got her a hearing with the boy. Then at a certain point she asked him: "Do you believe in God?"

"I don't know," he hesitated, ". . . I guess so."

"Would you or your parents mind if I talk about Him? I think it will help you."

The boy had no objection, nor did his parents, who were quite indifferent about the matter.

This teacher restricted her talks with the boy entirely to the basic notions of God as they appear for instance in the Declaration and in the talks of our great men. She felt that even this minimum would help to accomplish her purpose—a knowledge of God as a solicitous Father Who is interested in our lives and destinies, Who rewards our good actions and punishes our evil actions. In other words, she taught the boy only what he would learn if all the facts and facets of our traditions had been brought into the various classes he attended.

This approach accomplished the seemingly impossible. In a short time and with the ever-ready encouragement of the teacher, the boy changed radically. The energy he had spent in wrongdoing became channeled in another direction. Eventually he became a model student and leader in school affairs. He had caught some of the faith and charity of this farsighted teacher and he rebuilt his life on faith in God and love of his fellow men.

THE DIFFICULT CASES

There is no doubt that there are some cases a teacher meets where nothing will avail except a recourse to religious principles. Even in the mind of the child there is the conviction that unless there is a God, nothing means very much, life has no meaning, right and wrong have no meaning. The child, like the adult, needs a higher loyalty.

Counseling in schools is a very important phase of education. More and more of it is being done in an organized way. So much the better, provided that counseling services of this kind do not become divorced from spiritual and religious values. These values are needed in counseling perhaps more than anywhere else.

A Sacred Trust

The individual teacher can find his best opportunities to stress the religious values of our American heritage in his personal contacts with the students. If the student or his parents are willing, the teacher can inquire about his beliefs, his church affiliations. He can if he wishes, refer to the Ten Commandments, the Christian precepts of morality, particularly the obligations of charity or love of neighbor. He can encourage church attendance in a general way. He can mention God as a rewarder and punisher of our deeds. And so on. There is nothing in all of this that is not a part of American belief and practice.

It is good for teachers and counselors to use to the utmost the various scientific and psychological techniques that have been learned in recent years. But these can best be used in a spiritual context.

The ageless and universal truths about man as a creature created in God's image, endowed with inalienable rights and responsibilities, should be the basis for these scientific methods. Especially in the case of young people these higher values are necessary in order to give a meaning to life's problems—the struggle with temptation, life in community with others, and so forth.

Once again, in the case of the individual student, as in the case of our national life, it is a question of wedding the old and the new, the modern with the timeless. Any teacher who works on this basis will have better success in his relations with his students, and will long remain in their memories as a vital force for good in their lives.

The Homeroom Teacher

A certain intimacy between a good teacher and the students is bound to grow. It enables them to talk about things that ordinarily would remain unsaid. Teachers tell of many little incidents that happen from day to day in their homeroom class.

The following story comes from a kindergarten teacher:

One day the fire engines clanged past the school building. A little girl came over to the teacher with a worried look on her face and said: "Please pray. My Mommy always makes me pray when we hear the engines because it might be my Daddy. Please, can't we pray?"

The teacher turned to the class and said: "Elaine would like us to say a prayer that her Daddy, who is a fireman, will be safe. That might be his engine going to the fire right now." So the little tots shut their eyes while the teacher prayed: "God bless Elaine's Daddy and keep him safe." Elaine smiled happily and went back to play.

The matter could not have been dealt with more successfully.

In and out of class the subject of God will occasionally arise. It may be on the occasion of the death of a relative, of trouble at home or trouble in school. The teacher can use this knowledge of the pupil's family and of his beliefs to offer comfort or advice.

The question of the "equal creation" of all men by God is bound to come up in questions concerning race, creed, color, or the social or political differences of the students.

The various holidays of all faiths will affect the school schedule and can scarcely pass without a sympathetic and intelligent reference. Thanksgiving Day, Christmas, Yom Kippur, Passover, Easter, Memorial Day, and others are times when school is out for all or some of the students. A discreet word of explanation about them is in order.

And so it can be with many other extracurricular activities. The discretion and honesty of the teacher will guide him to incorporate all of this, while still keeping within the framework of our best traditions.

The suggestions submitted in this chapter are only a few of thousands that could be proposed. But these few may suggest many others to the teacher. Those who look into it will find that the field is rich.

nine

Fountainhead of Our Freedom

SINCE THE DECLARATION OF INDEPENDENCE DEPENDS
so much for its basic strength on both Natural Law and the revealed truths that have come down to us through the ages, it
is important that we should know (1) something of the setting in which this immortal document was prepared, (2) how
it invokes the authority of God in four different ways, and
finally (3) its significance for us today.

STORY OF THE DECLARATION OF INDEPENDENCE

The great story of the Declaration of Independence begins on
June 7, 1776, in Philadelphia. The Second Continental Congress had been in continuous session since May 10, 1775. No
recesses were called but when necessary the members were free
to absent themselves as they needed.

Jefferson had gone home to Monticello in December,
1775, and when he returned to Philadelphia in May, 1776, he
looked for lodgings. These he found on Market Street. They
were simple quarters on the second floor, comprising a parlor
and a bedroom. In the parlor he put his little folding writing
box constructed by Benjamin Randolph, his own cabinet-
maker, who made it according to Jefferson's personal specifications. This parlor and this writing box were to play an important part in the composition of the immortal document he
would pen within another month.

Nearly fifty years later he tried to reconstruct from memory the description of the house for a Dr. Mease of Philadelphia:

> At the time of writing that instrument [the Declaration] I lodged in the house of a Mr. Graaf, a new brick house, three stories high of which I rented the second floor consisting of a parlour and bedroom ready furnished. In that parlour I wrote habitually and in it wrote this paper particularly. . . . The proprietor Graaf was a young man, son of a German, and then newly married. I think he was a bricklayer, and that his house was on the S. side of Market street, probably between 7th and 6th and if not then the only house on that part of the street, I am sure there were few others yet built near it. . . . I have some idea, but very faint that it was a corner house. . . .

A. Nation's Will to Be Free

When Jefferson reached the Continental Congress, the subject of independence from Great Britain had already been debated. On May 18, the Virginia delegates (during the absence of Jefferson) had been instructed to propose a declaration of independence to the Continental Congress. Already Virginia had declared its independence of England. In fact in the middle of June, Jefferson was instructed to send a list of grievances to the Williamsburg convention to be incorporated into the Virginia declaration. This work was to serve him as a model to follow when preparing a similar document for the United Colonies.

The Decision

On June 7, Richard Henry Lee, a member from Virginia, gained the floor of the Congress. Standing, paper in hand, he faced the Congress and spoke in a deep and sonorous voice: "Resolved: That these United Colonies are, and of right,

ought to be free and independent States, that they are ab-
solved (freed) from all allegiance to the British Crown, and
that all political connection between them and the State of
Great Britain is, and ought to be totally dissolved."

John Adams fairly threw himself at President John Hancock in order to get immediate recognition: "I second the
resolution moved by the delegate from Virginia."

The resolution was put before the body, but it was decided that the issue was too momentous to decide that day.
Debate was postponed until the next morning.

The next day was Saturday. Debate raged all day long.
Adams and Lee led the fight for declaring independence. Rut-
ledge thought the time not yet ripe. Everyone knew what the
results of a declaration would be: certain war with Great
Britain and possible, even probable, defeat. Robert Livingston
said: "We must find some nation to help us. War is bound to
follow a declaration of independence. We must make ready
to fight such a war."

A statement of this kind, however, did not deter most of
the delegates, it only served to arouse them.

Dr. John Witherspoon, a Presbyterian minister who was
President of Princeton, as well as a member of the Congress,
never addressed his fellow members without a memorized
speech. Yet he now rose and said heatedly: "In my judgment,
the country is not only ripe for independence but it is in
danger of becoming rotten for want of it."

The argument went from side to side. Evening fell and a
decision was again put off until the following Monday.

The Committee of Five

It was agreed on Monday to postpone a vote on the resolution
until July 1. A committee of five, comprising Jefferson, Adams,
Franklin, Roger Sherman, and Robert Livingston, was appointed to draft a declaration.

The committee met, it is believed, at a place on Bristol Pike where Franklin was confined by an attack of gout. Jefferson was chosen chairman, and the views of the five on what the declaration should contain were outlined. Then Jefferson was asked to write up a first draft.

In his diary Adams dramatizes the episode and gives the reasons for Jefferson's selection:

ADAMS: (Jefferson proposed to me to make the draught. I said), I will not; you shall do it.
JEFFERSON: Oh no!
ADAMS: Why will you not? You ought to do it. I will not.
JEFFERSON: Why?
ADAMS: Reasons enough.
JEFFERSON: What can be your reasons?
ADAMS: Reason 1st; You are a Virginian and a Virginian ought to appear at the head of this business. Reason 2nd. I am obnoxious, suspected and unpopular; you are very much otherwise. Reason 3rd. You can write ten times better than I can.
JEFFERSON: Well, if you are decided, I will do as well as I can.
ADAMS: Very well, when you have drawn it up we will have a meeting.

The Masterful Pen

Jefferson set to work at once. Throughout the warm days of June he labored in his room on Market Street. He wrote, as he said later, "without reference to a book or pamphlet." A commentator of the day said, "He poured the soul of a continent into his manifesto."

When Jefferson had finished the original draft he passed it on to Franklin and Adams for their criticism. Very few changes were made. Jefferson wrote to Madison at a later date: "Their alterations were two or three only and merely verbal.

I then wrote a fair copy, reported it to the Committee, and from them, unaltered, to the Congress."

However, nineteen corrections in all appear on the first page of Jefferson's rough copy. It is certain that Franklin made two corrections and Adams, five. The original draft was then reported to the Committee and ended with a total of twenty-six changes and an addition of three paragraphs.

BIRTH PANGS OF A NEW NATION

On Friday, June 28, Jefferson presented the Declaration to Congress. Debate broke out again. Both sides measured their strength, one vote per colony. As the day wore on, tempers and temperature soared. The resolution was obviously getting nowhere. Providentially two incidents occurred to cool off the situation—a thundershower and a message from George Washington, already in command of the Continental Army, encamped near New York where it was threatened with defeat.

Yet John Hancock, President of the Congress, once again postponed the discussion on the declaration.

WHAT ONE VOTE CAN DO!

When the session had adjourned, John Adams approached a delegate from Delaware (two of the delegates from Delaware were split on independence), and said: "We need Delaware's vote. But Delaware has three delegates. Where is the third man?"

"He's in southern Delaware. What do you think of sending for him?" the delegate asked.

"He favors independence, I take it," countered Adams.

The man nodded assent.

"Then send for him at once," Adams cried, "and may Heaven speed his horse's feet."

The next day as the members were entering the Statehouse, a horse carrying a weary rider galloped up Chestnut Street. Cesar Rodney, the missing delegate, dismounted quickly and rushed into the Statehouse.

"You've made it," exclaimed one delegate, shaking his hand. "I hardly dared hope you would when I sent the messenger."

"Yes, I made it," Rodney replied. "I'd have come from the ends of the earth to vote for independence."

And vote for independence he did, casting the one vote needed to swing the Convention.

In short order a roll call was made for the consideration of Lee's resolution for independence. Twelve colonies (not including New York) voted in favor. It was July 2. John Adams called it the "most important day in the history of America."

A Momentous Session

For two days Jefferson's declaration was read and examined paragraph by paragraph. Changes were made, parts were eliminated, ideas were incorporated. Jefferson sat in his place and said nothing. Franklin, sitting down beside him tried to console him by saying: "I have made a rule for myself. It is to avoid whenever possible writing papers to be reviewed by a public body."

Franklin followed this with the jest about the hatter. This man had designed a sign containing detailed information about himself and his shop. After submitting the sign to his friends for criticism, everything was removed from it except the man's name and a picture of a hat turned upside down.

Jefferson smiled with resignation. Several years later he thus remembered the event:

The debate seemed as though it would run on interminably. The weather was oppressively warm and the room occupied by the delegates was hard by a livery stable, whence the horseflies swarmed thick and fierce, alighting on the legs of the members and biting hard through their thin silk stockings. Handkerchiefs in hand they lashed at the hungry pests to no avail. Finally the annoyance became intolerable, and the members made haste to bring the momentous session to a close.

On the whole, the declaration as Jefferson reported it, stood up well. Almost three-quarters of it remained untouched.

July 4, 1776

Early in the afternoon of July 4, the discussion ended. The revised copy was then read and a vote was taken. Twelve colonies voted for independence. The New York delegate, though in favor, still had to await instructions from home. No doubt, with the British in the harbor and George Washington just outside the city with the Continental Army, the New York legislature was in continuous session and preferred to decide for itself on the question of independence.

In any event it was done. With a majestic pronouncement the colonies had severed their ties with Britain and had become free and independent.

Post riders carried the eventful news to the thirteen colonies. Accompanying each was a copy of John Hancock's letter, dated July 6, addressed to the head of every assembly. Part of it reads:

Sir,

Although it is not possible to foresee the Consequences of human Action, yet it is nevertheless a Duty . . . to trust the Event to that Being who controls both Causes and Events. . . . The important Consequences to the American States from this Declaration of Independence considered as the Ground and Foundation of a future Government, will naturally suggest the Propriety of having it proclaimed in such a Manner as that the People may be universally informed of it."

The new nation had been started on its way, and this Declaration of Independence was to be its foundation, its framework. All that has come since has grown from this. No wonder John Adams wrote to his wife Abigail that the day "ought to be solemnized with pomp and parade . . . from one end of this continent to the other, from this time forward, forevermore.

On July 15 the New York Convention sent its resolution in favor of the act. Thus, the Declaration of Independence was rightly entitled "The Unanimous Declaration of the Thirteen United States of America." This marked the first known use of the term "United States of America."

THE FATEFUL SIGNING

Only John Hancock, the President, and Charles Thomson, the Secretary, signed the Declaration of Independence on the Fourth of July.

Hancock, the delegate from Massachusetts, signed first, and with gusto. Grasping the pen, he wrote his name in letters so sweeping that since that day "putting your John Hancock" on paper has become synonomous for a well-formed signature. And as Hancock wrote it, he exclaimed: "There! John Bull can read that without spectacles, and may he double his reward of five hundred pounds for my head. *That is my defiance.*"

Then, realizing the gravity of the moment, he added: "We must be unanimous—there must be no pulling different ways—we must all hang together."

"Yes," quipped Franklin, "we must, indeed, all hang together, or assuredly we shall all hang separately."

AND FIRST IN PRAYER

When George Washington, a deeply religious man, received word of the issuance of the Declaration of Independence, he met the solemnity of the occasion in a characteristic manner and wrote this prayer:

Almighty God:

We make our earnest prayer that Thou wilt keep the United States in Thy holy protection; that Thou wilt incline the hearts of the citizens to cultivate a spirit of subordination and obedience to government; and entertain a brotherly love and affection for one another and for their fellow citizens of the United States at large. And, finally, that Thou wilt most graciously be pleased to dispose us all to do justice, to love mercy and to demean ourselves with that charity, humility and pacific temper of mind which were the characteristics of the Divine Author of our blessed religion, and without a humble imitation of whose example in these things we can never hope to be a happy nation.

Grant our supplication, we beseech Thee, through Jesus Christ Our Lord, Amen.

Washington then ordered the Declaration of Independence read to the army in New York. The gilded lead statue of King George III on horseback, which stood in Bowling Green, was at once pulled down from its pedestal and melted into bullets for the use of the American troops. In all the colonies pictures of the King were destroyed, and the royal coat of arms was torn from public buildings.

Congress and the people were at one in their gratitude to God and dedication of their new nation to Him. The Declaration was read in all the Churches followed by thanksgiving services.

For Better or Worse

By August 2, the majority of the delegates were able to sign the Declaration of Independence. William Ellergy, a delegate from Rhode Island, has left us an interesting account of the signing:

I was determined to see how they all looked as they signed what might be their death warrant. I placed myself beside the secretary, Charles Thomson, and eyed each member closely as he affixed his name to the document. Undaunted resolution was displayed in every countenance. Although I taxed my powers of penetration, I could discover no trace of fear among them; all seemed impressed with the solemnity of the occasion.

GREATER LOVE THAN THIS . . .

The responsibility felt by each of these men meant a subordination of all their personal interests to the welfare of the new nation. But they could not stop—they could not give in.

This letter from John Adams to James Warren, written some three weeks after the signing of the Declaration of Independence, crystalized the perseverance of the Founding Fathers:

Mr. Sam Adams, between you and me, is completely worn out. I wish he had gone home six months ago, and rested himself. In plain English, he has been so long here, and his strength and spirits so exhausted, that a hundred such delegates here would not be worth a groat.

My own case is worse. My face is grown pale, my eyes weak and inflamed, my nerves tremulous and my mind weak as water. . . . A few months' rest and relaxation will recoup me, but this is absolutely necessary to that end.

MILLIONS FOR INDEPENDENCE

Charles Carroll of Carrollton, Maryland, a Catholic, was considered the wealthiest man to sign the Declaration of Independence. Carroll was thought to be taking a risk far greater than the others because of his wealth. John Adams wrote this praise of Charles Carroll:

. . . a gentleman of independent fortune, perhaps the largest in America . . . ; educated in some university in France, though

a native of America, of great abilities and learning, complete master of the French language, and a professor of the Roman Catholic
religion, yet a warm, a firm, a zealous supporter of the rights of
America, in whose cause he has hazarded his all.

When the signers of the Declaration of Independence
had gathered, John Hancock asked Charles Carroll if he would
sign it. "Most willingly," answered Carroll as he prepared to
put his name to the document.

"There goes a few millions," remarked John Adams who
was standing near by; and all agreed that few took a greater
risk than Charles Carroll.

Just as Carroll was signing, Hancock again remarked
jokingly: "There are so many Carrolls in Maryland, the English will never know who this one is; so you're safe."

By way of reply Carroll wrote, "Charles Carroll of Carrollton," thereby placing the name of his town beside his own
name, and said: "I don't want any mistake about this; there
is only one Carrollton."

He reflected well the spirit of the others. That some of
the signers later suffered recriminations for their courageous
stand is well illustrated in the story of Lewis Morris, the representative from New York in the Continental Congress. The
father of six sons and four daughters, he lived with his family
in a large, comfortable mansion surrounded by a thousand
acres of forest land.

After the Revolution broke out, the British burned his
woodland, wrecked his mansion, scattered his livestock, and
smashed the many miles of fences which protected his lands.

His family and tenants were driven out. For seven years
the family suffered great deprivations. The three oldest Morris
sons endured even greater hardships in the Continental Army.

But with all this suffering, Lewis Morris never regretted
putting his name to the document which fathered the new
republic. His sense of obligation and sacrifice was no greater

than that of the others who risked their all when they signed
the Declaration of Independence.

THE SOURCE OF THEIR STRENGTH

Who were these men who started our country? Were they
unusual in any way? Did they all possess extraordinary talents
that could never be duplicated? No, not at all. They were men
who could be found in any age, even though Gladstone, the
famous jurist of the time, said they were "a group unequaled
in the history of the world."

Many explanations can be given for the determination
and courage of the Founding Fathers. They were, for the most
part, deeply religious men, and their faith in God was certainly
one source of their strength.

One person who symbolized the essential spirit of the
Continental Congress was William Ellery of Rhode Island. A
lawyer and Congregationalist, Ellery was so intent upon their
purposes that he closed every speech he made with the words
from the psalmist, "The Lord reigneth."

John Page, a delegate of the Virginia Convention and a
lifelong friend of Jefferson, showed his deep satisfaction with
the new document by a short prayer, "God preserve the
United States."

The fascinating story of the origin of our Declaration of
Independence and of the men who drew it up impresses us
with the greatness of this document and the intrepid spirit of
these men.

It is important, however, to consider the deeper meaning
of this charter of our liberties, and the philosophy of life and
government to which it dedicates our nation.

GOD IN THE DECLARATION OF INDEPENDENCE

Too often in our classrooms the Declaration of Independence
is merely referred to in passing as if it were of historical in-

terest alone. Sometimes it is presented only as a declaration of grievances in rebellion against the British King.

And yet the greatest significance of the Declaration of Independence lies in the first few paragraphs which voice the American idea of government and life. Not to know these is not to know the very heart of America.

Abraham Lincoln made reference to this fact when he wrote:

> All honor to Jefferson—to the man, who in the concrete pressure of a struggle for national independence by a single people, had the coolness, forcast and sagacity to introduce into a merely revolutionary document an abstract truth, applicable to all men and all times, and so to embalm it there that to-day and in all coming days it shall be a rebuke and a stumbling-block to the very harbingers of reappearing tyranny and oppression.

The best scholars agree with Lincoln. The larger, second part of the Declaration rests on the first, just as its authors understood that the right to change a government rests on a natural God-given right.

In the following pages we outline a few ideas that are merely suggestive of a deeper treatment. There is a job to be done here. We leave it to the experts to explore the questions more thoroughly.

The essence of the Declaration is an appeal to God, the Author of life and of all human rights, to justify the rebellion of the Colonies against the King and Parliament of England.

In this real sense, we may say that God is the very cornerstone of American life and thought.

Actually, God is mentioned in the Declaration four times. Each mention of Him is made, not in a merely pious, offhanded way, but in a deliberate and significant manner.

FIRST REFERENCE TO GOD

In the first version of the Declaration of Independence, Jefferson wrote the name of God but once, but he did this in a very crucial way. This mention is in the first sentence:

When, in the course of human events, it becomes necessary for one people to dissolve the political bands which have connected them with another, and to assume, among the powers of the earth, the separate and equal station to which the *laws of nature and of nature's God* entitle them, a decent respect to the opinions of mankind requires that they should declare the causes which impel them to the separation.

It is plain that Jefferson justified this momentous severance of national relations by an appeal to the "law of nature." It was, in other words, an appeal to a "higher law," a law established by God through creation and instilled on the minds and in the hearts of men and in the nature of things.

To this "natural law" all are subject whether as individuals or as nations. It is the foundation of any justifiable revolution.

SECOND REFERENCE TO GOD

The second mention of God appears in a revision Jefferson made of his first draft. Here he wishes to emphasize that our fundamental liberties which we receive through this "natural law" derive ultimately from God. Thus, he rules out a sort of deism which would put everything in the laws of nature. We read:

We hold these truths to be self-evident—that all men are created equal; that they are *endowed by their Creator* with certain unalienable rights; that among these are life, liberty, and the pursuit of happiness.

In his first draft Jefferson had written: ". . . and from that equal creation they derive rights inherent and unalienable."

In his own hand he changed this phrasing to read: "endowed by their Creator with certain unalienable rights."

THE ROLE AND FUNCTION OF GOVERNMENT

This addition served to make more explicit Jefferson's proposition in the first paragraph, that our rights are founded in God through nature itself. We can understand in a graphic way by the following diagram:

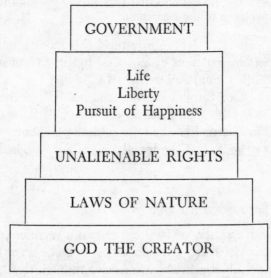

The dome of government in the United States must be built on this foundation of God-given natural rights. Such was the belief of Jefferson and his contemporaries in the colonies.

NATURAL RIGHTS FORM OF GOVERNMENT

Upon the idea of a natural higher law coming from divine law, from which flow certain inalienable rights, the authors of the

Declaration of Independence built the American concept of government. Under God the people were to be supreme; the state or government was to be their servant. The majority was destined to rule, but minority rights were to be safeguarded. The common good was to be sought, but individual rights were to be preserved. We read: "To secure these rights, governments are instituted among men, deriving their just powers from the consent of the governed."

THE RIGHT TO REBEL

Founded on the same basis of natural law is the right of rebellion against a tyrannical abuse of authority which would violate the rights of the individual, the minority, or the majority. The American Revolution, in which our nation was born, carried into effect this fundamental truth of God-given natural rights which are superior to all human institutions, legislation, or authority. We read in the Declaration:

. . . whenever any form of government becomes destructive of these ends, it is the right of the people to alter or abolish it, and to institute a new government, laying its foundations on such principles, and organizing its powers in such form, as to them shall seem most likely to effect their safety and happiness.

Thus, in these few incisive sentences written at the very beginning of the life of our nation all possibility of totalitarian dictatorship or of an omnipotent state was eliminated. A simple loyalty to these first principles of our government set forth in the Declaration of Independence will save us from the pitfalls of tyranny. But if recognition of our dependence on God should ever be stricken from our theory of government or our way of life, we would have reason to fear the suppression of our liberties and the deification of the state.

THIRD REFERENCE TO GOD

God is next mentioned in the Declaration at the beginning of the last paragraph. Jefferson had written,

> We, therefore, the representatives of the United States of America in General Congress assembled, do, in the name and by the authority of the good people of these States, reject and renounce all allegiance . . .

The "Committee of Five" left this unchanged.

But now it came to the Congress. They inserted after the words "Congress assembled," the phrase, *"appealing to the Supreme Judge of the world* for the rectitude of our intentions." Congress too, apparently, wanted to go on record as finding in God the justification for the new American Nation.

FOURTH REFERENCE TO GOD

In the last sentence of the Declaration the Congress did it again. Into Jefferson's copy they inserted after the words "support of this declaration" the phrase, "with a firm reliance on divine Providence . . ."

Thus they made a final act of prayerful faith in God, the Creator and Judge of the world and of men.

THE TEACHING OF THE DECLARATION OF INDEPENDENCE

God appears in this great document, then, as Creator, Judge, Provider, and the Source of all our basic rights: in other words, just as He is conceived of in the Judaeo-Christian tradition. He is woven inextricably not only into the texture of the document but into the fabric of our national philosophy of Government.

There is no doubt that our Founding Fathers firmly believed that a rejection of God would be a rejection of the American government as they understood it. They would certainly be deaf to any plea for a "secularist" or non-religious way of life such as is pleaded for by some circles of thought today.

In the Declaration of Independence alone we have an answer to those who would seek to banish God from our schools or any other public institutions. Just to read it in the classroom is to make a profession of faith.

The Declaration Today

Since the day it was written the Declaration of Independence has served us well. From its inspiration came our Constitution in 1787, the Bill of Rights in 1791, Jacksonian democracy in the 1820's, the humanitarian movement of the 1840's; it was the foundation upon which Lincoln depended in the War between the States.

No greater champion of the Declaration of Independence ever lived than Abraham Lincoln. In his address on February 22, 1861, which he delivered in Independence Hall in Philadelphia, he said:

. . . all the political sentiments I entertain have been drawn, so far as I have been able to draw them, from the sentiments which originated in and were given to the world from this hall. I have never had a feeling, politically, that did not spring from the sentiments embodied in the Declaration of Independence.

But most impressive of all are these words of the "lost speech" (1856) of the great Emancipator:

This was their lofty, and wise and noble understanding of the justice of the Creator to His creatures, to the whole great family of man. In their enlightened belief nothing stamped with the Divine image and likeness was sent into the world to be trodden on and degraded, and imbruted by its fellows.

Now, my countrymen, if you have been taught doctrines

which conflict with the great landmarks of the Declaration of Independence; if you have listened to suggestions which would take from its grandeur, and mutilate the symmetry of its proportions; if you have been inclined to believe that all men are not created equal in those inalienable rights enumerated by our charter of liberty; let me entreat you to come back. Return to the fountains whose waters spring close by the blood of the Revolution.

Think nothing of me—take no thought for the fate of any man whomsoever—but come back to the truths that are in the Declaration of Independence. Do not destroy the immortal emblem of humanity, the Declaration of Independence.

There is little doubt that it was Lincoln's firm devotion to the principles of the Declaration that gave him the force and courage to carry his country through a Civil War for the preservation of national unity.

In Woodrow Wilson's Day

It is interesting to note that President Woodrow Wilson, who saw us through the First World War and then set up the League of Nations, was faithful to the principles of the Declaration of Independence. He said: "Jefferson's Declaration of Independence is a practical document for the use of practical men. It is not a thesis for philosophers, but a whip for tyrants; it is not a theory of government, but a program of action."

Thus it is clear that every great American who fought for the rights of all as opposed to tyranny found both the spirit and the letter for his stand in the Declaration of Independence. We may also assume that any departure from these truths now or in the future would be a flight from freedom.

The Travels of a Document

For a hundred and one years after it was adopted and signed the Declaration of Independence had no permanent home. During its wanderings the document found shelter in ten cities and five states, twice narrowly escaping destruction by fire. In both the Revolutionary War and the War of 1812 it nearly fell into the hands of the British.

In 1894, the text dimmed by more than fifty years' exposure to light, and the signatures damaged by too frequent rolling of the parchment, the document was placed in a safe in the State Department library.

Later, in 1921, it was moved to the Library of Congress where it was for many years on exhibition in a shrine especially constructed for its preservation and safekeeping.

Finally, in 1952, the precious parchment was placed in the National Archives Building in Washington and encased in a special mechanical vault which lowers it to a bomb-proof shelter after exhibition hours.

WORK FOR ALL

There is a long road ahead before we can be sure that the principles of our charter of liberties are known and respected by all young Americans. We believe a greater effort is needed to attain this goal. Teachers, citizens, and legislators should do what they can to put the spotlight on the idea of God-given rights in this document.

One lawyer in the midwest introduced a bill into the legislature requiring that instruction be given in the schools on the entire Declaration of Independence. We quote the bill at length as a suggestion for teachers who would like to prepare a course of their own for their students, or others who hope to promote the teaching of the Declaration of Independence in schools.

This lawyer stated his case clearly in the opening passages of the law: that thorough teaching of the Declaration of Independence would be a step in the right direction in giving students an idea of their birthright and dignity and responsibility.

Here we quote a few sections from the proposed law:

1. "*Nature's God,*" means the Author of all nature.

2. "*Nature's law,*" means the fixed principles which govern the course of the planets and stars, the relation and sequence of the seasons, the orderly phenomena of chemistry and physics, and the growth and development of all life as well as the laws found within the dictates of man's reason.

3. "*All men are created equal,*" means the original bringing into existence of human life by the Creator, which self-evident truth makes all men equal as to their origin and right to life, liberty and the pursuit of happiness, in contrast to the foreign state ideologies that hold that men are not created at all but evolve necessarily through accident or chance or that certain races are created superior to others and can, therefore, subject inferior races accordingly.

4. "*That they are endowed by their Creator with certain inalienable rights,*" means that our forefathers held certain rights to be written into the nature and mind of man by the Creator, in contrast to foreign political philosophy that holds men to be born with no rights apart from the will of the State, which Creator-endowed rights were self-evident to our forefathers' reason which concluded that just as the sun was created for a definite purpose and with the inalienable right to live in accordance with that purpose, which philosophy the dictators reject and so deny the validity of inalienable rights as moral powers . . ."

5. "*Right to the pursuit of happiness,*" means the inalienable right written by the Creator in the nature of man which gives him the moral power to choose the work or vocation that he prefers, to acquire a home and property for himself and his loved ones, and to enjoy the blessings and gifts of a bountiful Creator as evidenced by the endless natural and inventive creations with which man is blessed.

Another section of this lawyer's bill is worthy of your attention. Section 10 reads:

10. "*Appealing to the Supreme Judge of the World for the rectitude of our intentions,*" means that these noble patriots saw

in the dictates of reason, laws written in the minds of man as well as in the phenomena of nature and that there exists a Just and Supreme Judge Who weighs character in the light of fair play and Who, recognizing the merits of a just cause, would not permit a dictator to overrule for long their inalienable rights provided they were men willing enough to fight for these rights.

This lawyer is just one man. What moved him was the will to get going and do something constructive. You too will find that the deeper your understanding of the Declaration of Independence the stronger and more determined will be your efforts to make it loved and respected by everyone.

Varying Interpretations

Not long ago I received a letter from a state education supervisor. In response to an inquiry of mine concerning the teaching of the Declaration of Independence he wrote: "The Declaration of Independence is presented simply as an historical document. The interpretation and philosophy present therein would vary with the teacher."

A mayor of a large Eastern town, who read the Declaration of Independence to the residents of the town at a July 4 celebration, left out every one of the four references to God as the source of our existence and rights, apparently with the notion that they were not an important part of the document.

The question is to what extent should the interpretation of the Declaration of Independence vary with the teacher? Jefferson considered it "an expression of the American mind which is written in terms so plain and firm as to claim their assent." And he expressed the hope that the principles in it would be "eternal." It is our job today to know what these "eternal principles" in the Declaration are. They made our country great, and made the Declaration itself an immortal document. Our least loyalty to both is to preserve the letter and the spirit of these ideas.

EVERYBODY'S JOB

Any alert citizen can do something to draw attention to the problem. A teacher, of course, can do most. But a student may request a fuller treatment of the Declaration of Independence. The average citizen can propose this to a School Board meeting, a P.T.A. meeting, and so forth.

It is up to you to see what you can do, and then proceed to do it.

ten

Part and Parcel of American Life

THIS CHAPTER PRESENTS A FEW EVENTS FOUND IN American history and tradition which indicate how deeply the spiritual has been woven into the fabric of American life.

The medium of American history is an important and fitting way to keep an awareness of God in the classrooms of America. The religious aspects of our history are matters of undeniable truth.

We mention only a limited number but these may prompt you to discover others for yourself. They are not hard to find, rather they are hard to avoid while studying the history of our great country. We are a religious people and our acts bear testimony to that fact.

Let us look at some of the better-known examples in our history.

FIRST SETTLEMENT IN VIRGINIA

The "Articles, Instructions, and Orders," dated November 20, 1606, and given to the London Company which established the permanent settlement in Virginia, make perhaps the most significant early example of the Christian purpose of American colonization. Here is a portion of it in its original archaic form:

And wee doe specially ordaine, charge, and require . . . that the true word and service of God and Christian faith be preached

143

planted and used not only within every [one] of the said several colonies, and plantations, but alsoe as much as they may amongst the salvage [sic] people. . . .

MAYFLOWER COMPACT

On a cold November morning in 1620, a tiny vessel, the *Mayflower*, approached Plymouth Rock. Aboard, forty-one men, women, and children were elated at the sight of land. Before stepping on firm ground the men gathered on deck to sign the Mayflower Compact. Long hours of discussion had gone into this record of their crystal-clear purpose, which reads:

> In the Name of God, Amen.
> We, whose names are underwritten, the loyal subjects of our dread Sovereign Lord King James, by the Grace of God, of Great Britain, France, and Ireland, King, Defender of the Faith, &c. Having undertaken for the Glory of God, and Advancement of the Christian Faith, and the Honour of our King and Country, a Voyage to plant the first colony in the northern parts of Virginia . . .

(Virginia was the goal of the Pilgrims, but bad weather and poor maps took them off their course and forced them to land at Plymouth Rock in Massachusetts.)

> . . . do by these presents, solemnly and mutually in the Presence of God and one another, covenant and combine ourselves together into a civil Body Politick, for our better Ordering and Preservation, and Furtherance of the Ends aforesaid . . .

They called upon God to witness the signing.

> . . . and by Virtue hereof do enact, constitute, and frame, such just and equal laws, Ordinances, Acts, Constitutions and

Offices from time to time as shall be thought most meet and convenient for the general Good of the Colony; unto which we promise all due Submission and Obedience. In Witness whereof we have hereunto subscribed our names at Cape Cod the eleventh of November in the Reign of our Sovereign Lord King James of England, France, and Ireland, the eighteenth, and of Scotland, the fifty-fourth. Anno Domini, 1620.

Thus the first written constitution in the new world was established under God with its purpose the perpetuation of His truths. Every American should be familiar with this outstanding document.

The Mayflower Compact, far from being an isolated instance, represents clearly the spirit and ideals of these earliest Americans. Throughout the history of the colonies a sense of personal and public responsibility to God continued.

FORERUNNERS OF THE DECLARATION OF INDEPENDENCE

The documents of the various colonies that were the forerunners of the Declaration of Independence, the Constitution, and the Bill of Rights always reflected a consciousness of the presence of God. For example, the Massachusetts Bill of Rights begins:

We, therefore, the people of Massachusetts, acknowledging with grateful hearts, the goodness of the great Legislator of the universe, in affording us, in the course of His Providence. . . .

CONTINENTAL CONGRESSES

As the course of the new nation was being charted and planned, the men who formed the First Continental Congress gave acknowledgement and tribute to God many times and asked His guidance in their great role.

Their first proclamation of prayer has come to be known as the Declaration of Dependence on God, and the following excerpts from it show why. It set aside July 12, 1775, as a day of fasting and prayer and as such it was the first enactment of a religious holiday. Since it reflects the mentality of the early Americans from a spiritual point of view, it is worth a slow and thoughtful reading.

As the great Governor of the world, by His supreme and universal providence, not only conducts the course of nature with unerring wisdom and rectitude, but frequently influences the minds of men to serve the wise and gracious purposes of His providential government; and it being, at all times, our indispensable duty devoutly to acknowledge His superintending providence, especially in times of impending danger and public calamity, to reverence and adore His immutable justice as well as to implore His merciful interposition for our deliverance:

This Congress, therefore, considering the present critical, alarming, and calamitous state of these Colonies, do earnestly recommend that Thursday, the twentieth day of July next, be observed by the inhabitants of all the English Colonies on this Continent as a day of public humiliation, fasting, and prayer; that we may, with united hearts and voices, unfeignedly confess and deplore our many sins, and offer up our joint supplications to the all-wise, omnipotent, and merciful Disposer of all events; humbly beseeching Him to forgive our iniquities . . .

The Declaration goes on to say:

That these colonies may be ever under the care and protection of a kind Providence, and be prospered in all their interests; that the divine blessing may descend and rest upon all our civil rulers, and upon the Representatives of the people, in their several Assemblies and Conventions, that they may be directed to wise and effectual measures for preserving the union, and securing the just rights and privileges of the Colonies; that virtue and true religion may revive and flourish throughout our land . . .

And it is recommended to Christians of all denominations to assemble for public worship, and to abstain from servile labor and recreation on said day.

Ordered, that a copy of the above be signed by the President, and attested by the Secretary, and published in the newspapers and in handbills.

Again in 1777, Congress issued this proclamation:

It is therefore recommended to the legislative or executive Powers of these UNITED STATES, to set apart THURSDAY, the eighteenth Day of December next, for SOLEMN THANKSGIVING and PRAISE.

A day of thanksgiving was also proclaimed in 1782 after the victory of the American armies and again in 1783 after the signing of the peace treaty with Great Britain.

Other days of prayer and thanksgiving have been set aside by various Presidents and Congresses since that time.

THE NORTHWEST ORDINANCE, 1787

In the history of westward expansion, the Ordinance of 1787 marked another step in the definition of our religious liberty. Its influence has been widely felt not only in the Middle West and Northwest but in the foundation of each new state. Looking back in 1859, Lincoln stated that "Congress traced their course by that Ordinance of '87." Article III of this document, which has had such a prominent part in shaping our history, reads:

Religion, morality and knowledge, being necessary to good government and the happiness of mankind, schools and the means of education shall forever be encouraged.

PRAYER IN CONGRESS

From the beginning of our history our lawmakers have worked under the guidance of prayer. This practice may be traced to the first Continental Congress. A member proposed that a prayer be read at the first session. The resolution was carried and the session opened with a reading from the Bible and a prayer for the protection of the people of America. From that day forward Congress has been regularly convened by prayer.

Following the precedent set by the national legislature, many state houses have opened their sessions with prayers. This practice is often followed down the line to the legislative branches of city and town government.

CHAPLAINS

In conjunction with the religious tone established in the first Congress, an official chaplain, the Reverend Mr. Jacob Duche, a minister of the Church of England, was elected on July 9, 1776. This practice of having a chaplain as an officer of each House and paying him a salary from the national treasury has continued ever since. The duties of the chaplains have remained almost unchanged to the present day. They include, in addition to the prayers at the opening sessions, the delivering of sermons at the Sunday service, conducting of funerals, officiating on days of public prayer and thanksgiving, and assisting in patriotic celebrations.

In 1854, an attempt was made to do away with the chaplaincies. The attack was based on Article 6 of the Constitution which stated that "no religious test shall ever be required as a qualification to an office of public trust under the United States." But, in rejecting the appeal, Congress made it clear that this reference was "to a class of persons entirely distinct from chaplains."

Public opinion was almost wholly in favor of continuing the chaplains. This was expressed in the words of Supreme Court Justice Story, who questioned "whether any free government can be permanent where the public worship of God and the support of religion constitute no part of the policy or duty of the State in any assignable shape."

In addition to chaplains in Congress and in the Armed Forces, the federal government has made provisions for chaplains in federal prisons, in the Veterans Administration hospitals, and in old soldiers' homes.

INAUGURATION SERVICES

In many ways the first presidential inauguration established precedents that are now almost taken for granted, and once again the religious element was not only present but paramount.

The full report on the inauguration of our first President, George Washington, in 1789, indicates that this occasion was intended to be a dedication of this country and its government to the service of God. It was moved by the United States Senate that there be a religious service in connection with the inauguration:

Resolved That, after the oath shall have been administered to the President, he, attended by the Vice President and the members of the Senate and the House of Representatives, shall proceed to St. Paul's Chapel, to hear divine service, to be performed by the Chaplain of Congress already appointed.

With slight changes the measure passed both Houses. Every inauguration, including that of President Eisenhower, has, almost without exception, taken on the same spiritual tone.

THE AMERICAN SEAL

Following the inauguration of George Washington, the Congress approved the design for the American Seal.

The history of the seal began on July 4, 1776, when the Continental Congress appointed Benjamin Franklin, Thomas Jefferson, and John Adams "a Committee to prepare a device for a Seal of the United States of America."

The committee decided upon Jefferson's proposal that one side of the seal contain a picturization of the children of Israel in the wilderness, "led by a cloud by day and a pillar of fire by night." The reverse side would include characteristic features of England, Scotland, Ireland, France, Germany, and Holland, the countries from which the majority of Americans had come; shields for each of the thirteen states, together with Liberty and Justice as supporters; and a crest showing "the Eye of Providence in a radiant Triangle whose Glory extends from the Shield and beyond the Figures."

The motto was to be *E Pluribus Unum* (One out of many).

A second committee took up the task of completing the design. Charles Thomson, Secretary to Congress, and William Barton of Philadelphia worked on it until their design was officially adopted in 1782. Not all the proposed ideas were incorporated in the design; but the two men retained the "Eye of Providence" and the motto *E Pluribus Unum*. Seven years later the design was approved by Congress.

An interesting research project for students would be the examination of various state seals and the meaning of their mottos. Among the outstanding ones are:

Colorado: *Nil sine numine* (Nothing without God).
Arizona: *Ditat Deus* (God enriches).
Connecticut: *Qui transtulit Sustinet* (He who has brought us here sustains us).

Florida: *In Deo Confidimus* (In God we place our trust).

Maryland: *Scuto Bonae Voluntatis Tuae Coronasti Nos* (Thou hast crowned us, as with a shield of Thy good will, Psalms 5:13).

South Dakota: Under God the people rule.

AMERICAN CURRENCY

A replica of the Great Seal of the United States is found on the one-dollar bill. Note the components of the design. The pyramid in the circle on the left symbolizes the strength of the Union. It was left unfinished to show that there would always be work to do for the preservation of the country. Above the pyramid the triangular Eye of Providence represents the Eye of God watching over us. Beneath the pyramid the words *Novus ordo seclorum* (A new order of the ages) signify that God's Providence is the foundation of our new Republic. *Annuit Coeptis* means "He [God] has favored our undertakings." The Roman numerals at the bottom of the pyramid are dated 1776, the year of the signing of the Declaration of Independence.

Our coins, too, reflect this acknowledgement of God. The story of the origin of the inscription "In God We Trust" on our coins can be told in any classroom to demonstrate our spiritual heritage.

In 1861, after seven months of civil war, Salmon P. Chase, the Secretary of the Treasury, received a letter from a Protestant minister, the Reverend Mr. M. R. Watkinson, a pastor in the small town of Ridleyville, Pennsylvania. The clergyman wrote:

One fact touching our currency has hitherto been seriously overlooked. I mean the recognition of the Almighty God in some form on our coins. What if our Republic were now shattered beyond reconstruction? Would not the antiquaries of succeeding centuries rightly reason from our past that we were a heathen nation?

He proposed a motto on the theme of God, Liberty, Law, and concluded his letter with these words,

From my heart I have felt our national shame in disowning God as not the least of our present national disasters.

Secretary Chase immediately recognized the merit of the Rev. Mr. Watkinson's suggestion. Despite many overwhelming problems in directing the finances of a country torn by civil war, he quickly sent off a letter to James Pollock, Director of the Mint, in Philadelphia. He wrote:

No nation can be strong except in the strength of God, or safe except in His defense. The trust of our people in God should be declared on our national coins.

Then, along the lines suggested by Mr. Watkinson, he continued:

You will cause a device to be prepared without unnecessary delay with a motto expressing in the fewest and tersest words possible this national recognition.

By the end of that year, 1861, a bronze pattern for a ten-dollar gold piece with the motto "God, Our Trust" had been submitted. "Our Country; Our God" was later suggested. And in 1864, "In God We Trust" first appeared on a United States coin, a two-cent piece. The final inscription had been proposed by Chase himself. From that day to the present our coins have borne this inscription recognizing our dependence, as a nation, on divine Providence.

Many of the early decisions of our government very definitely showed the influence of a religious policy. The actions of our lawmakers through the years have exhibited not only a very favorable attitude toward religion but in many instances have encouraged its practice. Following are a few of the many examples that could be used in a classroom to emphasize the great respect that has been shown religion and religious institutions by those who govern our land.

EXEMPTION FROM TAXES

In exempting church properties from taxation, the government has given a clear example of its attitude toward the practice of religion. This practice has continued since the early days of the republic.

BLASPHEMY LAWS

The showing of disrespect to God or to persons, to writings or to things considered holy, has been judged a serious offense by Jewish, ecclesiastical, and English common law. In line with this tradition, many statutes have been passed in this country condemning such displayed disrespect on the grounds that it is so offensive to respectable citizens that it is likely to disturb the public peace. Television, radio, and motion-picture codes today respect this same attitude toward religion.

REQUIRED OATHS

Recognizing the serious and sacred character of an oath, our lawmakers have made it a requirement that anyone holding public office in the United States must take one before assuming his duties. All Federal employees must also take this oath. It might be well for every American to read it over, ponder it, and try to live up to the letter and the spirit of it in every possible way. Here is the oath:

I, ———, do solemnly swear that I will support and defend the Constitution of the United States against all enemies, foreign and domestic; that I will bear true faith and allegiance to the same; that I take this obligation freely, without any mental reservation or purpose of evasion, and that I will well and faithfully discharge the duties of the office upon which I am about to enter, so help me God.

An oath is also required in courts of law and in the attesting of legal documents. All these conclude by calling on God to witness the truth of the statement: "So help me God."

CONSCIENTIOUS OBJECTORS

In bowing to religious creed or principle, the United States exempts certain men from compulsory military service when their faith prohibits them from participating in war.

DUELING

A sermon by Dr. Lyman Beecher in 1806 did much to influence public opinion and legislation against dueling. Here is an excerpt from that sermon:

Dueling is a great national sin. . . . Atheists may scoff; but there is a God—a God who governs the earth in righteousness— an avenger of crimes—the supporter and destroyer of nations; and as clay in the hand of the potter, so are the nations of the earth in the hand of God. . . . We are murderers, a nation of murderers, while we tolerate and reward the perpetrators of the crime.

CEMETERIES

In general, the State treats cemeteries and the remains of the dead with great respect. Cemeteries are regarded by common law as places of special sacredness—"holy ground." Disturbance of a church cemetery has been held by the courts to be a public nuisance, and, in 1892, the contemplated sale of the grave of George Washington's mother was forbidden as "a scandalous reflection upon a civilized Christian community."

FEDERAL FUNDS FOR RELIGIOUS EDUCATION

Many times in the history of our country the federal government and various religious groups have collaborated in the education of citizens. Bringing the Christian heritage to the American Indian has been a major concern. In 1803, a treaty with the Kaskaskia Indians recognized the essential work of the missioner. It stated:

> And whereas the Greater part of the said tribe have been baptized and received into the Catholic Church, to which they are much attached, the United States will give, annually, for seven years, one hundred dollars towards the support of a priest of that religion, who will engage to perform for said tribe the duties of his office, and also to instruct as many of their children as possible, in the rudiments of literature. And the United States will further give the sum of three hundred dollars, to assist said tribe in the erection of a church.

TREATIES

Note how the Treaty of Paris, the Treaty of the Netherlands, and other early treaties of our country had significant clauses in them expressing dependence upon God, safeguarding of religious freedom, and similar references.

INTERNATIONAL POLICY

The State Department recently announced plans to include more religious material in American information being sent abroad. Edward W. Barrett, former Assistant Secretary of State for Public Affairs, said:

Our campaign of truth can be made tremendously more effective through increasing the proportion of religious materials in the radio programs, pamphlets and motion pictures that we are sending to people of all religious faiths the world over.

The stories behind the writing of our national anthem and other patriotic songs, the first telegraph message, and the nickname "Old Glory" applied to the American flag, give additional evidence of the religious spirit of the early days of our country.

"The Star-Spangled Banner"

Our national anthem was composed in 1812 by Francis Scott Key, a thirty-four-year-old American attorney.

During the War of 1812, the British Army was approaching the city of Baltimore, which was being protected by American soldiers in Fort McHenry. After landing on the shores of the Patuxent River in Maryland, the English attacked on the night of September 13, 1814. Their fleet began to bombard Fort McHenry.

That night Key went aboard a British ship to obtain the release of an American who was being held prisoner. The intensity of the battle forced him to remain overnight. From the deck of the ship he breathlessly watched the siege of Fort McHenry all through the night while smoke and fire hovered over the city. As dawn broke he was overjoyed to see the American flag still waving over the fort.

Taking an old envelope from his pocket, he hastily scribbled the lines:

O say can you see, by the dawn's early light . . .

He had begun "The Star-Spangled Banner." On the boat back to Fort McHenry he completed the work, ending the last stanza with reverent praise of God:

Praise the Power that hath made and preserved us a nation.
  Then conquer we must, when our cause it is just   1 em
  And this be our motto—"In God is our Trust."

For 117 years this song was popular in its own right as a
patriotic hymn. On March 3, 1931, Congress passed a bill,
officially adopting it as our national anthem.

"BATTLE HYMN OF THE REPUBLIC"

Julia Ward Howe was visiting in Washington, D. C., in
December, 1861. Signs of war were everywhere. The railroads
were guarded by soldiers, and the streets were crowded with
men in uniform singing war songs, among them the stirring
tune, "John Brown's Body."

After hearing the song, Mrs. Howe found herself mentally
composing new words for the tune—words that would lift the
minds and hearts of the soldiers to God, words that would
remind them that "God's truth is ever marching on."

Her song turned out to be our great "Battle Hymn of the
Republic."

The words were published a short time later in the *Atlantic Monthly*, and soon all the North was singing the song.
It is said that the first time President Lincoln heard the new
hymn he was so moved that he cried out, with tears in his
eyes, "Sing it again!"

"AMERICA"

A music teacher, Lowell Mason, was eager to find a new
"song with a patriotic flavor" for his students to sing. Samuel
Francis Smith, a theology student at Andover, Massachusetts,
and a friend of Mason's, came across the music of "God Save
the King." He began to fit words to the music, unaware that
the music was that of the English national anthem. The

words, "My country 'tis of thee . . ." began forming in his
mind. In thirty minutes the song was completed!

Mason liked it immediately. He called it "a hymn of
praise. A lovely hymn for America and my boys and girls!"

The words of the final stanza give praise to God, the
Cause of our liberty:

> Our fathers' God to Thee,
> Author of liberty,
> To Thee we sing:
> Long may our land be bright,
> With freedom's holy light;
> Protect us by Thy might,
> Great God, our King!

Quite unknown to the Reverend Mr. Smith, Mr. Mason
had his students sing the hymn at a Fourth of July celebration
in the Park Street Church in Boston. Many people left the
ceremonies humming the music.

Four years later "America" was published and heard all
over the country.

THE FIRST TELEGRAPH MESSAGE

Spiritual awareness was not confined to those who formed
our government. It was rooted in the hearts of the people and
therefore appeared in every facet of American life. This is
clearly emphasized by the following historical event.

In 1839, when Morse had perfected his telegraph to the
point where he could send a message more than three miles,
he took it to Washington. He appealed unsuccessfully to Congress for an appropriation to continue his experiments.

Disappointed and dejected, Morse went to Europe and
tried to patent his invention. His applications in England and
Russia failed. France accepted the telegraph, but never paid
Morse.

He returned to Washington. On the last day of the congressional session in February, 1843, four years after his original appeal, Morse still had not received the necessary appropriation. Discouraged and broken in spirit, he packed his bag, paid his hotel bill, and bought a train ticket for home. On the way to breakfast, Morse met the daughter of a friend. Running up to him, she said breathlessly, "I have to congratulate you!"

"Congratulate me! What for?" asked Morse.

Then she told him. Congress had appropriated twenty-five thousand dollars for a telegraph line.

Overjoyed, Morse told the young woman that she would write the first message to go over the telegraph wire.

A little over a year later, in May, 1844, the wire was completed. It stretched from Washington to Baltimore. Alfred Vail, Morse's coworker, was at the Baltimore end of the wire. In Washington, Morse kept his promise to the young woman, who was on hand for the great occasion. She handed him a piece of paper. On it was written the first message ever to go over the telegraph. Morse tapped out the words: "What hath God wrought?"

A few minutes later the same words came back over the wire: "What hath God wrought?" Vail had answered with the same immortal message.

"OLD GLORY"

You may be one of the few Americans who know the fascinating story of how our flag got its nickname, "Old Glory."

One bitterly cold day in 1830, the *Charles Dagett* stood ready to set sail in Salem Harbor. The Captain, William Driver, was about to begin the ceremonies for the embarkation.

A sailor passed the flag to him folded in the form of a triangle and said: "Sir, in the days gone by it was the custom of sailors embarking on a journey to dedicate the flag to the Trinity—God, the Father; God, the Son; and God, the Holy Ghost. Then, after Benediction, the flag was unfurled and raised, and the sailors would shout, 'Glory! Glory! Glory!' "

As Captain Driver looked up at the flag being hoisted, he cried out: "To thee, let me call thee 'Old Glory.' "

Thirty years later, during the Civil War, the city of Nashville, Tennessee, fell to soldiers of the North. Ceremonies were planned to fly the Stars and Stripes, but the flag in use for the occasion was too small.

Captain Driver, still in possession of "Old Glory," was there. He offered the flag for the ceremony. A cry went up from the crowd. Someone shouted "Old Glory" and the famous nickname stuck. It has been the popular name for the American flag ever since.

HOLIDAYS

Much can be gained from a study of the holidays celebrated in this country. Of course the word *holiday* itself comes from the words *holy* and *day*. You will find it defined in the dictionary as "a consecrated day; a religious anniversary or festival."

Down through the centuries New Year's Day has been given religious observance to remind man that he has reached another milestone in life and has an opportunity to make a fresh start for the coming year. This day is observed in the United States as a nation-wide holiday.

Memorial Day, May 30, and Armistice Day, November 11, are special days on which to pay tribute to and pray for those who gave their lives for their country.

Christmas in the United States is regarded as perhaps the most important religious holiday of the year. As far as the policy of the government toward it is concerned, it is interesting to note that it is the only day of the year on which many public buildings, such as the Washington Monument, the Lincoln Memorial, and the Jefferson Memorial, are closed to the public.

In April, 1953, Senator Robert A. Taft gave these interesting statistics about the observance of Good Friday by the United States Senate: ". . . For the past six years the Senate has not met on Good Friday. Before that time, sometimes the Senate met on that day and sometimes it did not. In the thirty years preceding this year, the Senate was in session thirteen times and not in session seventeen times."

Just as the Christian holydays, Christmas and Good Friday, are respected by those in authority, the Jewish holidays have been recognized and their observance encouraged. In New York City in 1953, the Board of Education suspended its bylaws to permit eight thousand teachers, supervisors and clerks of the Jewish faith to observe Rosh Hashana holy days in September without loss of pay.

Most of the credit for establishing Thanksgiving as a national holiday is due to one woman, Sarah Hale, who was born in Newport, New Hampshire, on October 24, 1788. For forty years she edited a magazine known as *Godey's Lady's Book*, a publication which advocated advanced education for women, conducted departments devoted to domestic problems and fashions, and exerted a marked influence on the life of those times.

For seventeen years she actively campaigned through her magazine and in other ways for a national observance of Thanksgiving Day by all the states of the Union. There was, she claimed, no greater bond than rejoicing together over a common good.

Finally, in 1863, President Lincoln proclaimed the first National Thanksgiving Day, the twenty-sixth of November, 1863, and every year since then we observed Thanksgiving.

The true significance of the day is often overlooked, however, as the following story brings out.

During the month of November a teacher in a small city in Massachusetts asked her second grade students why they celebrate Thanksgiving Day. She was amused as well as alarmed by the answers she received:

"We eat turkey."

"Our friends come to visit us."

"It's the President's birthday."

"It's Columbus's birthday."

"The teachers want a day off."

"The janitor wants to clean the school."

"It's Christmas."

The teacher then related to the children the story of the First Thanksgiving, of how the Pilgrims having landed in America gave thanks to God for all the blessings He had given them.

Apparently the children had never heard this before and soon they told the teacher that they were going to thank God for being able to walk and play games, for having enough food to eat, for having good mothers and fathers—in short, for everything God had given them.

THE BIBLE

Another example of the respect for religion as evidenced in this country is the great attention paid to the distribution of the Bible in the early days, and the continued honor paid it ever since.

In the eighteenth century traveling conditions did not make it easy for the hard-working missionaries of the day to get around to all those in their charge. This made it of utmost importance to make the Bible available to the people.

In 1777, Congress took up the problem, proposing that the colonists print their own edition. The idea had to be temporarily abandoned, however, as there were few printing presses in the country at the time.

But the Founding Fathers did not give up. They passed a resolution that twenty thousand copies of the Bible be imported. Again the plan had to be abandoned, this time for lack of funds.

Finally Congress turned the matter over to the states, expressing regret that it could not afford to finance the purchase, but with the hope that the individual states would. The resolution read:

That it be recommended to each of the States who may think it convenient for them that they take proper measures to procure one or more new and correct editions of the Old and New Testament to be printed and that such states regulate their printers by law so as to secure effectually the said books from being misprinted.

Meanwhile, a Philadelphia printer, Robert Aiken, had succeeded in publishing a copy of the New Testament and appealed to Congress for funds to continue his work on the Old Testament in order to have a complete American edition of the Bible.

But Congress was blocked by the same lack of funds. A costly revolution was being fought. The best it could do was to give an official "stamp of approval" to Aiken's work.

Finally, not financial but legislative assistance was brought into the picture. Congress passed a resolution taking the import duty off the printing plates of a Bible, thus making it possible to bring them into the country.

Official Stamps

In 1952, further recognition was given this greatest of all "best sellers." In that year a three-cent United States postage stamp was issued to commemorate the five-hundredth anniversary of the printing of the first book, the Holy Bible, by Johann Gutenberg.

Such are a few of the outstanding facts and documents which serve to show the deeply religious strain that runs throughout our whole history and culture. We shall now turn to a few of our outstanding leaders who speak to us in this same vein.

eleven

They Were Men of Faith

THE FACTS AND INCIDENTS JUST MENTIONED, WHICH are so vital a part of America's past and present, were founded on a strong religious faith. Without this basis, our history would have been charted on a different course. This faith was evident in the men who made our history—our Founding Fathers and those who followed in their footsteps. We will do well to give a little thought and study to the religious beliefs and background of some of these men who have made such a mark in our history.

WILLIAM PENN

William Penn was a deeply spiritual man. From the moment that King Charles II granted him a charter in the new world, he was determined that the Commonwealth of Pennsylvania would have spiritual roots. His purpose was clearly explained in the first paragraph of the Charter of Privilege, written in 1701, as the framework of the Commonwealth. The opening sentence illustrates his abiding faith in God:

Almighty God, being Only Lord of Conscience, Father of Lights and Spirits, and the author as well as object of all Divine knowledge, faith and Worship, who only can enlighten the mind, and persuade and convince the understandings of people. In due reverence to His Sovereignty over the Souls of Mankind . . .

Penn's prayer for Philadelphia gives us another insight into the religious feeling of a great American. Written in 1664, it now appears on a bronze tablet in the Philadelphia City Hall:

. . . And thou, Philadelphia, the virgin settlement of this province, named before thou wert born; what love, what care, what service and what travail have there been to bring thee forth and preserve thee from such as would abuse and defile thee. O that thou mayest be kept from the evil that would overwhelm thee; that faithful to the God of thy mercies, in the life of righteousness thou mayest be preserved to the end. My soul prays to God for thee, that thou mayest stand in the day of trial; that thy children may be blest of the Lord, and thy people saved by His power.

Thomas Jefferson

A nominal Episcopalian, but a Unitarian in belief, Jefferson has been quoted to defend every and any position. But history cannot be converted. Jefferson was definitely a believer in God, in Christian morality, and in Natural rights springing from Divine creation.

His basic concept of man was evident in his actions from the beginning of his public career. At an early date Jefferson argued that the slave was a man created by God and consequently had the right to freedom just as much as anybody else. In his original draft of the Declaration of Independence, slavery was condemned as "cruel war against human nature itself, violating its most sacred rights of life and liberty." This was deleted in the final draft, but the well-known phrases on human equality and the inborn rights of life and liberty were retained.

This concept of man as a religious being was carried into Jefferson's ideas on education. He insisted that the teaching of religious truths be included in the curriculum of the University of Virginia which he headed. These are his words:

It was not, however, to be understood that instruction in religious opinion and duties was meant to be precluded by the public authorities, as indifferent to the interest of society. On the contrary, the relations which exist between man and his Maker, and the duties resulting from those relations, are the most interesting and important to every human being and the most incumbent on his study and investigation.

In developing his ideas on religious education, Jefferson proposed in 1814, that public funds in Virginia be used for the training of clergymen. Justice and foresight characterized his proposal. He stated that though each religious sect had its own religious services and program, theological students should be considered members of the University, "subject to the same regulations and entitled to the same privileges." Jefferson's policies guided the programs of his day and his influence has been felt to the present.

Carrying his ideas to the White House, Jefferson appropriated tax money both for the support of chaplains in the services and for the religious education of the Indians. A letter written by Jefferson gives another interesting insight into the judgment and spirit of the President. It concerns some nuns who apparently were disturbed about their property rights, and reads:

I have received, Holy Sisters, the letters you have written me, wherein you express anxiety for your property vested in your institution by the former Government of Louisiana.

The principles of the Government and Constitution of the United States are a sure guarantee to you that it will be preserved to you sacred and inviolate, and that your institution will be permitted to govern itself according to its own voluntary rules, without interference from the civil authority.

Whatever diversity of shade may appear in the religious opinions of our fellow-citizens, the charitable objects of your institution cannot be indifferent to any; and its furtherance of the wholesome purposes of society by training up its young members in the way they should go, cannot fail to insure it the patronage of the Gov-

ernment it is under. Be assured it will meet with all the protection
my office can give it.

GEORGE WASHINGTON

Throughout his life, the "Father of Our Country" was acutely
aware of the power of prayer and of the need for religion.
Speaking to his troops on May 2, 1778, of this need, he said:
"To the distinguished character of a Patriot, it should be our
highest glory to add the more distinguished character of a
Christian."

Several years later, on June 8, 1783, on the occasion of the
disbanding of the Army, he wrote to the governors of all the
states:

. . . I now make it my earnest prayer that God would have you,
and the State over which you preside, in his holy protection; that
he would incline the hearts of the citizens to cultivate a spirit
of subordination and obedience to government; to entertain a
brotherly affection and love for one another, for their fellow citizens of the United States at large, and particularly for their
brethren who have served in the field; and finally, that he would
most graciously be pleased to dispose us all to do justice, to love
mercy, and to demean ourselves with that charity, humility, and
pacific temper of mind, which were the characteristics of the
Divine Author of our blessed religion, and without an humble
imitation of whose example in these things, we can never hope to
be a happy nation. . . .

This portion of the letter to the governors has come to be
known as "George Washington's Prayer."

During his term as President of the United States, Washington set aside several days of prayer and thanksgiving. The
first one was on the occasion of the adoption of the Federal
Constitution. We quote a few lines from this Proclamation
of October 3, 1789:

. . . Now, therefore, I do recommend and assign Thursday, the twenty sixth day of November next, to be devoted by the people of these States to the service of that great and glorious Being, who is the beneficent Author of all the good that was, that is, or that will be; that we may then all unite in rendering unto Him our sincere and humble thanks for His kind care and protection of the people of this country previous to their becoming a nation; for the signal and manifold mercies, and the favorable interpositions of His providence, in the course and conclusion of the late war . . .

And, also, that we may then unite in most humbly offering our prayers and supplications to the great Lord and Ruler of Nations, and beseech Him to pardon our national and other transgressions . . . to protect and guide all sovereigns and nations . . . to promote the knowledge and practice of true religion and virtue . . .

Washington closed his presidential career as he had opened it, and the Farewell Address bears testimony to his abiding faith in the spiritual. We quote only a few lines here, but anyone would draw profit from an entire reading:

Let us with caution indulge the supposition that morality can be maintained without religion. Whatever may be conceded to the influence of refined education on minds of peculiar structure, reason and experience forbid us to expect that national morality can prevail in exclusion of religious principle.

ANDREW JACKSON

In the period of tension before the final outbreak between the North and the South, Jackson strove to emphasize the spiritual basis of America. In answer to the South Carolina Ordnance of Nullification in 1832, he prayed:

May the Great Ruler of nations grant that the signal blessings with which He has favored ours may not by the madness of party, or personal ambition be discredited and lost and may His wise Providence bring those who have produced this crisis to see the folly, before they feel the misery of civil strife, and inspire a return-ing veneration for that union, which, if we may dare to penetrate His designs, He has chosen, as the only means of attaining the high destiny to which we may reasonably aspire.

Abraham Lincoln

Few of the great historical figures have emphasized our depend-ence on Almighty God in a more powerful way than Abraham Lincoln. His actions testify to his ideals and his years as presi-dent are filled with examples of his belief in the spiritual man.

At a crucial point in the Civil War, Lincoln set aside March 30, 1863, as a day of fasting and prayer. The preamble of the proclamation read:

It is the duty of nations as well as of men to own their de-pendence upon the overruling power of God; to confess their sins and transgressions in humble sorrow, yet with assured hope that genuine repentance will lead to mercy and pardon; and to recog-nize the sublime truth, announced in the Holy Scriptures and proved by all history, that those nations only are blessed whose God is the Lord.

In that same proclamation he warned that—

Intoxicated with unbroken success, we have become too self-sufficient to feel the necessity of redeeming and preserving grace, too proud to pray to the God that made us . . .

On November 19, 1863, Lincoln delivered an address that has often been called the peak of American eloquence. The occasion was the dedication of a military cemetery at Gettys-burg, the scene of a terrible three-day battle some four months earlier.

One of the nation's greatest orators, Edward Everett, Secretary of State and Senator from Massachusetts, appeared on the speaker's platform before Lincoln. He gave a very lengthy account of the historic battle.

By contrast, Lincoln's address was so short that, according to reports, the photographer did not get his camera adjusted in time.

Newspapers of the day seemed to concentrate more on Everett's speech, because of its length, than on that of Lincoln. The greatness of Lincoln's speech was immediately recognized, however, by some. Everett himself wrote him: "I should be glad if I could flatter myself that I came as near the central idea of the occasion in two hours as you did in two minutes."

The original drafts of the Gettysburg Address in Lincoln's own handwriting are preserved in the Library of Congress. Neither of them contains the now famous words "under God," for these were inserted extemporaneously by the President as he was inspired by the deep significance of the occasion.

Perhaps one of the most widely felt decisions of Lincoln's term was the giving of the Emancipation Proclamation. Its story is known to all Americans, but the reasons for it should be clearly pointed out. When Lincoln issued it, he called it "a covenant with God," that is, an agreement with Him.

When Lincoln was about to issue this Proclamation, his Secretary of State, Seward, argued that it was not the right time for such a drastic step. Lincoln said: "I must sign it; I told the Lord I would."

Seward was taken aback and asked: "What is that you say, Mr. President?"

He replied: "I made a promise that if the Lord would give us victory and drive the enemy back into Virginia, I would emancipate the slaves; and I will do it."

Before placing his signature on the document, Lincoln in the closing sentence invoked "the considerate Judgement of mankind and the gracious favor of Almighty God."

Stories like these make the facts of history unforgettable to students and present a clear picture of the tenor of the times and the intentions of our national leaders.

These leaders and the ones following stood in the forefront of their times. Because of their influence our documents are filled with references to the Deity, "Christian" ideals, "the year of our Lord," the promotion of "religion" and of "religious freedom," "civic and religious liberty," the "worship of God," the provision for public prayer and thanksgiving to Almighty God, and so on. In most cases, these men showed by their utterances, their lives, and their support of some religious body, a desire to encourage religion.

George Mason was an Episcopalian and a firm believer in Divine Providence and the Natural Law basis of government.

Patrick Henry was an Episcopalian with Presbyterian connections. His religious convictions were strong. He frequently referred to God, to "holy religion," and he wrote a particularly religiously inspired will.

John Carroll of Maryland, a Catholic, was a devoted member of his church and equally a devotee of religious freedom for all denominations—something that did not yet exist universally in the colonies or states. A little-known statement of his tells of this:

When I signed the Declaration of Independence I had in view, not only our independence from England, but the toleration of all sects professing the Christian religion, and communicating to them all equal rights.

John Adams was a Congregationalist and made clear beyond any shadow of doubt his firm adherence to the Christian faith. In a letter to Jefferson, he wrote:

A patriot must be a religious man. The general principles on which the fathers achieved independence were the general principles of Christianity.

James Madison has been accused of some skepticism. His proclamation of days of fast and prayer, his frequent public references to the Almighty, gave witness to his real faith.

Alexander Hamilton was an Episcopalian and believed in Christianity as a basis of our government. He once proposed a society to support (1) the Christian religion, and (2) the Constitution of the United States.

Tom Paine was exceptional in that he was a deist. He was nevertheless a definite believer in God and in natural law. He was not at all, so some say, an atheist. He admitted, moreover, that government should protect religion.

There are many more we could mention: John Quincy Adams, Samuel Adams, William Livingston, John Jay, etc., who were all thoroughgoing Christians. It is reasonable to conclude, since easy to prove, that the Christianity of these leaders had a powerful influence on the views of man, the state, law, and ethics. It was this realization of the spiritual that was the main inspiration behind the Declaration and the Constitution, which was its political expression.

twelve

Cornerstone of American Government

FROM THE DAY THE DECLARATION OF INDEPENDEN-
dence was printed it was popularly acclaimed, and Jefferson,
who was considered its author, was soon hailed as a national
hero. Adams, and many others, however, were annoyed by the
praise Jefferson was receiving.

"There is not an idea in it," John Adams exclaimed, "but
what had not been hackneyed in Congress for two years before!"

This seemed a rather peevish statement for a man to
make almost forty-seven years after the signing of the Declaration of Independence. But John Adams cannot be dismissed
as a hothead, nor as one who did not know what he was talking about. Besides, he was talking about Thomas Jefferson, a
good friend of his.

Adams had been a member of the "Committee of Five"
that was appointed by the Second Continental Congress to
draft a declaration of independence, and he had assisted at the
whole proceedings.

Jefferson, according to him, was not the author of the
document. He had been chosen to draft it mostly because of
his writing ability. Adams wrote: "Mr. Jefferson came to Congress in June 1775 and brought with him a reputation for literature, science and a happy talent for composition. Writings of
his were handed about, remarkable for their felicity of expression."

But Adams, when writing to his friend Thomas Pickering in 1822 complained about the mistaken notion that the Declaration of Independence was Jefferson's. In this letter he declared: "The substance of it [the Declaration of Independence] is contained in the declaration of rights and the violation of these rights in the Journal of Congress in 1774. Indeed, the essence of it is contained in a pamphlet voted and printed by the town of Boston before the first Congress met, composed by James Otis."

A WORD FROM JEFFERSON

Jefferson was eighty years old when this debate had spread far and wide. He wrote to Madison about it the very next year (1823). He took no exception to Adams' and Pickering's contention that the ideas contained in the Declaration of Independence were a "commonplace compilation" and not his own invention. He wrote: "I know only that I turned to neither book nor pamphlet while writing it. I did not consider it as any part of my charge to invent new ideas altogether and to offer no sentiment which had ever been expressed before . . . In opposition, however, to Mr. Pickering, *I pray God that these principles may be eternal.*"

Jefferson then wrote to Henry Lee, Jr., an American general, commonly referred to as "Light Horse Harry." Apparently he wished to do his best to destroy the idea that he was the sole author of the Declaration of Independence. In this letter he stated that his intention in writing it "was to place before mankind the common sense of the subject in terms so plain and firm as to command their assent . . . It was intended to be an *expression of the American mind.* All its authority rests on the harmonizing sentiments of the day."

THE AMERICAN MIND AND ETERNAL PRINCIPLES

Three things stand out in this whole episode: (1) Jefferson was not the originator of the ideas in the Declaration of Independence; (2) it was the "expression of the American mind" of its time; and (3) its principles were considered to be "eternal principles."

Our aim in this section is to show that our American government and way of life is solidly built upon truths that have come down to us from the Judaeo-Christian tradition. It is to show that our form of government is founded not only upon the principles of revelation and the Inspired Word, but also upon the ageless concept of what has become known as the "Natural Law."

In seeking to know the *how* of God in education, it is also important to know the *why*.

Most Americans do not sufficiently realize how deeply religious our founding as a nation really was. In an age of crisis such as ours, we should take a closer look at our foundations, and be reinspired by the spirit of our Founding Fathers and by the principles laid down in the Declaration of Independence and the Constitution.

If this spirit was as clear to all of us as it should be, there would no longer be any problem about God in education. After all, the matter of God in education is only a part of a much greater question—God in life. If we today could understand God and His working through the Natural Law as clearly as our Founding Fathers did, our smaller difficulties on this score would disappear. We would understand that to cut God out of America and American education is to cut the heart out of both.

A Look Ahead

The issue is clear. As long as we remain faithful to our Judaeo-Christian traditions we shall keep our liberties. If we repudiate them we shall take the road to state dictatorship, as have all other nations which rejected God and His Natural Law. Experience proves that man must have an Absolute in his life, and so must nations. This Absolute is God and His Law. If these are denied they will be replaced by the omnipotent state, which makes itself a law unto itself.

GOD'S IMPRINT

A traveler was sitting outside his tent in the Sahara Desert one evening talking with his young Bedouin guide about the meaning of life. The guide said that despite his lack of schooling he was convinced that the whole universe was designed and ruled by an all-wise Being.

The traveler objected: "Nobody can know for certain that there is a God."

The lad pointed to a smooth stretch of sand across which there was a track of footprints. "When I see those footprints in the sand," he said, "I know for certain that some man has passed this way. Only a man could have made them."

Then he pointed to the fading colors of the glorious sunset in the west, and overhead to the dark blue sky in which the stars were coming out one by one. "And when I see the sun, and the moon, and the starry heavens in their beauty," he continued, "I know for certain that the Creator has passed this way. They are the footprints of God."

We might very well compare the Natural Law to the footprints which God, in the very act of creation, has impressed in Nature and in the heart of man.

In every generation and in every country, from the beginning of the human race, man has seen footprints of the Supreme Lawgiver, or "Nature's God," as the Founding Fathers referred to Him.

Individuals who have never had any contact with revealed religion show in many ways that they have instinctive notions of a moral law, to which all men in all times are bound.

NATIONS NOT EXCEPTED

This law, imprinted in the conscience of the individual, works on the wider level of societies and nations. Rulers and states are not exempt from following its precepts. In fact, we could well see the history of this law as mainly a struggle between tyranny and individual rights through the ages. Men from all times have always recognized "a higher law" which is superior to any state or any ruler.

A SYMBOL OF RESISTANCE

The story which illustrates the conflict between the law of conscience and the law of the usurping state perhaps better than any other is that of Antigone, as told by the great Greek playwright, Sophocles.

In this case, it was a woman whose name was Antigone. Her brother had fallen into disfavor with Creon, the King of Thebes, in Greece. When her brother died in battle, Creon ordered that he be left to lie unburied for the birds and dogs to desecrate.

Antigone knew in her heart that this was an unnatural and evil act, even though it was promulgated by the ruler of Thebes. Accordingly, she buried her brother.

She was then put on trial.

"Did you know of my order against doing this?" asked King Creon, infuriated because she had disobeyed his edict.

"I did," replied Antigone.

"Yet you dared to break my command?" questioned Creon.

"Yes," replied Antigone, "for it was not God who gave this order. I did not believe that your edicts had such force that you, a mere man, could thwart *the unwritten and unchanging laws of God. These are not matters of today or yesterday, but* are of all time. No man can tell at what time they appeared. In view of them I would not, through fear of human will, meet God's judgment. That I shall die, I know—how would I fail to know it?—as if you had never made an edict. And if before my time I die, I count it gain."

So convinced was Antigone that she had obeyed God's law that no amount of threatening could sway her. As she was being taken away to her death by the guards she cried: "Behold, oh Lords of Thebes, how I, the last remnant of a royal race, suffer because I am faithful to the Laws of Heaven."

THE HIGHER LAW

Antigone has been considered the heroine of all those who have given their lives in obedience to the "higher law" not recognized by the state. All through human history, even down to our own day, men, women, and children have courageously defied tyrannies which place themselves above the God-given law of nature.

But, what interests us more closely, it was to this "higher law" that our Founding Fathers appealed as a sufficient justification for declaring their independence from a ruler who had become tyrannical and a violator of this higher Natural Law. All of this they spelled out in detail in our Declaration of Independence, from which our nation was born.

WHAT IS THIS LAW?

Because of the great importance this law holds for us now and in our history, we would do well to obtain as clear an idea of it as possible, so as to be able to define it and see exactly how it works.

God created everything according to law. All His creatures are given a particular nature suited to the purpose for which they were created. In other words, everything has a law or set of laws governing all its activities in accordance with its purpose and nature.

For example, in the realm of inanimate things such as minerals, water, and the like, certain chemical and physical laws reign supreme and without exception. The laws of gravity, motion, energy, etc., completely explain all the movements of these bodies. They are, in short, their "laws of nature." Thus water must be wet; it must flow, freeze, or boil; rock must be of a certain composition.

In the animal or vegetative realm new laws are introduced because here there is life. Certain biological laws such as those of digestion, growth, and decay govern the nature of animals and plants. Thus a tree must grow, an animal must eat, and so on.

When we come to man we find in the first place that all these laws that govern the nature of minerals, vegetation, and animals hold good. This is because human nature is in part physical and animal. But these laws do not govern all of man. There are certain things man can do that can't be equaled by any of them. He is truly different.

The Real Difference

This is true because man has reason and is free. Having a spiritual soul, he has the power of free choice in his actions. He can *choose* to do some things, and he can *refuse* to do certain others.

The power of free choice, however, does not give man the power to act chaotically in choosing whatever pleases him most. He is restrained and guided by the Natural Law: that is, the fixed moral and spiritual laws formulated by Almighty God for mankind.

Mankind Has a Law

So we see that just as everything else in the universe has its own law in keeping with its nature, so man, although he is rational and free, has one too. It is his "law of nature." It is often referred to as the basic moral law. It is also called the "Natural Law" to distinguish it from that part of the moral law we receive from revelation or religion.

Definitions

Many attempts have been made to define this law and although everyone puts it in slightly different terms, all agree about its essential characteristics.

St. Thomas Aquinas defines it as "the participation of the rational creature in the Eternal law."

Our Declaration of Independence speaks of it as the "Laws of Nature and of Nature's God," and refers to it thus: "We hold these truths to be self-evident, that all men are created equal, that they are endowed by their Creator with certain unalienable rights."

President Eisenhower mentioned it in his Inaugural Address. He said: "This faith is an abiding creed of our fathers. It is our faith in the deathless dignity of man, governed by eternal moral and natural laws. This faith defines our full view of life. It establishes beyond debate those gifts of the Creator that are man's inalienable rights . . ."

Time magazine, in an article of March 9, 1953, entitled "Journalism and Joachim's Children," referred to it as a fact, namely, "that God's order in man's world includes a moral code, based on man's unchanging nature and not subject to man's repeal, suspension or judgment." It is indeed as good a definition as any other.

And there are many other definitions. All the great minds

of history recognized it and defined it. We might define it briefly as follows:

The Natural Law is the Eternal law which is written into man's nature by the Creator and which can be discovered by the proper use of man's reason.

WHAT ARE ITS CONTENTS?

While man-made laws are changeable and particular, the Natural Law contains only those fundamental rules of conduct that all men of all time must abide by. For example, its first principle is: *Good is to be sought and evil avoided.*

Here are a few of the secondary principles that men instinctively know in a rudimentary fashion even before the divine revealed law is communicated to them:

—God must be worshiped.
—Justice must be served.
—Stealing, murder, adultery, must be avoided.
—Parents must be honored.
—Pacts among nations must be respected.

The more particular the applications of the Natural Law become, the more man has need of revelation from God and the positive laws of society.

WHAT ARE ITS MAIN FEATURES?

There are three important characteristics of the Natural Law:

1. It is *universal*, applying to all times, to all men, whether as individuals, members of a group, or citizens of a nation.

2. It is *fixed and changeless*. Its applications may change, but its basic tenets can never vary. To admit the possibility of changing them would be to admit the possibility of changing man's nature or the purpose of human life.

3. Excepting the Revealed Law, Natural Law is the *highest law*. Because it was placed by God in man through creation, it stands above all man-made laws and statutes. Any law or statute conflicting with it is null and void. Any constitution or parliament that violates it is invalid, and any ruler who violates it does wrong.

For All Times and Places

Although our main purpose in considering the Natural Law is to prove that it is the basis of our government, it would be wrong for us to see it merely as an American matter, or even a Western civilization concept, or yet again just a Judaeo-Christian one. Since it is in man's very nature it is timeless and universal. It is as valid today as it has been from the beginning of time.

From Every Corner of the Earth

No better evidence of the universality of the Natural Law tradition can be had than from the last session of the Natural Law Institute, held at Notre Dame University in 1952. From this meeting we can see that the Law is in the tradition of every nation and that it can indeed serve as a common basis for all nations which want to remain free and responsible. This session of the Institute included a panel of five non-Christian leaders who represented their own individual cultures. We quote a small section from the remarks of each participant:

Dr. M. S. Sunderam, first secretary of education at the Embassy of India, said in his talk, "The Natural Law in the Hindu Tradition":

At no time in the history of man is a rediscovery of natural law more urgent than it is today. If the laws of men corrupt the soul of man besides dominating his body, man has the righteous duty to rebel against such laws and reassert the natural laws of his Maker.

Dr. Khalifa Abdul Hakim, director of the Institute of Islamic Culture in Lahore, Pakistan, told the five hundred legal scholars gathered there that—

When the present day materialism has had its day and people begin to realize a common spiritual basis as well, they may put their signatures to belief in one God as they have consented to believe in one world and one humanity.

Rabbi Solomon Freehof, of Rodef Shalom Temple, Pittsburgh, Pennsylvania, in his talk on "The Natural Law in Jewish Tradition," said:

If men believe that the law is essentially natural and God-given, then, with even a minimum of police power, order will reign . . . no tyranny will prevail.

Dr. Hu Shih, of Princeton University, and former Ambassador of China to the United States, spoke of the Confucian Canon which is based on—

. . . the universal principles of justice which, in the words of Aristotle, "all men, by a natural intuition, feel to be common right and wrong."

Dr. Daisetz T. Suzuki, of Claremont College, California, in his talk on "The Natural Law in the Buddhist Tradition," said:

Whatever we may argue about politics or economics, the moral laws being more fundamental, we cannot disregard them and live at peace with our neighbors.

Each of these representatives of various nations and cultures went on at length to say that Natural Law was at the heart of their heritage, and that today it is the only reasonable basis and hope of universal peace and freedom.

BACK HOME AGAIN

Natural Law then is part of the heritage of all mankind. But let us turn our attention to what it means to us in America. Its importance for our thinking cannot be exaggerated. For without this concept our very birth as a nation would make no sense. It is thanks to this concept that we sink our roots deep into the Judaic, Hellenic, Roman, and Christian sources of Western civilization. The point is well brought out by Herbert Agar in an article carried in the *New York Herald Tribune* on Sunday, March 8, 1952:

Upon it [Natural Law] the Roman stoics based their affirmation that all men are born free and equal, citizens of a universal commonwealth, children of God.

Upon it the later Roman jurists based their effort to build a universal legal code, applicable to everybody everywhere within the protection of the Roman Wall.

Upon it the Middle Ages based the hope of a Christian commonwealth wherein the several states would be the servants of man's freedom, not the masters, and each soul could seek its own salvation.

Upon it was built the English concept of the common law, discoverable by "the reasonable man."

And upon it was based the justification for the American Revolution.

The issue is clear. As long as we remain faithful to the Natural Law basis of government we shall keep our liberties. If we repudiate it we shall take the road to totalitarianism, as have all other nations that rejected it. Man must have an

Absolute in his life, and so must nations. This Absolute is God and His Law, which protect our freedom. If they are denied it will be the omnipotent state, a law unto itself, that will replace them; and this will destroy our freedom.

thirteen

American Roots Are Deep

TWO LAWYERS IN CHICAGO FELL INTO A DISCUSSION one day about the trend away from law and order throughout the world. One lawyer said that our only hope is to get back to the Ten Commandments.

"What have they got to do with it?" his companion countered. "They're just a bunch of customs that are out of date."

The first lawyer challenged him to look over the Ten Commandments and see which ones we could throw out and still keep our homes, businesses, and institutions intact.

The other man picked up the challenge and said he would have his answer ready the next time they were together.

It was not many days later that the two met again at their club.

"You really got me this time," said the skeptical one. "Do you know that I've been racking my brain for the last few days to find *just one* of those Commandments that we could do without and still keep things going. I must admit that I can't find a single one. And for the first time in my life I see that they sum up all law and order."

Practically the same thing happened on the other side of the world.

An old lady in China, who never before had heard of Christianity, was shown a copy of the Ten Commandments by a catechist. When the woman had read them over, her only comment was: "Why, these are very reasonable. I don't see how anyone could get on without them."

At first sight this Chinese woman instinctively recognized their reasonableness. God's law was written deep in her heart, even though she was unaware of it. The lawyer in Chicago made the same discovery.

EARLIEST ACKNOWLEDGMENTS

All primitive peoples had their basic law. They considered it to be of divine origin. And in this they were right, for it was God Who put it in their conscience.

The first explicit writing of the Natural Law came from Moses in the Ten Commandments. Although these are a product of Revelation, they are considered as a sort of divine confirmation of the law written in the hearts of all men.

Six centuries before Christ the Greek philosopher *Heraclitus*, the "philosopher of change," paid this tribute to the Natural Law. He wrote:

Wisdom is the foremost virtue, and wisdom consists in speaking the truth, and in lending an ear to nature and acting according to her. Wisdom is common to all . . . They who would speak with intelligence must hold fast to the (wisdom that is) common to all, as a city holds fast to its law . . . For all human laws are fed by one divine law.

The high-water mark of the Natural Law doctrine was in *Plato* and *Aristotle*. Plato made it the eternal ideas of God in man's mind. Aristotle was more realistic about it. He was even called by some the "father of Natural Law."

The *Stoics* were very clear in their ideas of it.

Even the great Greek poets and playwrights, *Homer*, *Sophocles*, *Xenophon*, and the others, referred to it in their works.

Roman Law

Through the Stoics the Natural Law philosophy passed into Roman law, that great masterpiece of early civilization.

Cicero can be considered the spokesman for the Roman jurists. Every American would profit from reading and reflecting on this magnificent passage of his.

There is in fact a true law—namely, right reason—which is in accordance with nature, applies to all men, and is unchangeable and eternal. By its commands this law summons men to the performance of their duties; by its prohibitions it restrains them from doing wrong.

Note how applicable Cicero's thoughts are to our times.

To invalidate this law by human legislation is never morally right, nor is it permissible ever to restrict its operation, and to annul it wholly is impossible. Neither the Senate nor the people can absolve us from our obligation to obey this law, and it requires no Sextus Aelius to expound and interpret it.

Cicero proceeds to point out in great detail the universality and timelessness of the Natural Law.

It will not lay down one rule at Rome, and another at Athens, nor will it be one rule today and another tomorrow. But there will be one law, eternal and unchangeable, binding at all times upon all peoples; and there will be, as it were, one common master and ruler of men, namely God, who is the author of this law, its interpreter, and its sponsor.

The man who will not obey it will abandon his better self, and, in denying the true nature of a man, will thereby suffer the severest of penalties, though he has escaped all the other consequences which men call punishment.

CHRIST AND NATURAL LAW

Christ gave to the Natural Law tradition a foundation and impulse it could not receive from earthly philosophers and thinkers. He did this by building His Divine Law, or Revelation, on it. In this way he safeguarded and strengthened it. He said, "I am not come to destroy, but to fulfill" (Matthew 5:17). Here he was referring to both the Mosaic Law and the Natural Law. Both Divine Law and Natural Law come from the one source, the Eternal Law, from God, the Supreme Lawgiver. "Thou shouldst not have any power against me, unless it were given thee from above," Christ said to Pilate (John 19:11).

Thus He showed that all true law comes from God, and that there cannot be any conflict between true laws, natural or divine; just as there can be none between faith and reason, nature and grace.

Also, Christ's revelation of the infinite value of the human soul and the supreme dignity of the human personality made it forever impossible for any state or ruler to justify a violation of the human rights founded upon Natural Law.

St. Paul, the great Apostle to the Gentiles, mentions the Natural Law. He wrote to the Romans: "When the Gentiles, who have not the law, do by nature those things that are of the law, these having not the law are a law to themselves: who show the work of the law written in their hearts" (Romans 2:14).

The Fathers of the Church, while chiefly concerned with the Divine Law, or Revelation, firmly adhered to the concept of a universal, timeless Natural Law and pointed out God as its basis.

St. Augustine regarded Natural Law as the Divine plan as manifested in man.

THE MEDIEVAL SCHOOLMEN

The Scholastic philosophers of the Middle Ages reached the highest peak in the history of the Natural Law doctrine. They gave much attention to investigating its meaning and its applications.

St. *Thomas Aquinas* more than anyone else showed what it contains, how it derives from the Eternal Law, and how it is of the essence of man. He went so far as to say: "We do not wrong God unless we wrong our own good" (*Contra Gentiles*, III, 122). This shows the great unity of the Divine and Natural Law in man.

He claimed that even God cannot change Natural Law. He wrote: "That God of necessity enacts and cannot alter that law which we call the natural law comes merely from the fact that His will cannot do away with His most perfect essence, that God cannot be at variance with Himself and cannot, as the Apostle says, deny Himself" (*De Veritate* p. 23).

This last point is important. The whole question of Natural Law, after St. Thomas, became a controversy over whether it is absolutely dependent on God and whether God Himself can change it. Two trends eventually developed; one true to the older tradition, and a new one in which Natural Law was separated from the idea of God.

THE LATER SCHOLASTICS

The old tradition was continued mostly through the Jesuit scholars, *Vittoria, Suarez,* and *Bellarmine.* These men further explored the Natural Law doctrine and applied it to positive law, especially international law. It was on these scholars that *Grotius,* the great Dutch Protestant legal philosopher, built his theories of Natural Law. As one commentator has said: "Hugo Grotius constitutes but a direct continuation of the great Natural Law tradition which stretches from St. Augustine to Suarez, and which culminated in St. Thomas" (Chroust, *Hugo Grotius and the Scholastic Natural Law Tradition*, p. 125).

A Turn for the Worse

In a certain sense Grotius marks the end of an era, even though some call him the "Father of Natural Law" and place him at the beginning of a new era. From his time on, the Natural Law tradition began to decay, slowly at first with the advent of *rationalism* and *extreme individualism*. With *Hobbes, Hume, Hegel, Locke, Rousseau,* and *Kant* it was already on the decline.

Finally with the advent of *positivism,* i.e., the doctrine in which there are no absolutes nor "higher law" of any kind, the Natural Law concept was to see its worst days. Not that the idea ever disappeared, but it had now lost its foundation on God and the nature of man. It could now be interpreted as the individual, the leader, or the majority wished. The end of this road is the denial of Natural Law. Its logical outcome was totalitarianism, and there can be little doubt that Hitler and Stalin were heirs to this tradition.

The Common Law

The English Common Law was that grouping of the laws which were common to the English realm. It was through *Henry de Bracton* and *Sir John Fortescue* that Common Law became heir to the Natural Law traditions of the Middle Ages. This heritage it maintained intact and safe from foreign influences down to the time of the American Revolution. In fact it was brought to America by the Pilgrims themselves.

Heinrich Rommen, in his book, *The Natural Law*, writes (p. 114):

This "destruction" of the idea of natural law at the hands of Hume was, in the Anglo-Saxon world, of less importance for the survival of the natural-law concept in jurisprudence than one might have expected. This fact must be attributed to the tenacity with which the spirit of the English common law retained the conceptions of natural law and equity which it had assimilated during the Catholic Middle Ages, thanks especially to the influence of Henry de Bracton (d. 1268) and Sir John Fortescue (d. cir. 1476).

Now, most of the Founding Fathers of the Republic were jurists, and they learned law from Common Law sources. This probably was how they learned the doctrine of Natural Law.

The two stalwarts of Common Law with whom they were all familiar were *Sir Edward Coke* (d. 1634) and *Sir William Blackstone* (d. 1780). They were the authorities from whom the Founding Fathers received their ideas of (1) Natural Law and Natural Rights, and (2) the right of rebellion against the violator of it.

Both of these jurists expressed their opinion on these two points. We feel it important that you read in their own words what later appeared in our own Declaration of Independence.

Coke wrote of Natural Law in this way:

The Law of nature was before any judicial or municipal law and is immutable. The law of nature is that which God at the time of creation of the nature of man infused into his heart for his preservation and direction; and this is the eternal law, the moral law, called also the law of nature.

On the right of revolution he wrote:

And it appears in our books, that in many cases, the common law will control acts of Parliament, and sometimes adjudge them utterly void; for when an act of Parliament is against common right and reason, or repugnant, or impossible to be performed, the common law will control it and adjudge such an action to be void.

Blackstone a century later conveys the same ideas. On Natural Law he said:

This will of his Maker is called the law of Nature . . . This law of Nature being coeval with mankind and dictated by God Himself, is superior in obligation to any other; no human laws are of any validity if contrary to this; and such of them as are valid derive all their force and all of their authority from this origin . . . Hence it follows that the first and primary end of human laws is to maintain these absolute God-given rights of individuals.

On the right to rebel he wrote:

Acts of Parliament that are impossible to be performed are of no validity; and if there arise out of them collaterally any absurd consequences, manifestly contradictory to common reason, they are, with regard to those collateral consequences, void.

On the influence of Coke and Blackstone on the Founders of the Republic we have the word of the renowned Constitutional authority, Dean Roscoe Pound, in his *Developments of Constitutional Guarantees of Liberty* (20 N.D. Lawyer, 347, 348, 1945):

So steeped were the Eighteenth Century colonial lawyers in Coke's teachings, for Coke's *Institutes* were the most authoritative law books available to them, and they were dealing with a tradition and not a code, that the controversial literature of the era of the Revolution, if it is to be understood, must be read or interpreted by a common law lawyer.

Indeed he must be a common law lawyer of the Nineteenth Century type, brought up to read and reread Coke and Blackstone until he get the whole feeling and atmosphere of those who led resistance to the home government.

Or again we have the testimony of the well-known jurist, Clarence Manion, who in his article, "The Natural Law Philosophy of the Founding Fathers," said this (quoted in *Natural Law Institute Proceedings*, 1947, vol. I, p. 9): "The natural law expounded by Coke in the Seventeenth Century, and by

Blackstone in the Eighteenth, met colonial specifications perfectly."

THE END OF '76

Some critics have tried to see the Declaration of Independence and the natural rights idea as a mere rationalization or afterthought, used to justify an unnecessary rebellion.

This is easy to disprove since we find a belief in the natural God-given rights admitted and accepted by the Founders and their contemporaries *before the Revolution* itself.

To give an idea of how widespread was the Natural Law philosophy at the time of the Declaration of Independence, we cite a few of the views of some important figures. It will take you only a few moments to read brief excerpts from these great authorities of early America.

Already in 1764, *James Otis* of Boston, whose influence in those days is acknowledged by all, wrote:

That the common good of the people is the Supreme law, is of the law of nature, and part of that grand charter given to the human race (though too many of them are afraid to assert it) by the only Monarch in the Universe Who alone has a clear and indisputable right to absolute power because He is the only one who is Omniscient as well as Omnipotent.

In 1774, *Alexander Hamilton* went on record to say:

The fundamental source of all your errors, sophisms, and false reasonings, is a total ignorance of the natural rights of mankind—were you once to become acquainted with these, you would never entertain a thought that all men are not by nature entitled to equal privileges. You would be convinced that natural liberty is a gift of a beneficent Creator to the whole human race, and that civil liberty is founded on that.

James *Wilson* (1742–1798), commonly referred to as "the philosopher of the Constitution," and one of the few signers of both the Declaration of Independence and Constitution, wrote much about the Natural Law. We quote some of it:

> . . . that our Creator has a supreme right to prescribe a law for our conduct, and that we are under the most perfect obligation to obey that law, are truths established on the clearest and most solid principles . . . [God] being infinitely and eternally happy in Himself, His goodness alone could move Him to create us, and give us the means of happiness. The same principle that moved His creating moves His governing power. What is the efficient cause of moral obligation—of the eminent distinction between right and wrong? . . . I give it [the question] this answer, the will of God. This is the Supreme Law . . . The law of nature is universal . . .

George Mason, who was the author of the Virginia Declaration (which preceded the writing of the Declaration of Independence), and to whom it is granted Jefferson owed most in writing our Declaration, was a well-known devotee of Natural Law. In 1772 he wrote:

> The laws of nature are the laws of God, whose authority can be superseded by no power on earth. A legislature must not obstruct our obedience to Him from whose punishments they cannot protect us. All human constitutions which contradict His laws we are in conscience bound to disobey.

Two years before Blackstone was published, John Adams wrote:

> . . . Liberty, the unalienable, indefeasible rights of man . . . were never so skillfully and successfully consulted as in that most excellent monument of human art, the common law of England.

And it is the same case with the others: Patrick Henry, James Madison, the Carrolls, Pinckney, and the rest. They, too, adhered to the same ideas as the foregoing.

From Moses to 1776

The rest of the story is told in Chapter 9, on the Declaration of Independence. The "eternal principles" which were an expression of the "American mind" were the principles of Natural Law which came down from the beginnings of human history to the very writing of our Declaration of Independence and Constitution.

The draft of the Declaration containing the Natural Law basis of our government was presented to the Continental Congress and examined line by line by all members. The Natural Law philosophy was maintained, and as we saw, two further references to God were included. Thus our nation sinks its roots deep into the Judaeo-Christian heritage of some four thousand years. It was the choice of this tradition which has kept for us our liberties in the face of an encircling enslavement.

The Source of Sources

The greatest source of the Divine and Natural Law basis of our nation was Christianity itself. Even if most of the founders had not been jurists and trained in Common Law (which they were), they would have arrived at a Natural Law position by direct contact with the primary source of the whole Hebraic-Christian tradition: the *Old and New Testaments*. That these are the greatest sources of our Western and American democratic traditions cannot be seriously doubted.

The Old Testament, containing the Ten Commandments, the preaching of the Prophets, and the books of Wisdom, has served as a basis of Christian morality and of Western civilization from the beginning. Ideas of one God, Justice, and Divine Providence were first given to the world by the Hebrew people.

The influence of the New Testament in the formation of our national mentality and in the building up of our democratic way of life is immeasurable. Certainly, without Christianity, democracy could never have·existed on any stable or permanent basis. The reasons for this are plain.

If we were to try to summarize the essentials of our democratic way of life, we might list the following:

1. Preservation of the basic rights of individuals and minorities as God-given.
2. Equality of all men before the law.
3. Personal and civic liberties.
4. The role of government as servant of the people.
5. A rule of law rather than of men.

Now these social or political goals presuppose certain others of a profounder nature which are found in their fullness and vigor in the Gospels. Among others they are as follows:

1. The infinite worth of every human person.
2. The equality of all men in the Creation by a just and good God.
3. The possibility of freedom and self-control through truth and virtue.
4. Charity, or love of neighbor, as the fulfillment of the law.
5. Justice, whose sanction is a Provident God Who will reward and punish all for their deeds.

It is upon these spiritual bases that our civic and political doctrines rest. Without them our way of life would be cut off from its sources and would decline and die. The great French-Jewish philosopher, *Henri Bergson*, remarked that one could say *"that democracy is evangelical in essence and that its motive power is love."* We have no reason to believe that our Founding Fathers received their main inspiration from any other source. It was this inspiration that stemmed from a belief that God is the basis of Natural Law and natural rights.

Once again, the great French-Christian philosopher, *Jacques Maritain*, when writing about the founding of our nation, said (*Man and the State*, p. 183):

Far beyond the influences received either from Locke or the XVIIIth Century Enlightenment, the Constitution of this country is deep-rooted in the age-old heritage of Christian thought and civilization. Paradoxically enough, and by virtue of the serious religious feelings of the Founding Fathers . . . peerless is the significance, for political philosophy, of the establishment of the American Constitution at the end of the XVIIIth Century. This Constitution can be described as an outstanding lay Christian document tinged with the philosophy of the day. The spirit and inspiration of this great political Christian document is basically repugnant to the idea of making human society stand aloof from God and from any religious faith . . .

WERE THEY CHRISTIAN MEN?

To speak of Christianity as a source of inspiration would be in vain unless we could show in actual fact that the Founders of our nation were in fact men of deep faith. Were they Christian-minded men?

The answer to the question is a most emphatic yes. Practically all of the Founding Fathers were religious-minded men, most were churchgoers, and very many, particularly those who had most to do with the founding of our nation, were pious men.

AN UNWRITTEN CHAPTER

This fact often comes as a surprise to many. It did to Anson Phelps Stokes, D.D., LL.D., former secretary of Yale University and former Canon of Washington Cathedral, who set out to investigate all the religious influences affecting our country from the beginning, and who studied the question most exhaustively. He spent twelve years at this and finally published, in 1950, three large volumes, comprising three thousand pages, entitled *Church and State in the United States*. In volume I, page 514, he wrote:

Much less recognized, but equally clear, is the conviction of the founders of the vital importance of religion to the new nation. I expected, before I began this study, to find this to be true as far as President Washington and some of his associates were concerned; but I have been surprised at the mass of evidence to support the claims of religion in a republic as expressed by men like Thomas Jefferson and Benjamin Franklin, who have often been classed as freethinkers. Even Thomas Paine was not an atheist. And the various provisions to encourage religions which we have quoted from the early days of the United States government are cumulative and convincing . . .

The founders saw clearly and definitely that without religion a democratic government could not succeed. If men are all, as the Declaration of Independence stated, "created equal" and "endowed by their Creator with certain unalienable rights," the maintenance of communion with that Creator, which is the heart of religion, would seem both logical and vital.

This has been a chapter in American history that has been for the most part unwritten. Most have learned a mass of facts about economic, military, or geographic America, but very little about religious America.

In 1907, J. Franklin Jameson, the president of the American Historical Association, wrote, as quoted in Sweet's *Religion in the Development of American Culture* (p. vii):

Of all the means of estimating American character . . . the pursuit of religious history is the most complete. He who would understand the American of past and present times, and to that end would provide himself with data representing all classes, all periods, all regions, may find in the history of American religion the closest approach to the continuous record he desires.

Some of the Facts

We shall here give just a very brief idea of the religious status of the Founders. It will be of interest and importance to know something in this regard about the three following groups: (1) the signers of the Declaration of Independence; (2) the members of the Constitutional Convention; (3) other ranking figures of this period who exerted much influence on our beginnings.

The Signers of the Declaration of Independence

There were 56 members in the Continental Congress who signed the Declaration of Independence. A breakdown of their religious affiliation is as follows:

Episcopalians	36
Presbyterians	6
Baptists	1
Quakers	1
Catholics	1

(Some authorities credit the Quakers with 2 and the Presbyterians with 5.) Thus, 45 of the 56 were churchgoers. All the rest were believers and were sympathetic to Christian truth and morality.

The Members of the Constitutional Convention

Of the 39 signers of the Constitution, only 6 had signed the Declaration of Independence. We might inquire, therefore, about the religious status of those who framed our Constitution. And we find little difference in the religious picture here;

these men were as Christian-minded as the signers of the Declaration.

On this subject we can do no better than quote the authority, William Warren Sweet, in *Religion in the Development of American Culture* (p. 85):

Numerous studies dealing with the political and economic factors in the making of the Constitution have appeared over the years, but there has been little attention given to the religious influences in the framing and adoption of the fundamental law of the land. The framers of the Constitution represented a cross-section of the American religious bodies of that day. Of them, nineteen were Episcopalians, eight were Congregationalists, seven were Presbyterians, two were Roman Catholics, two were Quakers, one a Methodist, one a Dutch Reformed while Edmund Randolph was a deist, though he later became a communicant of the Episcopal Church.

All the others were Christian theists, even though some were not completely orthodox in their beliefs.

To understand the Constitution correctly it must be seen as a political expression of the Natural Rights philosophy of the Declaration of Independence. All provisions in it and the Bill of Rights aim at protecting the God-given individual and minority rights mentioned in the Declaration of Independence. The entire new Constitution was an attempt to reduce to concrete application the Natural Rights idea contained in the Declaration of Independence.

THE FRAMERS OF THE STATE CONSTITUTIONS

It is equally important to know of the thoughts and beliefs of the framers of the state constitutions, for in those days our government was highly decentralized. Real power lay in the hands of the state legislatures.

And it is the same story here. The framers of their constitutions were in the great majority Christian churchgoers (mostly Protestant), showing open favor to religion. They opened their sessions with prayer, enforced respect for Sunday, used the name of God in their constitutions (all except two), exempted churches from taxation, and encouraged religion and religious bodies in general. Besides mentioning God in their constitutions, many states use the very terms of the Declaration of Independence about natural rights.

THE EDUCATION OF THE FOUNDING FATHERS

Another point of interest and value in connection with our thesis concerns the education of the founders. Here we find another source of their beliefs in the Natural Law concept of government.

The main sources of their education were the academies, colleges, and universities. In these were taught the scholastic theses and traditions that were the backbone of education throughout the previous thousand years.

1276 OR 1776?

The points of comparison between the universities and colleges of the colonial period, and of the period extending till the end of the eighteenth century and those of the Middle Ages are remarkable.

In our early schools Latin held a privileged position in the curriculum. Mostly all the college men could read and speak it, and public disputations in Latin were held at the commencements.

Scholastic philosophy, with a particular emphasis on the questions of God, the Natural Law, and ethics was taught. For example, we find discussed the questions of freedom of the will, Natural Law, conscience, necessity of revelations, the occurrence of miracles, man's rights and duties, man's last end, etc., in the same Latin terminology as of hundreds of years before.

The leading colleges and universities of that day, Harvard, William and Mary, Yale, Kings College (Columbia), the College of Pennsylvania (University of Pennsylvania), the College of Rhode Island (Brown), all taught theses that have been described by experts as "pure scholastic formulas."

There can be hardly any doubt that this training contributed to the harmony of opinion among the Founding Fathers which found expression in our early documents and practices, in the Articles of Confederation, the Declaration of Independence, the Constitution of the United States and those of the various individual states. For most signers of the Declaration of Independence were college men, and many others taught themselves from college sources.

To sum up, the Founding Fathers of our nation were heirs to the Natural Law philosophy that lies at the base of our government, as expressed in the Declaration and Constitution. Their knowledge came from several sources: from the Common Law which they knew well; from Christian beliefs; and from their education. In light of all this it is easy to understand how the "eternal principles" of the Declaration of Independence were "an expression of the American mind" as well as a product of Christian tradition.

The Choice Before Us

As far back as the early eighteenth century, a trend toward skepticism and distrust in reason and in the immutable order of nature began to challenge the age-old tradition of Natural Law. This movement rejected any objective or absolute law and finally put the basis of law in the will of the majority, or in social convention.

One could now see very plainly two forces opposing one another. On one hand there was the Natural Law tradition which went back to Judaeo-Christian sources and to Roman and Greek law and philosophy, and which became the foundation of Western civilization as well as the main source of the American Declaration of Independence and Constitution.

The other movement was a revolt against this traditional one which took the forms of relativism or atheistic materialism, denying all higher law and values that do not spring from man himself and nature.

This second destructive trend came too late, thank God, to affect substantially the founding of our nation. Its influence was restricted to the Continent.

However, this relativism came to the United States later. Its adherents have been very frank in admitting their disagreement with the philosophy of the Declaration of Independence and the Bill of Rights. They ridicule the notion of a Natural Law. For them all is change, all is relative. There is no higher law or sanction anywhere. The state is absolute.

IN OUR SCHOOLS AND COURTS

These ideas have found their way into our schools and universities.

One well-known educator, for example, ridiculed Jefferson's idea that the majority can be wrong.

One of our famous jurists defined truth as the majority vote that can lick all others. Very consistently he concluded that in the face of two contending ideas he could see no remedy but force. Therefore this view maintains "might makes right."

Another professor called Natural Law an illusion. Still another called the idea of government by law an absurd dogma.

One student was told in class that he should never again mention Natural Law because it was "antiquated, discredited, and dead as a dodo."

There are many other examples, but these few give an idea of how often we have tended to believe and practice one thing in our country and teach another in our schools.

STILL A VITAL ISSUE

Harold McKinnon wrote in his paper entitled "Natural Law and Positive Law" (quoted in *Natural Law Institute Proceedings*, 1947, Vol. I, p. 85): "In American jurisprudence, natural law is both a foundation and a stumbling block. It is a foundation, because it lies at the root of our juristic tradition. It is a stumbling block, because it is rejected by the prevailing philosophy."

IDEAS HAVE CONSEQUENCES

During the last war, one professor in England saw clearly how it all came about. Professor Hobhouse wrote (quoted in *Understanding Europe*, by Christopher Dawson, p. 189): "In the bombing of London, I had just witnessed the visible and tangible outcome of a false and wicked doctrine the foundations of which lay, I believe, in the book before me [Hegel's *Philosophy of Right*]."

The important thing to point out here is that Hegel and his followers denied Natural Law. Thus many interpreters see most of modern totalitarianism as arising from this denial. Hegel and Hobbes, the great deniers of Natural Law, are considered by many as the godparents of modern dictatorships.

THE REVIVAL OF NATURAL LAW

Etienne Gilson, the renowned French philosopher, has said: "The Natural Law always buries its undertakers." It seems that whenever it is put out the front door of our schools or courts it slips in the back door. Never is it downed for long; throughout history it has always come back to assume its rightful place. Natural Law always comes back just because it is natural and men think in terms of it. It cannot fade because, as Jefferson thought, it is eternal.

DOING SOMETHING ABOUT IT

Essential as it is for every citizen to understand well the underlying philosophy of our government, it is even more important for each of us to take practical steps to see that it is restored to the mainstream of American life, to our schools in particular. Every student in every school has a right to know these truths. The very survival of our liberties depends on them.

fourteen

A Lesson from the Nazis

During the postwar trials of nazis in germany in 1946, a former high official of the Third Reich confessed that he had taken part in the coldblooded murders of two and one-half million persons by the Nazis.

One American investigator, astounded at the casual manner in which the defendant admitted these atrocities, asked: "Do you believe in God?"

"Most emphatically not!" the Führer's disciple replied.

In countries the world over, where God has been deliberately rejected by atheistic rulers, the value of human life is soon belittled.

More than three thousand years ago the Hebrew Psalmist gave a warning which still holds true today: "The fool hath said in his heart: 'There is no God'" (Psalms 13:1).

A Bitter Lesson

We, of this generation, have no excuse not to learn from a terrible experiment that has taken place in our own times. We have a unique opportunity to study the speedy rise and the speedier fall of an atheistic state, which succeeded thoroughly and quickly in eliminating both Natural and Divine Law, from all phases of a school system that had previously recognized God. That state substituted instead the brutal laws of those who would defile and debase their fellow men. Since all of this happened within the past thirty years, it offers in modern perspective a stark and dramatic reminder of how important it is to be eternally vigilant in all that concerns the training of the young.

EDUCATION IN ERSATZ RELIGION

Ersatz is a useful German word meaning "substitute"; something which is put in place of the real thing.

Hitler and his Nazi followers knew that man needs to believe in something greater than himself. They perverted this instinct away from God and channeled it toward a substitute concept: "*Das Volk*," the mystical German People. An attempt was made to attribute divine power to Hitler. His book, *Mein Kampf* ("My Struggle"), became the Bible of the new belief.

Pagan Germanic gods became the objects of worship for young and old alike. The Golden Rule gave way to Hitler's dictum that "what is good for Germany is right; what is bad for Germany is wrong."

Young people were taught that they were the children of the State; not the children of God. Instead of honoring their parents, the children were encouraged to spy and report on them. In school, youngsters who had ended their childish letters with "*Grüss Gott*" learned to write "*Heil Hitler!*" instead. (Thus, a common greeting containing the word God was replaced by one containing the word Hitler.) Heathen tribalism gradually replaced Christianity in some phases of life. Kindness was considered weakness; brutality became a virtue.

EDUCATION IS ALWAYS FIRST ON THEIR LIST

Those who would enslave man concentrate first on the schools as the most effective place to deform and debase impressionable minds. Thus they quickly eliminate all teaching that reminds the human being that he is made in God's image, and that his rights come from his Creator.

In this process of atheizing any school system, those who are intent on evil find that their most valuable assistants are often well-meaning persons who have no intention of being accomplices but who are unable to distinguish between the use and the abuse of academic freedom.

Many who willingly identified themselves with the Nazis found out too late the terrible mistake they had made. An example of one who felt this belated revulsion was Hans Frank, the former Nazi governor of Poland. Before he went to the gallows he begged God's pardon and offered his life in atonement for his sins. Here is part of his testimony:

&§ We [the Nazis] did not imagine at the start of our road that turning away from God could have such destructive and deadly consequences and that unavoidably we would become involved in guilt more deeply all the time. Thus, we have come to shame in our estrangement from God and had to perish.

Then he concluded with this stirring plea:

I implore my people that it should not continue in this direction, not even one step, for Hitler's way was the way without God, and the road away from Christ, and in the final outcome the road of political stupidity, of disaster and death.

Sincere as it was, his repentance at the gallows could not restore to life the millions who had suffered cruel deaths, replace the property blasted and lost by war, or tie together the homes broken up by the world conflict.

These words can be a warning to us to be vigilant against the accidental or deliberate exclusion of God from the classroom. Since the totalitarians make God Number 1 on their liquidation list, we who live in a democracy should direct our first efforts toward restoring God to His rightful place in the education of our children.

A Look at the Record

That you may be well aware of the anti-God and anti-religious nature of Nazi teaching, you should glance over some of the following specific Nazi directives and instructions.

We do little more than list them. They speak for themselves.

The Nazi Concept of Education

Here are a few statements that show how completely totalitarians eliminate allegiance to God and substitute the false god of the Almighty State. The first is from Alfred Rosenberg, *Myth of the Twentieth Century* (p. 636):

The pre-requisite of all German education is the acknowledgment that it is not Christendom which has brought us civilization but that Christianity owes its lasting values to the Germanic character.

From "Neo-pagan Movement in Germany," by Lewis Spence. *The Quarterly Review*, July, 1940 (pp. 75–76):

It is particularly impressed upon teachers that no hope of a life to come or any idea of salvation must be allowed to obtrude itself upon the child's consciousness. "We are fighting," it is claimed in one of these publications, "as our ancestors said, for the fashioning of the world by the side of the gods"—that is, the German gods, not the God of an effete and outworn Christianity.

From Konrad Heiden, *A History of National Socialism* (p. 355):

[National Socialism] has put an end to the sovereignty of the intellect by forbidding inquiries after the why and the wherefore, and insisting by means of rubber truncheons, revolvers, and concentration camps upon a submission that is not otherwise justified.

"The chief purpose of the school," so the Nazi concept ran, "is to train human beings to realize that the State is more important than the individual; that individuals must be willing and ready to sacrifice themselves for Nation and Fuehrer." Herr Frank, Reich Cabinet Minister, said in a speech at Tubingen, October, 1936:

"The ideas of Adolf Hitler contain the final truths of all scientific knowledge" (from *Revolt Against Pity* by Dr. A. Guirdham, p. 21).

From *Revolution of Nihilism* by Hermann Rauschning (p. 28):

❧ Hostility to the things of the spirit, indifference to truth, indifference to the ethical conceptions of morality, honor, and equity . . . are not excrescences but the logical and inevitable outcome of the National Socialist philosophy, of the doctrine of violence.

From the same book (p. 81):

❧ The doctrine of violence states that "spiritual assets . . . have no intrinsic authority, no value in themselves; there is nothing that counts except force . . . it is virtually a duty for every member of the elite to undergo training in brutality."

PARENTS ARE SILENCED

We have seen how the Nazis tried to transfer natural devotion from God to the State. In the following statements we can see how they tried to transfer authority over the child from the parent to the all-powerful State.

Baldur von Schirach, Nazi Youth Leader, wrote ("*Das Junge Deutschland*," April, 1940, quoted in *Revolt Against Pity* by Dr. A. Guirdham, p. 13):

୶ A parent who keeps her children away from the Hitler Youth Movement abuses her parental power. This will be taken from her in so far as it affects the enrollment of children into the Hitler Youth.

Von Schirach devised a catechism for the spiritual education of German youth. In it he says (ibid., p. 14):

୶ If a child asks its mother for reassurance, "Am I yours?" the mother must answer, "No, you belong to the Fuehrer." . . . The lives of all German youths belong solely to Hitler.

Konrad Heiden, in A History of National Socialism (pp. 327–328), quotes Hitler's speech at Erfurt, Germany:

୶ If there are still to be found in our generation individuals who feel incapable of adapting themselves to the changed conditions, we will take their children from them and educate them to be serviceable to the German nation.

By the time six million children from the age of eight onward had been enrolled, their leaders could boast (William Teeling, "Youth on the Rhine," in Friends of Europe publications ⚹15, p. 7):

୶ They are becoming completely independent of their parents and showing loyalty only to the State.

LIFE BECOMES CHEAP

One of the most tragic results of removing God from the schools is that life becomes cheap. The saving concept that each individual is important because of his divine origin is lost. How openly the doctrine of the worthlessness of man is taught in the schools is evident from educational directives in any totalitarian state. A few such directives as the following will

give you some idea of how debasing this policy can become:
Nietzsche in his *Der Antichrist* (p. 62) wrote:

The equality of souls before God, this lie . . . this anarchist bomb of a conceit, which has become the last revolution, the modern idea and principle of the destruction, of the whole social order—this is Christian dynamite.

In an article, "Hitler and Arms," J. L. Garvin, editor of *The Observer* of London, summarized a Nazi manual written for the use of students by Professor Ewald Banse of Brunswick Technical High School (quoted in *Friends of Europe*, publication ⚡1, pp. 7–8):

Life being given, and sufficiently continued, is not a personal possession, but belongs to the State and the "race" . . . Women when their new-born babies are put into their arms must firmly contemplate the ultimate destruction of these infants. Babies of all nations are brought forth to kill each other periodically when mature. The dying warrior must shed his blood as in glad libation to his "National God."

Alfred Rosenberg, in his *Myth of the Twentieth Century*, wrote on page 169 (quoted in "Germany's National Religion," p. 13 of *Friends of Europe*, ⚡13):

A nation led by honor and duty would not maintain the lazy and the criminals, but would eliminate them.

Ernst Bergmann, in his book, *The German National Church*, wrote on page 72 (quoted in "Germany's National Religion," p. 20 of *Friends of Europe*, ⚡13):

This kind of Christianity was sheer brain disease of the human race, a mental affliction (pneumatose), which lasted thousands of years. Helplessly we struggle with the problems. All that Man can do now that he is freed of "dementia Christianity" is—

to become a beast again. As an animal, Man has today to begin
again.

From *The Revolution of Nihilism* by Hermann Rauschning (pp. 23, 28):

&s Man is not a logical being, not a creature guided by
reason or intelligence, but a creature following his instincts and
impulses, like any other animal.

In regard to the spiritual worth of the human being Hitler
had this to say:

&s To the Christian doctrine of the infinite significance
of the human soul and of personal responsibility, I oppose with
icy clarity the saving doctrine of the nothingness and insignifi-
cance of the human being.

On another occasion Hitler showed how anxious he was
to put this weird theory into practice for he said:

&s Look at these young men and boys! What material!
I shall eradicate the thousands of years of human domestication.
Brutal youth—that is what I am after—I want to see once more
in its eyes the gleam . . . of the beast of prey. With these I can
make a new world!

An official Nazi Party statement on May 5, 1940, said that
the Nazis had no interest in women beyond the child-
bearing age, and that the Reich was not concerned with "helping sick mothers with wretched children, but only those
mothers whom we think by our aid will be led to full useful-
ness" (from *Revolt Against Pity* by Dr. A. Guirdham, p. 11).
Guirdham quotes Herr Darrow, once Nazi Minister of
Agriculture, on Nazi plans regarding defeat of England (*Revolt Against Pity*, p. 24):

Able-bodied men will be exported as slaves to the continent. The old and weakly will be exterminated. All men remaining in Britain will be sterilized. A million or so young women of the Nordic type will be segregated in a number of stud farms, where with the assistance of picked German sires they will, during a period of ten or twelve years, produce nearly annually a series of Nordic infants to be brought up in every way as Germans.

In the Nazi system of things there was no place for the mentally defective, the physically weak, or those with incurable disease. Those who are molded in the belief that man is nothing more than a refined brute, without eternal destiny and with responsibility to no one beyond the omnipotent state, easily accept the gas chambers and horror murders of Dachau and Buchenwald.

DEGRADATION OF WOMEN

It took long centuries of slow, difficult training to raise the level of women to the dignified and respected one they now enjoy. The Nazis set out to undo this progress of centuries. Christian teachings on the sanctity of the home and marriage, the importance of the human soul, the value of premarital chastity, all were thrown overboard. Christian marriage ceremonies gave way to the new-style "German marriage." No secret was made of "the inferiority of women." Girls were persuaded with considerable shrewdness to like their state of degradation.

Sex was the most important subject in the education of Nazi girls. It was introduced early and realistically into their training, so that they would think of their primary function in life as being "breeders of soldiers."

Unmarried girls in their teens were urged to have children. Some of the finest summer resorts in Germany were turned into "baby farms" where pregnant girls were welcomed as true and loyal Germans. They were housed "in beautiful homes, usually attractive hotels and health resorts." When the children were born, they became the wards of the State and were brought up under its constant supervision.

The Nazi's perverted concept of "morality" was frankly explained by a teacher of eugenics at a girls' school in Frankfurt am Main. She said:

ఆ§ All of us women can now enjoy the rich emotional experience of having a baby by a healthy young man without the restricting ties of the old-fashioned marriage.

Heinrich Himmler, chief of the SS and the Gestapo, told German girls "of pure blood" that they had—

ఆ§ A wartime duty which lies beyond marriage and has nothing to do with it. This is to become mothers of children by soldiers who leave for the front.

The SS magazine *Schwarze Korps* put it this way:

ఆ§ The number of births of best blood must not be allowed in this war to sink below normal peacetime figures. A girl who here dodges her highest duty is as great a traitor as the soldier who deserts his flag. SS men! Show that you are ready not only to give your lives for your country, but to give her far more lives before you die!

UNDERMINING OF ALL RELIGION

The Nazis knew they could make little headway in brutalizing the young as long as Christianity and Judaism were constantly reminding them that as children of their Father in heaven, each of them had an eternal destiny, and that the role of the state was to protect their God-given rights.

They therefore made a ceaseless effort to ridicule and remove every religious influence, as these authoritative statements indicate:

Clara Leiser refers to this directive on pages 45 and 46 of her book, *Lunacy Becomes Us:*

We must avoid rituals reminiscent of church ceremonies. These ceremonies are dead. Our National Socialist ideology is not a substitute but a new creation. Christmas festivals in Protestant parish houses are as divorced from our ideology as the singing of Christmas hymns.

The Nazi Primer, Official Handbook for Schooling the Hitler Youth, says on page 9:

➤ The Christians, above all the Roman Church, reject the race idea with the citation 'before God all men are equal.' All who have the Christian belief, whether Jews, bush niggers, or whites, are dearer to them and more worthwhile than a German who does not confess Christianity. The one binding bond, above and beyond all restrictions, is the Belief which alone brings salvation.

Dr. A. Guirdham, on page 20 of his book, *Revolt Against Pity,* quotes Rosenberg as having said:

➤ The supreme values of both the Roman and the Protestant Churches represent a negative Christian attitude . . . they stand in the way of the vital powers of the Nordic race and they must yield. This is the significance of the present religious conflict.

Article XXX of church regulations, quoted in the *Manchester Guardian,* May 6, 1938, states that Clara Leizer wrote on page 46 of her book *Lunacy Becomes Us:*

➤ Starting with the day of the establishment of the National Church of the German Reich, the Christian Cross is to be removed from all the churches and cathedrals inside the frontiers of the Reich and its colonies, and is to be replaced by the immortal symbol of Germany—the Swastika.

German boys were taught to say: "Let Christ rot and the Hitler Youth march on!" (from *What Hitler Wants,* by E. O.

Lorimer, p. 148). Christmas, the Hitlerites discovered, did not commemorate the birth of Christ; it really originated with Wotan, a German god. Good Friday was dedicated to Baldur, another pagan German deity.

WORSHIP OF THE STATE

Realizing that men must worship a false god if they do not revere the True One, the Nazis made a supreme effort to set up gods of their own with no standards except those tolerated by the Nazis themselves. Hitler's ersatz religion tried to identify God with Germany. Baldur von Schirach, German youth leader, preached "the Divine Law that is called Germany." Hitler tried to parody Christ's words when he told his followers: "Let the children come with me, for they are mine." On all sides the new paganism was stuffed down German throats with such expressions as:

    ∾ "The German Faith Movement acknowledges only one Lord, Adolf Hitler."
    "Christ was great, but Hitler is greater."
    "To Thee, O My Leader, belong our hearts and our souls."
    "Fuehrer, my Fuehrer, my Faith and my Light."
    "Fuehrer, to Thee I owe, alone, my daily bread."
    "Adolf Hitler is the visible personal expression of what in our youth was represented as 'God.'"
    "I have never felt the Divine power of God as near as in the greatness of our Fuehrer."

    In their own words they reveal themselves: Herr Robert Ley, Nazi Minister of Labor, said in a speech at Ludwigshaven, July 9, 1937, quoted in *Revolt Against Pity*, by Dr. A. Guirdham, p. 21:

    ∾ Everything springs from Adolf Hitler. His faith is our faith, and therefore our daily creed runs, "I believe only in Adolf Hitler."

Ley also said (ibid., p. 20):

&§ The Fuehrer is for the German people today what once was, according to the Christian message of 2,000 years ago, the Messenger of God.

The Nazi Primer, Official Handbook for Schooling the Hitler Youth, quotes from Goebbels on page 257:

&§ The Nazi party is a political church, where for hundreds of thousands of years German people will be trained to be true National Socialists. We are the political pastors of our people.

E. O. Lorimer quoted from *Mein Kampf* on page 111 of *What Hitler Wants*:

&§ The sole earthly criterion of whether an enterprise is right or wrong is its success.

And he quoted from what Goebbels said at Stuttgart, September 4, 1938:

&§ The methods by which a people forces its way upwards are of no moment; only the goal which is reached is important.

A Warning for Us

At most, these are only a few samples of the Nazi position on education. Why should the Nazis, you may ask, devote so much time and attention to the education of their younger generation? The answer is that they knew that the school-children of one day would be the national leaders of the next. If they could be cast in the Nazi mold early in life, their rulers believed they would never abandon paganism. An earlier German, Bismarck, said: "What you want in the life of a nation, first put into the schools of that nation."

You may say: "Well, that was Nazi Germany, but that's all dead and gone. What possible bearing can it have on American schools today?"

True enough, the recent Nazi anti-God teaching is buried under the ruins of Germany. And there seems little chance of a similar catastrophe happening in our country. Yet there is still a tendency on the part of some American educators to eliminate God, to refer to the Ten Commandments as out of date or old-fashioned, to teach that "there is no difference between right and wrong." This is certainly inching closer and closer to the same point of view as that held by Hitler. He put it much the same way when he said, "The Ten Commandments have lost their validity . . . there is no such thing as truth, either in the moral or in the scientific sense."

Same Debasing Pattern

In every country the pattern is the same. The aim of the anti-God group is always to debase man, not to elevate him. Today, for instance, millions of young Chinese minds and hearts are being impressed over and over again with the idea that they are mere animals, little different from monkeys or other brute forms of life.

What was imposed on the Germans by the Nazi educational system a few years ago, has again been imposed on East Germany today under the Communists. And in fact, the same thing is being forced on China by the Communists.

Here is a passage from a Communist textbook recently introduced in China (*General Book of Knowledge*, Book 7, Lesson 25):

In very ancient times, man and monkeys were not different. Later man gradually learned to use his two hands to work, to use his hands to manufacture things. Thus man differed from the monkeys and other animals . . . Man is able to produce through his labors, other animals cannot produce through their labors . . .

This paragraph is typical of countless others. Note that twice in this brief paragraph the child is told that man is the same as "other animals." How long can a young person withstand such a subtle, relentless attack upon his receptive mind? Surely it is only a matter of time before the staunchest of those who are exposed to this constant repetition of "You are nothing but an animal" begin to act like animals. Once people lose respect for themselves, they quickly lose respect for others.

It is true that the most thorough indoctrination in such animalistic views can never completely extinguish an individual's deep-seated conviction of his true worth—the Nazi leaders who turned to God in repentance on the gallows demonstrated this fact to the world.

Yet history has also shown us that an individual can be temporarily deranged by a constant appeal to his animal instincts. For a time at least, he becomes an easy tool in promoting immorality, hatred, thievery, destruction, death, and the crimes that degrade both the individual and the nation.

Before It Is Too Late

In most nations people find out too late that a complacent attitude toward error can have disastrous results.

If the gradual weakening and eventual elimination of respect for Almighty God is the aim of any and every force that would destroy human freedom, then it should be our aim to work tirelessly for the proper recognition of God in all American education, public as well as private. Leading the way in this all-important effort should be the teacher.

Educators who love God and country far outnumber those who do not. And yet each of us, as a free American, is the custodian of our national heritage, our devotion to

God, and the fundamental beliefs on which our country was founded. Each of us passes this inheritance on to our children, and in this way the inheritance is perpetuated from one generation to the next. This is the one big chain that binds us all together.

But what happens when the chain is broken? What happens when a break occurs between the parent who holds the heritage and the child waiting to receive it? In this event, both parent and child are left dangling at loose ends. The parent's store of knowledge, religion, and tradition perishes with him. The child is deprived of an inheritance which should be his. By weakening the connection, the anti-God forces hope to wipe out tradition and heritage in one or two generations.

It is not enough that we sit back and do nothing. We must act, immediately and positively, to repair the damage and safeguard the God-given heritage which is rightfully ours and our children's.

We often think of the commentary of one American university professor now taking an active part in restoring God to the classroom, who said: "If the German professors had fought Nazism hard enough in the early days, fewer of them would later have died in the concentration camps."

A CHALLENGE TO ALL

Any impairment of truth in the classroom constitutes a challenge for each teacher, parent, student, and all who participate in the blessings of American freedom. These blessings did not come easily. They had to be fought for. To retain them we must be willing to fight just as hard.

Each of us has individual rights and responsibilities in this field. What each one does—or fails to do—can have far-reaching effects on freedom in our country and in the world.

We would be disloyal to God and country if we closed our eyes to the slow steady trend in American education that would eliminate from all grades of teaching everything that would even remind the young of a moral order based on the laws of God. When God is put out, sooner or later the Devil takes over. Disaster becomes inevitable.

The new president of the British Association for the Advancement of Science, Professor A. V. Hill, in his inaugural speech, pointed out to scientific men that it is necessary "to convince ourselves humbly that we are just like others in having moral issues to face." He stressed that trying to improve the lot of man by scientific methods alone, without a moral basis was a perilous illusion. He further emphasized that the Nazis, by abandoning faith in the sanctity of the human individual and of moral law, opened the way to catastrophe.

Dare we trifle with that same disaster that sooner or later has visited all peoples who have rejected their Maker? The issues are momentous. The stakes are big. The enemies of freedom are playing for keeps. The penalties for tolerating mistakes in the training of youth today are disastrous and greater effort than ever must be made to prevent possible catastrophe.

Better to Prevent

Not long ago I saw a large sign hanging over the entrance to an automobile repair shop. It read: "We Specialize in Collisions." In a way it seems to sum up a tendency of our day to wait until disaster strikes and then start repairing the damage. How much more sensible and profitable if we would "specialize" in preventing catastrophes. The old adage still holds true in our day: "An ounce of prevention is worth a pound of cure."

Don't spend valuable time and effort trying to fix the blame for our ills. It is more important to do something about curing them. See in your schools a powerful instrument to work with home and church to restore in men a sense of personal responsibility to God in every phase of public and private life.

You Are Needed

You must decide for yourself what you will do by yourself or through organizations to detect and correct the beginnings of the moral cancer that has already started to blight America. You can play an important role. But more than passing notice must be given if the cure is to be complete and thorough. Cancer of any kind has a way of taking advantage of the slightest neglect and bringing about fatal results.

What are the "warning signals" in American life today that you or anybody else can observe for yourself?

Breakdown of the Home

Anything that undermines the sanctity of the home is promoting the results the Nazis sought. In a free society, the home—the family—has always been the basic social unit. Our form of government depends on the permanence of marriage and the home for its very survival.

Yet today the United States has the highest divorce rate in the world—four hundred thousand each year.

Six million children in our country come from broken homes.

One hundred thousand illegitimate babies are born every year.

One million children suffer personality disorders.

Another four hundred thousand are brought into court each year on charges of juvenile delinquency.

Treason As Never Before

One of the most disturbing developments is the spread of treason and disloyalty in a country that has been so bountiful to the average citizen.

For more than 175 years, Benedict Arnold enjoyed the dubious distinction of being the only famous traitor in American history. Suddenly today his treachery has been duplicated too often in the spheres of influence, and the safety and well-being of the entire American people have been endangered.

It may have been these highly gifted traitors that Justice of the Supreme Court, Robert Jackson, had particularly in mind when he said: "It is one of the paradoxes of our times that modern society needs to fear . . . only the educated man."

THE INCREASE OF DISHONESTY

Cheating in schools and the spread of immorality and dope rings, serious as they are, are probably no more than the first outward signs of worse things to come, unless effective action is taken to give American youth the respect for God's moral law to which they are entitled.

Until this is done, the increasing acceptance of dishonesty as shown in the following remarks of college students will continue to grow. More and more are saying: "If you can cheat and get away with it, that's all right. Cheating is the only thing to do today."

Recounting even a few of our increasing social ills should spur us all to take greater interest in our schools. Each of us should seek every opportunity to strengthen them for the big task that they alone can do.

Dr. Oliver C. Carmichael, president of the Carnegie Foundation for the Advancement of Teaching, said that:

&S . . . the recent revelations of low standards in high places . . . should surely be sufficient to arouse the American people and to shock educational leaders into a reexamination of their goals and methods . . . These are but symptoms of a collapse of moral and spiritual values which should stir to action parents of children, leaders in public affairs, schools, colleges and churches.

One of the surest ways to protect our nation against the terrible fate that has befallen many nations in our day is to single out the one factor—God—that the totalitarians scrupulously screen out of all their schools and give Him due recognition in our entire educational system.

Section Four

The following chapters take the form of an appendix. They contain supplementary material that may prove useful for reference. They illustrate in a practical way that recognition of God and the moral law is part of the very fabric of American life.

fifteen

The Heart of Our Country

No MATTER WHERE PEOPLE MAY LIVE IN THIS great land of ours, they turn their eyes toward Washington in peace and in war. Quite rightly, they expect to find there the top leadership of our nation. For that reason, Washington commands the attention and respect of all Americans.

Relatively few Americans will ever have the great and thrilling opportunity of a personal visit to Washington. And the few who do visit that city may never notice the many tributes to the Almighty to be found there.

The capital of our great nation offers a wealth of information and inspiration that should make every citizen proud of his country. For students in particular, there are countless reminders of the deep and solid roots from which America draws its great strength of spirit. None of these should be overlooked if the coming generation is to possess that complete and well-balanced sense of patriotism that is a requisite for our continuance as a free nation.

In no other place in the United States are there so many, and such varied, official evidences of deep and abiding faith in God on the part of government as there are in Washington. There are lasting tributes both to our national leaders and to the great people that distinguish America for spiritual values above its material might.

In this chapter we point out additional reminders in Washington that reaffirm the proposition that our country is

231

founded on religious principles. We also attempt to show that the continuance of freedom depends on our restoring the same spiritual consciousness to the mainstream of American life today that made possible these monuments and tributes of the past.

First Glimpse of Washington

A visitor entering Washington by train sees the words of Christ from the Gospel of St. John (8:32) prominently inscribed above the main arch leading into Union Station. Here, at the very entrance to the seat of government of the United States, are the words: "The truth shall make you free."

Nearby is another inscription cut into enduring stone, the words from the Eighth Psalm of the Old Testament: "Thou hast put all things under his feet."

A third inscription reiterates the spiritual theme: "Let all the ends thou aimest at be thy country's, thy God's, and truth's."

All three inscriptions acknowledge the dependence of our Republic upon the guiding hand of Almighty God.

On Capitol Hill

Throughout the majestic capital city similar inscriptions testify to the religious faith of our forefathers. Since these evidences are part of our national history, it would help every student to have his attention called to them in the classroom.

In the Capitol, overlooking Washington from its famous "Hill," we find the lawmakers working in the Senate and House of Representatives. Prominently displayed for all to see is the quotation from the Book of Proverbs (4:7): "Wisdom is the principal thing: therefore get wisdom, and with all thy getting, get understanding."

The Library of Congress

The visitor to the Library of Congress will see a quotation
from the Old Testament which reminds each American of
his responsibility to God. It reads: "What doth the Lord require of thee, but to do justly and love mercy and to walk
humbly with God" (Micah 6:8).

Another Scriptural quotation also prominently displayed
in the lawmakers' library preserves the Psalmist's acknowledgment that all nature reflects the order and beauty of the Creator: "The heavens declare the glory of God, and the firma-
ment showeth his handiwork" (Psalms 19:1).

Underneath the statue of History in the Library of Congress are Tennyson's prophetic lines:

> One God, one law, one element   6ems
> And one far-off divine event,
> To which the whole creation moves.

Additional proof that American national life is God-
centered comes from this Library inscription: "The Light
shineth in the darkness and the darkness comprehendeth it
not" (John 1:5).

In the Library's second-floor East Hall an anonymous
inscription assures all Americans that they do not work alone:
"For a web begun God sends thread."

The Original Copy of the Declaration of Independence

One of the most hallowed documents in the Nation's Capitol
is the Declaration of Independence. As we have already seen
in this book, it contains the basic philosophy of our government according to which God is the source of our rights. The
original document is in the National Archives Building where
it is displayed to the public in a newly constructed, bomb-
proof vault.

The Washington Monument

One of the most impressive and beautiful sights in Washington is the Washington Monument rising 555 feet above the ground. When it was being built, citizens and organizations were permitted to donate blocks of stone with signatures of appropriate quotations.

Starting from the top of the Monument, we find three Bible quotations on the twenty-fourth landing. One donated by the Methodist Church of New York reads: "The memory of the just is blessed" (Proverbs 10:7).

The Sunday-school children of the Methodist Church of Philadelphia contributed a stone with the inscription: "Train up a child in a way he should go, and when he is old, he will not depart from it" (Proverbs 22:6).

The third stone carries these words of Christ: "Suffer the little children to come unto me and forbid them not, for of such is the kingdom of heaven" (Luke 18:16).

Twice in the Monument appear the words: "Holiness to the Lord" (Exodus 28:36). One of these inscription stones was given by the Grand Lodge of Freemasons of Pennsylvania. The second is anonymous.

Among many similar expressions throughout the Monument, we find this one from the City of Richmond, Virginia, on the eighteenth landing: "*Tuum nos sumus monumentum*" ("We are Thy monument").

The City of Boston placed a stone slab on the fifteenth landing which reads: "*Sicut patribus sit Deus nobis*" ("As God was to our fathers may He be unto us").

Baltimore's contribution on the twelfth level reads: "May heaven to this union its beneficence . . ."

The Indiana Lodge of Odd Fellows has a sixth-landing gift reading: "In God We Trust."

The United Sons of America provided the inscription: "God and Nature's Land."

THE LINCOLN MEMORIAL

Near the Washington Monument is the Lincoln Memorial, a nation's tribute to its martyred Civil War president. This massive shrine pays homage to the greatness of a simple and heroic man whose very life was offered on the altar of liberty.

The gentleness, power, and determination of Lincoln come to us clearly through the features chiseled in granite by the sculptor. We can almost hear him speak the words that are cut in the wall by his side:

. . . that this nation under God shall have a new birth of freedom, and that government of the people, by the people, for the people, shall not perish from the earth.

In his Second Inaugural Address the great President made liberal use of the words *God, Bible, prayers, Providence, Almighty,* and *Divine Attributes.*

Then the address goes on:

. . . as was said three thousand years ago so it still must be said, "The Judgments of the Lord are true and righteous altogether."

With malice toward none, with charity for all, with firmness in the right as God gives us to see the right let us strive on to finish the work we are in, to bind up the nation's wounds, to care for him who shall have borne the brunt of battle and for his widow and his orphan—to do all which may achieve and cherish a just and lasting peace among ourselves and with all nations.

JEFFERSON MEMORIAL

At the south end of the Tidal Basin stands the classic memorial to Thomas Jefferson. On the frieze encircling the hall are

Jefferson's words: "I have sworn upon the altar of God eternal hostility against every form of tyranny over the mind of man."

On a panel near the statue we find in Jefferson's words a forceful and explicit warning that removing God from this country will destroy it. Here he says:

God who gave us life gave us liberty. Can the liberties of a nation be secure when we have removed a conviction that these liberties are the gift of God? Indeed I tremble for my country when I reflect that God is just, that his justice cannot sleep forever. Commerce between master and slave is despotism. Nothing is more certainly written in the book of fate than that these people are to be free. Establish the law for educating the common people. This it is the business of the State to effect and on a general plan.

Jefferson foresaw that times would change in this country, but he believed in changeless truths which would persist through any age. He held that the dignity of man came from God. His memorial in our nation's capital is a constant reminder that respect for man is based upon his close relationship to God.

Pausing here for a moment, let us reflect that Washington, Jefferson, and Lincoln, the giants of America, had this in common—they all paid repeated and public tribute to this nation's dependence on God.

SUPREME COURT

In the United States Supreme Court, the highest court in the land, we see ample evidence that our courts are conducted according to belief in the Almighty. Thus we find in the Supreme Court tribunal such phrases as "Divine Inspiration," "truth," "safeguard of the rights of the people," "defense of human rights," and "liberty and peace."

At the Pentagon

Just outside of Washington we find the Pentagon, the world's largest office building and the center of the American Armed Services. Flanking the main entrance are two signs which read: "Worship Daily according to Your Faith."

Catholic, Protestant, and Jewish religious services are held at the Pentagon, and members of the three faiths are urged to attend.

The military leaders, too, recognize the necessity for strong spiritual training. General of the Army Omar Bradley said: "This country has many men of science, too few men of God. It has grasped the mystery of the atom, but rejected the Sermon on the Mount."

As a lifetime soldier who has seen countless thousands of young Americans in uniform, he further observed: "This shocking apathy to the conditions of their schools and the sterility of the curriculum is responsible even today for the political immaturity, the economic ignorance, the philosophical indifference, and the spiritual insolvency of so many young men."

Monuments and Statues

In Washington stands the statue of Francis Asbury, a Methodist bishop and pioneer who died in 1816. The statue, erected with the permission of Congress in 1924, carries the inscription: "His continuous journeying through cities, villages and settlements from 1771 to 1816 greatly promoted patriotism, education and religion in the American Republic."

Other monuments to religion include those of James Cardinal Gibbons given by the Knights of Columbus and a statue of Saint Joan of Arc donated to the capital by a French Women's Society.

The nuns who in Civil War days attended the wounded and dying on battlefields are commemorated in a Washington statue with the inscription: "They comforted the dying, nursed the wounded, carried hope to the imprisoned, gave in His name a drink of water to the thirsty."

UNKNOWN SOLDIER

Before leaving Washington, let us make our final stop at the National Cemetery in Arlington, Virginia. Here are peaceful ranks of Crosses and Stars of David, reminding us that our government has given its fallen men back to the God Who gave them life.

The Tomb of the Unknown Soldier stands for all those fallen in battle who could not be idenitfied; members of all sects, faiths and religions.

And here once more we find the acknowledgment of God's divine power in the eloquent words:

"Here lies in honored glory, an American soldier, known but to God."

BASIC AMERICAN CONCEPTS

Since our greatest leaders have shown no doubt about God's proper place in the American birthright, would we dare to do less?

As we go through Washington, we cannot help reflecting on the tendency in American education during the last few decades to lose sight of God. Have we not, as individuals, been too complacent and blind to the fact that complete education requires teaching of our religious background as the very essence of true Americanism? Can we in conscience allow our schools to drift away from the basic concepts that gave vigor and purpose to life in this country?

One way to help correct this defect is to spread far and wide a knowledge of the many testimonials to faith found in the very center of our nation. Each and all of them reveal what has been and still is in the hearts of our people.

sixteen

The Pattern Set by the Armed Services

IN DISCUSSING SOME PROBLEMS OF EDUCATION, IT might be interesting to note the direct and specific pattern set by the United States government for the moral training of servicemen.

The departments of the Army and the Air Force, in August, 1951, published a forthright booklet entitled, *Duty-Honor-Country*.* The pamphlet provides an outline for instructors whereby they may instill into the men a sense of individual moral responsibility.

We read in the foreword:

To achieve this purpose, the character development programs stress, by every available means, the moral principles that sustain the philosophy of American freedom, particularly as it is set forth in the opening paragraph of the Declaration of Independence. That philosophy regards man as a creature of God. As such, each individual in the armed services is accountable and responsible to his Creator for the way he performs his civic and his military duty, for the maintenance of his own and the Nation's honor, and for the quality of the service he renders to his country as a member of the honorable profession of arms.

*You can secure a copy of this 98-page booklet by sending 35 cents to the U. S. Government Printing Office, Washington, D.C., and referring to it as the Department of the Army Pamphlet No. 16–5, titled *Duty-Honor-Country*. Three additional booklets in this series, under the same title *Duty-Honor-Country*, and listed No. 16–6, No. 16–7, No. 16–8, are also obtainable at 35 cents each. All were published by order of the Secretaries of the Army and the Air Force by the authority of General J. Lawton Collins, Chief of Staff, U. S. Army, and General Hoyt S. Vandenberg, Chief of Staff, U. S. Air Force.

240

In order that you may have some of the information first-hand we quote at length from this official booklet.

If you are a parent you will readily recognize that it includes the very principles that you cherish in the home, that you would like to have in the schools, and that you are glad to know are in the Armed Forces.

If you are a teacher it will provide a ready-made formula that you can bring right into the classroom. *It is something that is officially approved by your government.*

If you are a student it is well for you to be familiar with the sound instruction provided for young people in the Armed Forces. You have a right to the same moral guidance in your school. If it is not at present supplied, there are many legitimate steps you can personally and individually take to see that you and your fellow students have the advantage of the same or similar instruction as part of your birthright as an American.

SOMETHING MISSING

The Armed Forces presume that when a young man or woman enters any branch of the Service the groundwork for further character training has already been rooted by the training of the home and school. They, unlike business, the professions, or other spheres of activity, are in a position to continue this character training. Yet reports from many in the Armed Services reveal that the moral preparation given in our schools today is so inadequate that it is presenting an enormous problem for those in charge of training our servicemen.

One Air Force captain at a training base in Texas said that he found most recruits deficient in basic moral principles. After reading Christopher literature on the importance of increasing the number of teachers of high character and competence, he decided he would try to supply what was lacking by becoming a college teacher as soon as he completed his time in the service.

It Couldn't Be Clearer

The foreword to this booklet leaves no shadow of doubt that moral training is not only prescribed teaching, but that it is the business and personal responsibility of all officers to see that it is not isolated or sidetracked. It is to be presented as a continuing and vital force in the mainstream of military training:

1. Formal instruction in morality is a staff responsibility of the chaplain. Nevertheless, morality cannot be taught successfully by the chaplain alone.

2. Formal disapproval is given to the teaching of any theory which is contrary to the American doctrine that "regards man as a creature of God." Neither can morality be taught successfully . . . in an atmosphere of contradiction by other instructors.

3. Sound morality must underlie all military instruction, formal and informal.

4. The moral implications of all instruction must be clear, first of all, to the instructor.

You would have to read this booklet for yourself to appreciate fully the many valuable points it presents. A few paragraphs quoted here will give you some idea of its content and force of spirit.

Morality Depends on Principles

On page 3 we find under the heading, "Morality is a Prerequisite of Duty," this emphatic statement:

No one can and will develop a sense of duty unless he has a high regard for moral principles, for morality is the cement which holds man together in units and groups. Moral principles are those rules in life which help us to respect the other man and to work together with others in the performance of our daily tasks.

We read a striking paragraph on page 5 concerning the important part conscience plays:

Because of this close relationship between morality and sense of duty the poet Wordsworth once called duty the "stern daughter of the voice of God." The "voice of God" in each of us is conscience. You and I have a way of knowing what is right and what is wrong. Our conscience is quick to make us feel very uncomfortable when we walk out on a job, for example, for when we let other people down. Conscience prefers to have us do our duty. A sense of duty consists of letting our conscience be our guide.

On page 13 servicemen are reminded that "honor always has moral overtones."

Used in this way "honor" has to do with the practice of virtue, but is distinguished from "virtue" in its general sense by applying to specific virtues pertaining to certain professions. Military honor has to do with courage and faithfulness, while business honor, let us say, is a term used to connote primarily honesty and trustworthiness. But in either case—in all instances, as a matter of fact—the word "honor" carries overtones of moral obligation.

WE ALL NEED GUIDANCE

On page 19 there is specific recommendation under the heading, "Follow God's Moral Law":

Then how shall we know what is right? This is where the Moral Law steps in to guide us. In it are set forth the principles by which we can live with the assurance that what we do will be right, just, and true. For if we love God above all things and our neighbor as ourselves there can be no doubt about the quality of our behavior.

Honor requires of us that we develop a fine sense of our individual moral obligations. That can come only from a constant practice of high principle in the performance of our duty.

On page 29 it states, "America's Dependence Upon God Is Expressed in Thanksgiving Day Proclamations":

It is not difficult to demonstrate that America officially recognizes its dependence on God. Every Thanksgiving Day, for example, the President of the United States calls upon the citizens of this country to repair to their respective houses of worship in order to give thanks to Almighty God for the blessings of the year just passed and to implore Him for His protection and benediction in the year to come.

OUR ROOTS ARE SPIRITUAL

On page 31 there is a potent paragraph, "The Role Religion and Morality Have Played in Shaping Our National Life":

This was in keeping with the spirit expressed in the words of the Northwest Ordinance, another of our freedom documents: "Religion, morality, and knowledge being necessary to good government and the happiness of mankind, schools and the means of education shall forever be encouraged." This is an official statement of the spirit which motivated many of the early settlers. Those people took along their religion; they built churches wherever they went. This accounts for the fact that in our history there has lived through all these years a kind of idealism which is derived from religious truths. This has done much to keep us a covenant nation. After all, what is said publicly and officially by our elected representative is guided by what people are thinking and doing in local communities.

On page 46 before presenting the three versions of the Ten Commandments it is stated explicitly, "The Best Known Rules for Living Are the Ten Commandments":

They read quite simply; but, if you apply yourself to them seriously you will discover that, although there are just 10 of them, they cover most of the serious problems of life. Beginning with

THE PATTERN SET BY THE ARMED SERVICES 245

the attitude we should be showing toward God, they go on to describe the relationship we ought to have with other people.

Keeping First Things First

On page 55 we read under the heading, "The Highest Knowledge is to Know God":

> What, do you suppose, is the highest and best thing in life to know? To know the multiplication table helps us in our daily problems. To know a second language helps us when we get to a country where that language is spoken. Knowing how a car works helps us to get on our way when it breaks down . . . But is that the greatest good one can know? We dare say that there is something better to know than all this. The finest use for this part of the soul is to know God, our Creator.

On page 59 we are told, "The Bible Helped to Start Our Country Off in the Right Way":

> Do you know how large a part this Book played in getting our country off to a right start? Here are some words from Daniel Webster's Bunker Hill address:
> "The Bible came with them (the colonists). And it is not to be doubted that to the free and universal reading of the Bible in that age men were much indebted for their own views of civil liberty. The Bible is a book of faith, and a book of doctrine, and a book of morals, and a book of religion of especial revelation from God; but it is also a book which teaches man his own individual responsibility, his own dignity, and his equality with his fellow man."

On a Solid Foundation

The sound, sensible position taken by the Army is well summed up on page 83 under the heading, "Moral Principles Are Decided by God's Rules," and which reads as follows:

Of all the moral perversions one hears there is none to match the remark, "It's not wrong as long as I don't get caught." That slogan is fashioned on the center anvil of the devil's hottest workshop. He has put a great deal of planning and cunning into the device of getting people to believe and repeat such a vicious lie.

Is it right to kill someone as long as I can get away with it? Hitler said it was right; and Europe still suffers in agony. Is it right to steal if I can get by? The Communists say so; and the world is frightened at the shadow this philosophy has cast over the lives of all of us. Getting by or getting caught has nothing to do with the rightness or wrongness of an action. Moral issues are not decided by the policeman's knock at the door. They run much deeper.

seventeen

Each President Paid Tribute to God

ALL OF OUR PRESIDENTS FROM GEORGE WASHING-
ton up to and including Dwight D. Eisenhower, although
differing in many of their ideas and policies, were consistent
in recognizing the dependence of this nation on Almighty
God.

This is revealed in a study of the Inaugural Address of
each President. Each and every one has declared his belief in
the existence of God, that we have duties and obligations
toward Him, and that this nation owes Him a debt of gratitude for the many blessings He has showered upon it.

It is possible in this limited space to present only excerpts
from the Inaugural Addresses. Those wishing to get the full
setting would do well to consult the original speeches.

PRESIDENT GEORGE WASHINGTON
(1789–1797)

. . . it would be peculiarly improper to omit in this first official act my fervent supplications to that Almighty Being Who
rules over the universe, Who presides in the councils of nations, and Whose providential aids can supply every human
defect, that His benediction may consecrate to the liberties
and happiness of the people of the United States a Government instituted by themselves for these essential purposes, and
may enable every instrument employed in its administration
to execute with success the functions allotted to his charge.

247

In tendering this homage to the Great Author of every public and private good, I assure myself that it expressed your sentiments not less than my own, nor those of my fellow-citizens at large less than either.

. . . I shall take my present leave; but not without resorting once more to the benign Parent of the Human Race in humble supplication that, since He had been pleased to favor the American people with opportunities for deliberating in perfect tranquility, and dispositions for deciding with unparalleled unanimity on a form of government for the security of their union and the advancement of their happiness, so His divine blessing may be equally conspicuous in the enlarged views, the temperate consultations, and the wise measure on which the success of this Government must depend.

PRESIDENT JOHN ADAMS
(1797–1801)

Relying, however, on the purity of their intentions, the justice of their cause, and the integrity and intelligence of the people, under an overruling Providence which had so signally protected this country from the first, the representatives of this nation, then consisting of little more than half its present number, not only broke to pieces the chains which were forging the rod of iron that was lifted up, but frankly cut asunder the ties which had bound them, and launched into an ocean of uncertainty.

And may that Being who is supreme over all, the Patron of Order, the Fountain of Justice, and the Protector in all ages of the world of virtuous liberty, continue His blessing upon this nation and its Government and give it all possible success and duration consistent with the ends of His providence.

PRESIDENT THOMAS JEFFERSON
(1801–1809)

. . . enlightened by a benign religion, professed, indeed, and practiced in various forms, yet all of them inculcating Honesty, truth, temperance, and gratitude and the love of man; acknowledging and adoring an overruling Providence, which by all its dispensations proves that it delights in the happiness of man here and his greater happiness here-after . . .

And may that Infinite Power which rules the destinies of the universe lead our councils to what is best, and give them favorable issue for your peace and prosperity.

PRESIDENT JAMES MADISON
(1809–1817)

. . . to avoid the slightest interference with the rights of conscience or the functions of religion, so wisely exempted from civil jurisdiction . . .

In these my confidence will under every difficulty be best placed, next to that which we have all been encouraged to feel in the guardianship and guidance of that Almighty Being Whose power regulates the destiny of nations, Whose blessings have been so conspicuously dispensed to this rising Republic, and to Whom we are bound to address our devout gratitude for the past, as well as our fervent supplications and best hopes for the future.

PRESIDENT JAMES MONROE
(1817–1825)

If we persevere in the career in which we have advanced so far and in the path already traced, we cannot fail, under the favor of a gracious Providence, to attain the high destiny which seems to await us.

Relying on the aid to be derived from the other departments of the Government, I enter on the trust to which I have been called by the suffrages of my fellow-citizens with my fervent prayers to the Almighty that He will be graciously pleased to continue to grant us that protection which He has already so conspicuously displayed in our favor.

With full confidence in the continuance of that candor and generous indulgence from my fellow-citizens at large which I have heretofore experienced, and with a fine reliance on the protection of Almighty God, I shall forthwith commence the duties of the high trust to which you have called me.

PRESIDENT JOHN QUINCY ADAMS
(1825–1829)

. . . in the career upon which I am about to enter, I appear, my fellow-citizens, in your presence and in that of Heaven to bind myself by the solemnities of religious obligation to the faithful performance of the duties allotted to me in the station to which I have been called.

I shall look for whatever success may attend my public service; and knowing that "except the Lord keep the city the watchman waketh but in vain," with fervent supplications for His favor, to His overruling providence I commit with humble but fearless confidence my own fate and the future destinies of my country.

PRESIDENT ANDREW JACKSON
(1829–1837)

And a firm reliance on the goodness of that Power whose providence mercifully protected our national infancy, and has since upheld our liberties in various vicissitudes, encourages me to offer up my ardent supplications that He will continue to make our beloved country the object of His divine care and gracious benediction.

Finally, it is my most fervent prayer to that Almighty Being before whom I now stand, and who has kept us in His hands from the infancy of our Republic to the present day, that He will so overrule all my intentions and actions and inspire the hearts of my fellow-citizens that we may be preserved from dangers of all kinds and continue forever a united and happy people.

PRESIDENT MARTIN VAN BUREN
(1837–1841)

. . . I should not dare to enter upon my path of duty did I not look for the generous aid of those who will be associated with me in the various and coordinate branches of the Government; did I not repose with unwavering reliance on the patriotism, the intelligence, and the kindness of a people who never yet deserted a public servant honestly laboring in their cause, and, above all, did I not permit myself humbly to hope for the sustaining support of an ever-watchful and beneficent Providence.

Beyond that I only look to the gracious protection of the Divine Being whose strengthening support I humbly solicit, and whom I fervently pray to look down upon us all. May it be among the dispensations of His providence to bless our beloved country with honors and with length of days.

PRESIDENT WILLIAM HENRY HARRISON
(1841)

We admit of no government by divine right, believing that so far as power is concerned the Beneficent Creator has made no distinction amongst men, that all are upon an equality, and that the only legitimate right to govern is an express grant of power from the governed.

He (the American citizen) claims them because he is himself a man, fashioned by the same Almighty hand as the rest of his species and entitled to a full share of the blessings with which He has endowed them.

I can conceive of no more sublime spectacle, none more likely to propitiate an impartial and common Creator, than a rigid adherence to the principles of justice on the part of a powerful nation in its transactions with a weaker and uncivilized people whom circumstances have placed at its disposal.

PRESIDENT JOHN TYLER
(1841–1845)

My earnest prayer shall be constantly addressed to the all-wise and all-powerful Being who made me, and by whose dispensation I am called to the high office of President of this Confederacy, understandingly to carry out the principles of that Constitution which I have sworn "to protect, preserve, and defend."

In conclusion I beg you to be assured that I shall exert myself to carry the foregoing principles into practice during my administration of the Government, and, confiding in the protecting care of an ever watchful and overruling Providence, it shall be my first and highest duty to preserve unimpaired the free institutions under which we live and transmit them to those who shall succeed me in their full force and vigor.

PRESIDENT JAMES K. POLK
(1845–1849)

In assuming responsibilities so vast I fervently invoke the aid of that Almighty Ruler of the Universe in whose hands are the destinies of nations and of men to guard this Heaven-favored land against the mischiefs which without His guidance might arise from an unwise public policy.

With a firm reliance upon the wisdom of Omnipotence to sustain and direct me in the path of duty which I am appointed to pursue, I stand in the presence of this assembled multitude of my country-men to take upon myself the solemn obligation . . .

. . . I enter upon the discharge of the high duties which have been assigned me by the people, again humbly supplicating that Divine Being who has watched over and protected our beloved country from its infancy to the present hour to continue His gracious benedictions upon us, that we may continue to be a prosperous and happy people.

PRESIDENT ZACHARY TAYLOR
(1849–1850)

In all disputes between conflicting governments . . . the dictates of religion direct us to the cultivation of peaceful and friendly relations with all other powers.

. . . the goodness of Divine Providence has conducted our common country. Let us invoke a continuance of the same protecting care . . . and let us seek to deserve that continuance . . .

PRESIDENT MILLARD FILLMORE
(1850–1853)
(No inaugural—completed predecessor's term)

On the occasion of the death of President Taylor, President Fillmore said in transmitting a message to Congress: "I have to perform the melancholy duty of announcing to you that it has pleased Almighty God to remove from this life Zachary Taylor, late President of the United States. . . ."

PRESIDENT FRANKLIN PIERCE
(1853–1857)

. . . Standing, as I do, almost within view of the green slopes of Monticello, and, as it were, within reach of the tomb of Washington, with all the cherished memories of the past gathering around me like so many eloquent voices of exhortation from heaven, I can express no better hope for my country than that the kind Providence which smiled upon our fathers may enable their children to preserve the blessings they have inherited.

PRESIDENT JAMES BUCHANAN
(1857–1861)

In entering upon this great office I must humbly invoke the God of our fathers for wisdom and firmness to execute its high and responsible duties in such a manner as to restore harmony and ancient friendship among the people of the several States and to preserve our free institutions throughout many generations.

These I shall not attempt to portray, because I feel an humble confidence that the kind Providence which inspired our fathers with wisdom to frame the most perfect form of government and union ever devised by man will not suffer it to perish until it shall have been peacefully instrumental by its example in the extension of civil and religious liberty throughout the world.

PRESIDENT ABRAHAM LINCOLN
(1861–1865)

If the Almighty Ruler of Nations, with his eternal truth and justice, be on your side of the North, or on yours of the South, that truth and that justice will surely prevail by the judgement of this great tribunal of the American people.

Intelligence, patriotism, Christianity, and a firm reliance on Him who has never yet forsaken this favored land are still competent to adjust in the best way all our present difficulty.

With malice toward none, with charity for all, with firmness in the right as God gives us to see the light, let us strive on to finish the work we are in, to bind up the nation's wounds, to care for him who shall have borne the battle and for his widow and his orphan, to do all which may achieve and cherish a just and lasting peace among ourselves and with all nations.

PRESIDENT ANDREW JOHNSON
(1865–1869)

Toil and an honest advocacy of the great principles of free government have been my lot. Duties have been mine; consequences are God's. This has been the foundation of my political creed . . .

My past public life, which has been long and laborious, has been founded, upon a great principle of right, which lies at the basis of all things.

PRESIDENT ULYSSES S. GRANT
(1869–1877)

This [attaining the greatest good for the greatest number in the State] requires security of person, property, and for religious and political opinions, in every part of our common country, without regard to local prejudice.

. . . I ask the prayers of the nation to Almighty God in behalf of this consummation.

PRESIDENT RUTHERFORD B. HAYES
(1877–1881)

Looking for guidance of that Divine Hand by which the destinies of nations and individuals are shaped, I call upon you, Senators, Representatives, judges, fellow-citizens, here and everywhere, to unite with me in an earnest effort to secure to our country the blessings, not only of material prosperity, but of justice, peace, and union—a union depending not upon the constraint of force, but upon the loving devotion of a free people; and that all things may be so ordered and settled upon the best and surest foundations that peace and happiness, truth and justice, religion and piety, may be established among us for all generations.

PRESIDENT JAMES GARFIELD
(1881)

With unquestioning devotion to the Union, with a patience and gentleness not born of fear, they have followed the light as God gave them to see the light!

I shall greatly rely upon the wisdom and patriotism of Congress and of those who may share with me the responsibilities and duties of administration, and, above all, upon our efforts to promote the welfare of this great people and their Government I reverently invoke the support and blessings of Almighty God.

PRESIDENT CHESTER A. ARTHUR
(1881–1885)
(No inaugural—completed predecessor's term)

On the occasion of General Sherman's retirement, Arthur said on February 9, 1884: "The President deems this a fitting occasion to give expression in this manner to the gratitude felt toward General Sherman by his fellow-citizens, and to the hope that Providence may grant him many years of health and happiness in the relief from the active duties of his profession."

PRESIDENT GROVER CLEVELAND
(1885–1889, 1893–1897)

And let us not trust to human effort alone, but humbly acknowledging the power and goodness of Almighty God, who presides over the destiny of nations, and who has at all times been revealed in our country's history, let us invoke His aid and His blessing upon our laborers.

. . . I am sure my gratitude can make no better return than the pledge I now give before God and these witnesses of unreserved and complete devotion to the interests and welfare of those who have honored me.

Above all, I know there is a Supreme Being who rules the affairs of men and whose goodness and mercy have always followed the American people, and I know He will not turn from us now if we humbly and reverently seek His powerful aid.

PRESIDENT BENJAMIN HARRISON
(1889–1893)

Entering thus solemnly into covenant with each other, we may reverently invoke and confidently expect the favor and help of Almighty God—that He will give to me wisdom, strength, and fidelity, and to our people a spirit of fraternity and a love of righteousness and peace.

PRESIDENT WILLIAM McKINLEY
(1897–1901)

In obedience to the will of the people, and in their presence, by the authority vested in me by this oath, I assume the arduous and responsible duties of President of the United States, relying upon the support of my countrymen and invoking the guidance of Almighty God.

Our faith teaches that there is no safer reliance than upon the God of our fathers, who has so singularly favored the American people in every national trial, and who will not forsake us so long as we obey His commandments and walk humbly in His footsteps.

PRESIDENT THEODORE ROOSEVELT
(1901–1909)

My fellow citizens, no people on earth have more cause to be thankful than ours, and this is said reverently, in no spirit of boastfulness in our own strength, but with gratitude to the Giver of Good who has blessed us with the conditions which have enabled us to achieve so large a measure of well-being and of happiness.

PRESIDENT WILLIAM HOWARD TAFT
(1909–1913)

Having thus reviewed the questions likely to recur during my administration, and having expressed in a summary way the position which I expect to take in recommendations to Congress and in my conduct as an Executive, I invoke the considerate sympathy and support of my fellow-citizens and the aid of the Almighty God in the discharge of my responsible duties.

PRESIDENT WOODROW WILSON
(1913–1921)

The feelings with which we face this new age of right and opportunity sweep across our heartstrings like some air out of God's own presence, where justice and mercy are reconciled and the judge and the brother are one.

God helping me, I will not fail them, if they will but counsel and sustain me!

In their ardent heat we shall, in God's Providence, let us hope, be purged of faction and division, purified of the errant humors of party and of private interest, and stand forth in the days to come with a new dignity of national pride and spirit.

I pray God I may be given the wisdom and the prudence to do my duty in the true spirit of this great people.

PRESIDENT WARREN G. HARDING
(1921–1923)

But with the realization comes a surge of high resolve, and there is reassurance in belief in the God-given destiny of our Republic.

But here are a hundred million with common concern and shared responsibility answerable to God and country.

PRESIDENT CALVIN COOLIDGE
(1923–1929)

Peace will come when there is realization that only under a reign of law, based on righteousness and supported by the religious conviction of the brotherhood of man, can there be any hope of a complete and satisfying life. Parchment will fail, the sword will fail, it is only the spiritual nature of man that can be triumphant.

America seeks no earthly empire built on blood and force. No ambition, no temptation, lures her to thought of foreign dominions. The legions which she sends forth are armed, not with the sword, but with the cross. The higher state to which she seeks the allegiance of all mankind is not of human, but of divine origin. She cherishes no purpose save to merit the favor of Almighty God.

PRESIDENT HERBERT HOOVER
(1929–1933)

This occasion is not alone the administration of the most sacred oath which can be assumed by an American citizen. It is a dedication and consecration under God to the highest office in the service of our people. I assume this trust in the humility of knowledge that only through the guidance of Almighty Providence can I hope to discharge its ever-increasing burdens.

I ask the help of Almighty God in this service to my country to which you have called me.

PRESIDENT FRANKLIN DELANO ROOSEVELT
(1933–1945)

In this dedication of a Nation we humbly ask the blessing of God. May He protect each and every one of us. May He guide me in the days to come.

Almighty God has blessed our land in many ways. He has given our people stout hearts and strong arms with which to strike mighty blows for freedom and truth. He has given to our country a faith which has become the hope of all peoples in an anguished world.

PRESIDENT HARRY S. TRUMAN
(1945–1953)

We believe that all men have a right to equal justice under law and equal opportunity to share in the common good. We believe that all men have the right to freedom of thought and expression. We believe that all men are created equal because they are created in the image of God.

People everywhere are coming to realize that what is involved is material well-being, human dignity, and the rights to believe in and worship God . . .
With God's help, the future of mankind will be assured in a world of justice, harmony and peace.

PRESIDENT DWIGHT D. EISENHOWER
(1953–)

We are summoned by this honored and historic ceremony to witness more than the act of one citizen swearing his oath of service, in the presence of God.

In our quest of understanding, we beseech God's guidance.

This is the work that awaits us all, to be done with bravery, with charity, and with prayer to Almighty God.

eighteen

Forty-seven State Constitutions Recognize God

WE PRESENT HERE EXCERPTS FROM THE PREAMbles to the forty-seven State Constitutions (the Bill of Rights in the case of Oregon) which acknowledge our dependence upon God. You will see that on the whole our State Constitutions are miniature Declarations of Independence. Some of them use the very words of the Declaration itself. And practically all call attention to the fact that our rights and liberties stem from God.

ALABAMA
(Adopted in 1901)

We, the people of the State of Alabama, in order to establish justice, insure domestic tranquillity and secure the blessings of liberty to ourselves and our posterity, invoking the favor and guidance of Almighty God, do ordain and establish the following Constitution and form of government for the State of Alabama.

ARIZONA
(Adopted in 1912)

We, the people of the State of Arizona, grateful to Almighty God for our liberties, do ordain this Constitution.

263

ARKANSAS
(Adopted in 1874)

We, the people of the State of Arkansas, grateful to Almighty God for the privilege of choosing our own form of government, for our civil and religious liberty, and desiring to perpetuate its blessings and secure the same to ourselves and posterity, do ordain and establish this Constitution.

CALIFORNIA
(Adopted in 1879)

We, the people of the State of California, grateful to Almighty God for our freedom, in order to secure and perpetuate its blessings, do establish this Constitution.

COLORADO
(Adopted in 1876)

We, the people of Colorado, with profound reverence for the Supreme Ruler of the Universe, in order to form a more independent and perfect government; establish justice; insure tranquillity; provide for the common defense; promote the general welfare and secure the blessings of liberty to ourselves and our posterity; do ordain and establish this Constitution for the "State of Colorado."

CONNECTICUT
(Adopted in 1818)

The people of Connecticut acknowledging with gratitude, the good providence of God, in having permitted them to enjoy a free government, do, in order more effectually to define, secure, and perpetuate the liberties, rights and privileges which they have derived from their ancestors, hereby, after a careful consideration and revision, ordain and establish the following Constitution and form of civil government.

DELAWARE
(Adopted in 1897)

Through Divine goodness, all men have by nature the rights of worshiping and serving their Creator according to the dictates of their consciences, of enjoying and defending life and liberty, of acquiring and protecting reputation and property, and in general of obtaining objects suitable to their condition, without injury by one to another; and as these rights are essential to their welfare, for the due exercise thereof, power is inherent in them; and therefore all just authority in the institutions of political society is derived from the people, and established with their consent, to advance their happiness; and they may for this end, as circumstances require, from time to time alter their Constitution of government.

FLORIDA
(Adopted in 1887)

We, the people of the State of Florida, grateful to Almighty God for our constitutional liberty, in order to secure its blessings and to form a more perfect government, insuring domestic tranquillity, maintaining public order, and guaranteeing equal civil and political rights to all, do ordain and establish this Constitution.

GEORGIA
(Adopted in 1887)

To perpetuate the principles of free government, insure justice to all, preserve peace, promote the interest and happiness of the citizen, and transmit to posterity the enjoyment of liberty, we, the people of Georgia, relying upon the protection and guidance of Almighty God, do ordain and establish this Constitution.

IDAHO
(Adopted in 1890)

We, the people of the State of Idaho, grateful to Almighty God, for our freedom, to secure its blessings and promote our common welfare, do establish this Constitution.

ILLINOIS
(Adopted in 1870)

We, the people of the State of Illinois—grateful to Almighty God for the civil, political and religious liberty which He hath so long permitted us to enjoy, and looking to Him for a blessing upon our endeavors to secure and transmit the same unimpaired to succeeding generations—in order to form a more perfect government, establish justice, insure domestic tranquillity, provide for the common defense, promote the general welfare, and secure the blessing of liberty to ourselves and our posterity, do ordain and establish this Constitution for the State of Illinois.

INDIANA
(Adopted in 1851)

To the end that justice be established, public order maintained, and liberty perpetuated: We, the people of the State of Indiana, grateful to Almighty God for the free exercise of the right to choose our own form of government, do ordain this Constitution.

IOWA
(Adopted in 1857)

We, the people of the State of Iowa, grateful to the Supreme Being for the blessings hitherto enjoyed, and feeling our dependence on Him for a continuation of those blessings, do ordain and establish a free and independent government, by the name of the State of Iowa, the boundaries whereof shall be as follows. . . .

KANSAS
(Adopted in 1863)

We, the people of Kansas, grateful to Almighty God for our civil and religious privileges, in order to insure the full enjoyment of our rights as American citizens, do ordain and establish this Constitution of the State of Kansas, with the following boundaries. . . .

KENTUCKY
(Adopted in 1891)

We, the people of the Commonwealth of Kentucky, grateful to Almighty God for the civil, political and religious liberties we enjoy, and invoking the continuance of these blessings, do ordain and establish this Constitution.

LOUISIANA
(Adopted in 1921)

We, the people of the State of Louisiana, grateful to Almighty God for the civil, political and religious liberties we enjoy and desiring to secure the continuance of these blessings, do ordain and establish this Constitution.

MAINE
(Adopted in 1820 and 1876)

We, the people of Maine, in order to establish justice, insure tranquillity, provide for our mutual defense, promote our common welfare, and secure to ourselves and our posterity the blessings of liberty, acknowledging with grateful hearts the goodness of the Sovereign Ruler of the Universe in affording us an opportunity, so favorable to the design; and, imploring His aid and direction in its accomplishment, do agree to form ourselves into a free and independent State, by the style and title of the State of Maine, and do ordain and establish the following Constitution for the government of the same.

MARYLAND
(Adopted in 1867)

We, the people of the State of Maryland, grateful to Almighty God for our civil and religious liberty, and taking into our serious consideration for best means of establishing a good Constitution in this State for the sure foundation and more permanent security thereof, declare. . . .

MASSACHUSETTS
(Adopted in 1790)

We, therefore, the people of Massachusetts, acknowledging, with grateful hearts, the goodness of the great Legislator of the universe, in affording us, in the course of His providence, an opportunity, deliberately and peaceably, without fraud, violence, or surprise, of entering into an original, explicit, and solemn compact with each other; and for forming a new Constitution of civil government, for ourselves and posterity; and devoutly imploring His direction in so interesting a design, do agree upon, ordain, and establish the following Declaration of Rights, and Frame of Government, as the Constitution of the Commonwealth of Massachusetts.

MICHIGAN
(Adopted in 1909)

We, the people of the State of Michigan, grateful to Almighty God for the blessings of freedom, and earnestly desiring to secure these blessings undiminished to ourselves and our posterity, do ordain and establish the Constitution.

MINNESOTA
(Adopted in 1857)

We, the people of the State of Minnesota, grateful to God for our civil and religious liberty and desiring to perpetuate its blessings and secure the same to ourselves and our posterity, do ordain and establish this Constitution.

MISSISSIPPI
(Adopted in 1890)

We, the people of Mississippi in convention assembled, grateful to Almighty God, and invoking His blessing on our work, do ordain and establish this Constitution.

MISSOURI
(Adopted in 1945)

We, the people of Missouri, with profound reverence for the Supreme Ruler of the Universe, and grateful for His goodness, do establish this Constitution for the better government of the State.

MONTANA
(Adopted in 1889)

We, the people of Montana, grateful to Almighty God for the blessings of liberty, in order to secure the advantages of a State government, do in accordance with the provisions of the enabling act of Congress, approve the twenty-second of February A.D. 1889, ordain and establish this Constitution.

NEBRASKA
(Adopted in 1875)

We, the people, grateful to Almighty God for our freedom, do ordain and establish the following declaration of rights and frame of government, as the Constitution of the State of Nebraska.

NEVADA
(Adopted in 1864)

We, the people of the State of Nevada, grateful to Almighty God for our freedom, in order to secure its blessings, insure domestic tranquillity, and form a more perfect government, do establish this Constitution.

NEW HAMPSHIRE
(Adopted in 1784)

Every individual has a natural and unalienable right to worship God according to the dictates of his own conscience, and reason . . . morality and piety, rightly grounded on evangelical principles, will give the best and greatest security to government, and will lay, in the hearts of men, the strongest obligations to due subjection; and the knowledge of these is most likely to be propagated through society by the institution of the public worship of the Deity.

NEW JERSEY
(Adopted in 1844)

We, the people of the State of New Jersey, grateful to Almighty God for the civil and religious liberty which He has so long permitted us to enjoy, and looking to Him for a blessing upon our endeavors to secure and transmit the same unimpaired to succeeding generations, do ordain and establish this Constitution.

NEW MEXICO
(Adopted in 1912)

We, the people of New Mexico, grateful to Almighty God for the blessings of liberty, in order to secure the advantages of a State government, do ordain and establish this Constitution.

NEW YORK
(Adopted in 1895)

We, the people of the State of New York, grateful to Almighty God for our freedom, in order to secure its blessings, do establish this Constitution.

NORTH CAROLINA
(Adopted in 1876)

We, the people of the State of North Carolina, grateful to Almighty God, and the Sovereign Ruler of Nations, for the preservation of the American Union and the existence of our civil, political and religious liberties, and acknowledging our dependence upon Him for the continuance of these blessings, to us and our posterity, do, for the more certain security thereof and for the better government of this State, ordain and establish this Constitution.

NORTH DAKOTA
(Adopted in 1889)

We, the people of North Dakota, grateful to Almighty God for the blessings of civil and religious liberty, do ordain and establish this Constitution.

OHIO
(Adopted in 1851)

We, the people of the State of Ohio, grateful to Almighty God for our freedom, to secure its blessings and promote our common welfare, do establish this Constitution.

OKLAHOMA
(Adopted in 1907)

Invoking the guidance of Almighty God in order to secure and perpetuate the blessings of liberty; to secure just and rightful government; to promote our mutual welfare and happiness, we the people of the State of Oklahoma, do ordain and establish this Constitution.

OREGON
(Adopted in 1859)

All men shall be secured in the natural right to worship Almighty God according to the dictates of their own consciences.

PENNSYLVANIA
(Adopted in 1874)

We, the people of the Commonwealth of Pennsylvania, grateful to Almighty God for the blessings of civil and religious liberty, and humbly invoking His guidance, do ordain and establish this Constitution.

RHODE ISLAND
(Adopted in 1843)

We, the people of the State of Rhode Island and Providence Plantations, grateful to Almighty God for the civil and religious liberty which He hath so long permitted us to enjoy, and looking to Him for a blessing upon our endeavors to secure and to transmit the same unimpaired to succeeding generations do ordain and establish this Constitution of Government.

SOUTH CAROLINA
(Adopted in 1895)

We, the people of the State of South Carolina, in convention assembled, grateful to God for our liberties, do ordain and establish this Constitution for the preservation and perpetuation of the same.

SOUTH DAKOTA
(Adopted in 1889)

We, the people of South Dakota, grateful to Almighty God for our civil and religious liberties, in order to form a more perfect and independent government, establish justice, insure tranquillity, provide for the common defense, promote the

general welfare and preserve to ourselves and to our posterity
the blessings of liberty, do ordain and establish this Constitution for the State of South Dakota.

TENNESSEE
(Adopted in 1870)

That all men have a natural and indefeasible right to worship
Almighty God according to the dictates of their conscience;
that no man can of right, be compelled to attend, erect or
support any place of worship, or to maintain any minister
against his consent; that no human authority can, in any case
whatever, control or interfere with the rights of conscience;
and that no preference shall ever be given, by law, to any religious establishment or mode of worship.

TEXAS
(Adopted in 1876)

Humbly invoking the blessings of Almighty God, the people
of the State of Texas, do ordain and establish this Constitution.

UTAH
· (Adopted in 1895)

Grateful to Almighty God for life and liberty, we, the people
of Utah, in order to secure and perpetuate the principles of
free government, do ordain and establish this Constitution.

VERMONT
(Adopted in 1793)

That all men have a natural and unalienable right, to worship
Almighty God, according to the dictates of their own con-

sciences and understandings, as in their opinion shall be regulated by the word of God; and that no man ought to or of right can be compelled to attend any religious worship, or erect or support any place of worship, or maintain any minister, contrary to the dictates of his conscience, nor can any man be justly deprived or abridged of any civil right as a citizen, on account of his religious sentiments, or peculiar mode of religious worship; and that no authority can, or ought to be vested in, or assumed by, any power whatever, that shall in any case interfere with, or in any manner control the rights of conscience, in the free exercise of religious worship. Nevertheless, every sect or denomination of christians ought to observe the sabbath or Lord's day, and keep up some sort of religious worship, which to them shall seem most agreeable to the revealed will of God.

VIRGINIA
(Adopted in 1902)

That religion or the duty which we owe to our Creator, and the manner of discharging it, can be directed only by reason and conviction, not by force or violence; and, therefore, all men are equally entitled to the free exercise of religion, according to the dictates of conscience; and that it is the mutual duty of all to practice Christian forbearance, love and charity towards each other.

WASHINGTON
(Adopted in 1889)

We, the people of the State of Washington, grateful to the Supreme Ruler of the Universe for our liberties, do ordain this Constitution.

WISCONSIN
(Adopted in 1848)

We the people of Wisconsin, grateful to Almighty God for our freedom, in order to secure its blessings, form a more perfect government, insure domestic tranquillity and promote the general welfare, do establish this Constitution.

WYOMING
(Adopted in 1889)

We, the people of the State of Wyoming, grateful to God for our civil, political and religious liberties, and desiring to secure them to ourselves and perpetuate them to our posterity, do ordain and establish this Constitution.

nineteen

The Beginnings and Development of Our Schools

UNTIL RELATIVELY RECENT TIMES EDUCATION BE-longed to the home and church. The child was taught by parents or tutors employed by them, and the church was the teacher of the parents and tutors. We well may say that in Western civilization the church was the mother of education.

The appearance of the state on the educational scene came late, and due to very definite causes. The reason was not a dissatisfaction with the work of the parents or the church. Less again was it with the idea of separating education from religion. The role of the state became necessary because of new circumstances which made education too great a task for the parents, the private schools or the church.

Principal among these new developments were (1) the growth of popular education, (2) the multiplication of religious sects, and (3) the expansion of secular knowledge. On the more general side we might include, also, the progressive secularization of culture throughout the world, and the growth of the modern national state.

EUROPEAN INFLUENCE

All these developments took place in Europe, and although our interest does not lie in that direction we must understand that our American system of education is an offshoot of European education. The same patterns existed here as there;

and it is necessary to understand the general background to know whence our system came, and what our aims should be.

When our forefathers came to America they brought old-world patterns of education with them, so that the first teachers in America were the family and the church. Then came the private religious schools; next came private religious schools aided by the state; and finally, the exclusively state-supported and -controlled schools. These latter did not monopolize American education, however. They were established alongside the private schools. From the beginning our system was pluralistic, consisting of public, private, and church schools.

In this chapter we are interested mostly in the origin and development of the public-school system. We shall see that there, too, until very recently, the purpose and intent of those who started this system was not to exclude religion from it but to eliminate sectarian instruction, while keeping as much religion as was possible without violating the rights or sensitivities of any children or their parents.

New England

Education in America at first made its greatest strides in Massachusetts. Both early church education and later public school education developed there more quickly and on a wider scale than elsewhere.

When the Puritans settled in New England they desired to establish religious commonwealths as nearly as possible like Calvin's city-state at Geneva. The cornerstone was religion and education. To the minister more than to anyone else fell the task of fostering and preserving learning.

Education was considered important because it advanced the cause of religion. Practically all Protestant sects maintained that an educated clergy was necessary in order that the Bible might be fully understood. Education was provided for youth in order to enable them to learn to read the Bible, which was considered the source of truth and virtuous living.

The first school in New England was the home. Parents taught their children to read the Bible, the elementary principles of religion, and their civil duties. Early in the history of New England the home gave way to town and dame schools. These taught reading, writing, arithmetic, church doctrine, and rules of conduct. Subject matter was largely drawn from the Scriptures. Ministers chose the textbooks with a view toward instilling the doctrines of Puritanism in the minds of pupils. The *New England Primer*, for example, abounds in religious allusions, prayers, and religious verses. No schoolmaster was ever appointed, nor any woman permitted to keep a dame school, without the consent and approval of the ministers. Often, ministers themselves were the schoolmasters.

Around 1640, parents and masters of apprentices were somewhat remiss in performing their educational duties. As the result of appeals by ministers, the General Court of Massachusetts in 1642 directed officials of every town to see to it that parents taught their children "to read and understand the principles of religion and the capitall lawes of the country" and to instruct them "in learning and labor and other employments . . . profitable to the Commonwealth." The passage of this law marked the first time among English-speaking people that a state legislative body ordered that all children be taught to read. It was the first time the state acted to control education.

Five years later church authorities were still dissatisfied with the character of education in the Bay Colony. They appealed again to the General Court which passed the famous law of 1647. In the preamble the law stated that it was "one chief object of ye ould deluder, Satan, to keep men from the knowledge of ye Scriptures." Therefore, the Court ordered every town of fifty or more families to appoint a teacher to instruct children in reading and writing. Teachers were to be paid by the parents (tuition fees) or by the inhabitants in general (tax levy) in whatever way each town might determine. Every town of one hundred or more families was to provide a grammar school. This legislation laid the cornerstone for our present day tax-supported school system.

MIDDLE COLONIES

The Dutch-established parochial schools in New York were under the control of the Dutch Reformed Church. They had been extended to nearly all the settlements of the colony by the time of the English conquest. The schoolmaster was always an official of the church—usually the minister; sometimes, the sexton. Children were taught to read and write, a little figuring, the catechism and prayers. All except children of the poor paid fees to the schoolmaster.

Most Pennsylvania schools in the colonial period were founded by churches or private individuals. Here, as elsewhere, emphasis was placed on reading, writing, arithmetic, and religion. And here, too, clergymen were usually the teachers. Quakers, Lutherans, Presbyterians, Moravians, Mennonites— settled in Pennsylvania—believed in the necessity of learning to read the Bible as a means of salvation. Education was, therefore, important to religion. A law passed in 1683, requiring parents to teach their children to read and write so that they might be able to read the Bible by the time they were twelve years of age, was vetoed by the Crown. Another compulsory education law was later enacted, but dropped when enforcement proved difficult. Parochial schools remained as chief centers of education.

THE SOUTH

In the South, widely separated farms and plantations made the establishment of an effective school system all but impossible.

Parents taught their own children. In some cases, tutors were employees and some of the wealthier planters sent their children abroad to school. A common practice was for several planters to co-operate in building a schoolhouse and in paying a teacher for instructing their children. Out of such community enterprises grew the "old Field Schools," frequently attended by rich and poor alike. There were a few endowed parish schools providing instruction for poor children. Most private schools were taught by ministers of the Anglican Church.

THREE TYPES

By the close of the colonial period three types of educational practice existed in America:

1. In New England there was a state system of compulsory public school education, originally Calvinistic in principle; the state acted as collaborator of the church.

2. In the Middle colonies there was a system of parochial schools.

3. In the South there was no state supervision except caring for orphans and children of the poor; there were tutors in the home and private pay schools.

In all three types, religion was inseparable from education.

HIGHER EDUCATION

Higher education, like elementary education, had a religious purpose in the colonial era. Harvard, the first college in the colonies, was authorized by the General Court of Massachusetts in 1636 and endowed two years later by John Harvard, a Charleston minister. Its purpose, clearly stated in the charter, was "the advancement of all good literature, artes and sciences" and "all other necessary provisions that may conduce to the education of the English and Indian youth of this Country in knowledge and godliness." Harvard was founded "*in Christi gloriam*" ("to the glory of Christ") and dedicated "*Christo et Ecclesiae*" ("to Christ and the Church"). It definitely aimed to educate men for the ministry.

Sixty-five years later, ten Congregational ministers founded Yale College to educate men "fitted for publick employment both in Church and Civil state." The first president of King's College, later to become Columbia University, stated its chief purpose was "to teach and engage the children to know God in Jesus Christ, and to love and serve him, in all sobriety, godliness, and righteousness of life, with a perfect heart and a willing mind."

Six other colleges were established in the colonial era, all of them, except one, under church auspices: Dartmouth (1769), Congregationalist; William and Mary (1693), Anglican; The College of New Jersey, now Princeton (1746), Presbyterian; Queen's College, now Rutgers (1766), Dutch Reformed; Rhode Island College, now Brown (1764), Baptist; the Philadelphia Academy, now the University of Pennsylvania (1751), non-sectarian.

Religion and education walked hand in hand during the days when the foundations of America were being laid. Our country was built by men who believed in God and His moral law. They wrote their faith in our important documents, modeled their lives upon it, and infused it into our schools. Slowly, and to the degree necessary, the state, usually by invitation, lent a hand. Even then the state acted as co-operator, and often as the "servant" of the church, which it recognized as the supreme teacher.

RELIGION AND EDUCATION ON THE WESTERN FRONTIER

By the end of the first third of the nineteenth century about
a third of the people of the United States lived on the Western frontier beyond the Alleghenies. It was practically impossible to speak of education there without speaking of religion.

In April, 1828, the *Quarterly Journal of the American
Education Society* said (pp. 64–65):

> More schools and colleges efficiently conducted, and a larger
> number of educated ministers of the gospel, and a healthful tone
> of moral feeling, are . . . wanted at the West. Christians must use
> their utmost exertions to plan their institutions of learning and
> religion in the Western States . . . We want to see a public sen-
> timent made "vital in every part" by the all-pervading influence of
> the religious principle . . . to develop intelligent, industrious, and
> virtuous freemen.

In this period, Dr. Lyman Beecher used to tell his audi-
ences, "Education, intellectual and religious, is the point on
which stands our destiny."

Professor William W. Sweet, in his book, *Religion on the
American Frontier* (p. 9), observes that "almost every Presbyterian preacher in the West" was a schoolmaster.

The first schools in Detroit, Michigan, and in Vincennes,
Indiana, were opened by Catholic missionaries.

No less than sixteen colleges and universities in the Mid-
dle West were founded under religious auspices—among them,
Washington and Jefferson, Ohio University, Western Reserve,
Ohio Wesleyan, Dennison, Notre Dame, and Northwestern.

Clergymen were prominent as educators. Most colleges
had clergymen as presidents. A Congregational minister, the
Rev. John D. Pierce, "led the educational movement in the
Middle West along the general lines laid down by Horace
Mann." The Reverend Gabriel Richard, a Catholic priest, was

one of the founders, and vice president of the University of Michigan in 1817. He taught in six of its thirteen departments. Ohio's first state superintendent of public instruction was Samuel Lewis, "a licensed local preacher in the Methodist Church." Boards of trustees of Ohio's academies "were chosen mainly from leaders in the churches."

After 1843, the Reverend Theoron Baldwin was so actively engaged in educational work in the West that he was called "the father of Western colleges." He was secretary of the "Western College Society." It has been said that "no other organization was so effective in aiding the development of higher educational facilities in the West."

During the 1850's and 1860's the Reverend Pierre De Smet, a Jesuit missionary, was characteristically known as "a zealous apostle of religion and education in the West."

In 1849 the Reverend Samuel Willy went to California and became president of the board of trustees of the College of California. Later, he "was one of the leaders in founding the state university."

Dr. Henry P. Van Dusen, in his book, *God in Education* (p. 43), says that "of the 207 colleges established before the Civil War, 180 were denominationally sponsored, 21 were state universities, 6 were under public or semi-public but not religious auspices."

The close relation between religion and education was so much a part of American life that a visitor to our shores, in 1831–33, Alexis de Toqueville, wrote:

I have known of societies formed by the Americans to send out ministers of the Gospel into the new Western States to found schools and churches there, lest religion should be suffered to die away in those remote settlements, and the rising States be less fitted to enjoy free institutions than the people from which they emanated.

Education on America's frontier was in the hands of people who believed in God. They took responsibility for it, built the schools, and did the teaching.

BEGINNINGS OF THE PAROCHIAL SCHOOL

The causes of the transition from private schools were many. On the whole it was a historical phenomenon. America was growing in size and in diversity. The older molds were bound to crack. It became obvious that private education could no longer do the job alone. The state came in to fill in the parts that were being left unattended. Neither then nor now has the state ever considered itself a rival or monopolist in the field of education. Then as now, in theory and in practice our system was pluralistic.

By 1825, foreign immigration was becoming a factor in changing American life. It not only increased our population; it also changed the religious complexion of the country. Previously, there had been a marked degree of religious uniformity in America. But the new immigration altered that. Sectarian schools—in which the religion of a sect was taught—were found unsatisfactory for children who belonged to different religious groups. Part of the solution of this problem seemed to lie in the establishment of non-sectarian, state-controlled and -supported schools.

Part of it lay in the establishment of parochial schools to provide for the needs of large numbers of Catholic immigrants from Europe who came to the United States after 1820.

Desiring to take care of the spiritual and educational wants of these immigrants, and believing that education could not be divorced from "religion and sound morals," the Catholic Church's First Plenary Council of Baltimore in 1852 exhorted "bishops . . . to see that schools be established in connection with all the churches of their dioceses."

A contributing cause to their development was the practice of reading the King James version of the Bible in the public schools, which emphasized the Protestant point of view. Catholics regarded this as unfair to their children. They sought to correct the situation by making provision for parochial schools.

Briefly, this is how parochial schools were begun on a country-wide basis.

They are a recognized, valid, and accepted part of our educational system. In the United States today some four million pupils are enrolled in nearly fourteen thousand religious or parochial elementary and high schools which are maintained by Catholics, Lutherans, Seventh Day Adventists, Episcopalians, Reformed Churches, Mennonites, Jews, and others.

Another cause for the shift to public education was the increase in American population which required an even greater number of schools. Only the state had financial resources sufficient to provide them—and eventually it did.

On the continent the followers of the movement known as the Enlightenment, and later of the French Revolution, militantly preached the secularist way of life. Although their influence was not great in America, whose Revolution was a conservative one, it was felt by a few who pressed for the elimination of religion from social living.

Meanwhile the modern state was growing in size and in self-awareness. It tended to absorb more of the functions usually left to individuals and private groups. Education was sure to come under its compass.

Thus, public schools appeared in America because the circumstances of our national development demanded them—not because of "a deliberate or wanton violation of the rights of the Church." Moreover, the new public schools were not hostile to religion. Everyone agreed they would teach belief in God. The public schools were non-sectarian, but had a distinct Protestant character. They were by no means unreligious.

No National Education

The Constitution of the United States made no provision for a nation-wide system of education. Learning, when the Constitution was framed, was regarded largely as a local matter and was left to the several states to handle as they saw fit. By 1800, there were sixteen states in the Union, and of these seven had defined in their constitutions the state's duty in respect to education. As might be expected the New England states, with their state-control tradition, were the most explicit in the matter. The Middle states, with their parochial-school setup, were much less emphatic, while the Southern states and the new states of Kentucky and Tennessee completely ignored it.

Although the constitutions of many of the states contained no specific references to education, almost all the states in a very short time were legislating general school laws. These laws, however, were negative in character, since they left the working out of education to the local communities. The states aimed at supporting education and preserving the good of all.

The Founding Fathers were not, as a group, interested in a national system of education. They preferred to leave it to the states. Notable exceptions in this regard were Washington and Jefferson. The one thing they were all agreed on was that education should be religious in aim and spirit. We include below the few references made to education by our leaders in early America.

In his Farewell Address Washington warned:

Of all the dispositions and habits which lead to political prosperity, Religion and Morality are indispensable supports . . . Whatever may be conceded to the influences of refined education on minds of peculiar structure, reason and experience forbid us to expect that national morality can prevail in exclusion of religious principle.

The Northwest ordinance of 1787 has the same sentiments. (See chapter 10.) This was an ordinance that was to be the guiding rule for all our Western acquisitions. The Southwest Ordinance was also built upon it. Daniel Webster said it was "so wise and liberal in spirit" that he doubted "whether one single law of any lawgiver, ancient or modern, has produced effects of more distinct, marked and lasting character." It is interesting to note that Jefferson was one of its principal drafters. This Ordinance declared: "Religion, morality, and knowledge being necessary to good government and the happiness of mankind, schools and the means of education shall forever be encouraged . . ."

Thomas Jefferson founded the University of Virginia and took great pride in this accomplishment. Despite his much touted and supposed affinity for the idea of a narrow interpretation of separation of church and state, he suggested a school of theology in the University at state expense.

The Growth of the Public-School System

Most of the Founding Fathers had died by the time the problem of universal, free, and non-sectarian tax-supported schools was faced. The struggle for these schools began at the close of the first quarter of the nineteenth century. "In 1850 they were becoming an actuality in every Northern State." Massachusetts was the first to act. In 1826–27 it passed legislation forbidding the teaching of the doctrines of any sect in the public schools. New Jersey followed in 1844. Then twenty-one more states. "Seventeen other states have included such measures on their admission into the Commonwealth of States."

In principle, the public schools were *non-sectarian*. Doctrines of particular denominations could not be taught in them. But public schools were not *unreligious*. Doctrines common to all denominations could be taught. Not only so, they were taught—and educators insisted that they be taught.

Prayers, reading of the Bible, and the precepts of morality were included in all curricula.

For example, the Massachusetts School Laws of 1827 stated: "The school Committee shall never direct to be purchased or used in any of the town schools, any books which are calculated to favor the tenets of any particular sect of Christians."

This provision of the law was not directed against teaching religion in the public schools but only against the teaching of the tenets of a particular sect.

Horace Mann, who before anyone else can claim the title of founder of the public-school system, became secretary of the Massachusetts State Board of Education in 1837. He had a controversy with the American Sunday School Union which wanted to place their books in the public school libraries. Mann opposed this because of the sectarian bias of the books, not because he was hostile to teaching religion in the schools. The committee appointed to investigate the matter reported to the State Board of Education:

While the Legislature requires the children in our common schools to be taught the principle of piety and virtue and prohibits the propagation of sectarian views, it cannot in truth be said that the Legislature or the Board of Education are regardless of the religious instruction of the children and youth of the commonwealth. On the contrary, the facts prove that Massachusetts still retains and cherishes the great principles of freedom that were cherished by her Puritan ancestors . . .

Horace Mann himself vigorously defended religious instruction in the schools. In his final report to the State Board of Education, he said:

I avail myself of this, the last opportunity which I may ever have, to say in regard to all affirmations or intimations that I have ever attempted to exclude religious instruction from the schools, or to exclude the Bible from the schools, or to impair the force of that volume, that they are now, and always have been, without substance or semblance of truth. Our system earnestly inculcates all Christian morals; it founds its morals on the basis of religion; it welcomes the religion of the Bible; and in receiving the Bible, it allows it to do what it is allowed to do in no other system, to speak for itself.

In 1917 the Massachusetts constitution was amended to make "the prohibition of sectarian teaching statutory." But again this provision was aimed against "denominational" teaching, not "the teaching of the elements of Christianity."

During the Hayes-Tilden presidential campaign in 1876, the Republican platform called for an amendment to the constitution forbidding "the application of any public funds or property for the benefit of any school or institution under sectarian control." James G. Blaine had submitted the same amendment "in a strengthened form" to Congress on August 14, 1875. It failed to get the necessary two-thirds vote. But even this amendment was "not to be construed to prohibit the reading of the Bible in any school or institution."

Most state constitutions prohibit the teaching of sectarianism in the public schools—the particular tenets of a sect. The emphasis is on the prohibition of sectarianism, not religion.

Clyde Lamont Hay, in The Blind Spot in American Education, has said (p. 34):

No law has ever been passed by any state forbidding the use of the Bible in the public schools, but the exclusion of the Bible in the schools of some of our states has been brought about through interpretations of the law by the courts or by Attorneys General.

An Important Difference

Thus it appears that those who first advocated the exclusion of sectarian teaching in the public schools did not mean to exclude the teaching of religion. As proof may be cited the provisions of some state constitutions which require the reading of the Bible in the public schools even though they do exclude sectarianism. Massachusetts is a case in point. New York, Iowa, Indiana, West Virginia, Florida, and Mississippi have passed laws that forbid the exclusion of the Bible from the public schools.

From our earliest days down to our own twentieth century the voice is clear which calls for the preservation of the religious spirit and aim of our public schools. If the schools were cut off from the churches, there was no intent to cut them off from religion or from God.

In recent years some few, but zealous, people who are hostile to religion have invoked a false and un-American principle of separation of church and state in their efforts to eliminate all teaching of belief in God from our state-supported schools. They try to make "separation of church and state" mean what it never meant in American history—that the state has no interest in religion as such and must look with disfavor on its presence in state-supported institutions.

These modern secularists have been influential in educational circles and have succeeded to a great extent in bringing about their aim—the elimination of God from the classroom. Fortunately, there has been during the last few years a healthy and vigorous reaction against this secularistic trend. Attempts of many sorts to restore religion to education are now afoot.

The way we propose in this book is only one small answer to a great problem. We believe that if today we learn more about our American beginnings and development we will not abandon the field so easily to the articulate minority of such recent appearance which would have us renounce our traditions and culture.

We might well conclude with the straightforward words which Nicholas Murray Butler, president of Columbia University, uttered in 1934:

The separation of church and state is fundamental in American political order, but so far as religious education is concerned, this principle has been so far departed from as to put the whole force and influence of the tax-supported schools on the side of one element in the community—that which is pagan and believes in no religion whatever.

377.10973
K29a